A COMPARATIVE STUDY OF WH-WORDS IN CHINESE EFL TEXTBOOKS, ELICITED NATIVE AND NON-NATIVE SPEAKER DATA AND WRITTEN NATIVE AND NON-NATIVE SPEAKER CORPORA

FEIFEI ZHANG

authorHOUSE®

AuthorHouse™
1663 Liberty Drive
Bloomington, IN 47403
www.authorhouse.com
Phone: 1 (800) 839-8640

Published by AuthorHouse 06/12/2015

ISBN: 978-1-5049-1085-9 (sc)
ISBN: 978-1-5049-1086-6 (e)

Print information available on the last page.

DEDICATION

To my parents, with love

Contents

List of Tables

List of Figures

Abstract

This study presents a corpus-based analysis of the use of "wh" sentences by language learners, in language textbooks and in authentic written discourse. It focuses on the polysemeous nature of "wh" words, which can be used as interrogatives, declaratives and to introduce subordinate clauses.

The analysis of "wh" sentences in EFL textbooks showed that there are more prototypical examples at low proficiency levels. When teaching the interrogative, textbooks focus almost exclusively on grammatical words, particularly at the beginners' level.

The analysis of "wh" sentences elicited from Chinese speaking learners of English and Expert users of English suggested that the prototypical structure is very strong in both sets of data, although native speakers tend to use more prefabricated chunks of language.

The analysis of "wh" sentences from native speakers and non-native speakers' written corpora suggested that subordinate clauses are strongly present in both corpora, except for the word "why" in non-native speakers' data. The use of different words occurring immediately after "wh" words in the two corpora can be explained by (1) the relatively small vocabulary size of the L2 speakers; (2) non-native speakers' lack of awareness of restricted collocations; (3) L1 transfer; (4) over/under-generalization of rules and (5) textbooks.

Acknowledgements

I would like to express my deepest gratitude to my supervisor, Dr. Jeannette Littlemore, for her careful guidance and inspired encouragement throughout the entire study of my work, without whom I would not have been able to complete this study. Many thanks are due to the lecturers in the Centre for English Language Studies at the University of Birmingham for their inspiring and enlightened help with my academic writing.

A great number of friends and colleagues have given me help and encouragement during the preparation of this dissertation. Many thanks are due to Joe Bennett for his organization of Friday research seminars which gave me many inspiring ideas and opinions. I also would like to express my appreciation to my personal friends Anna, Peggy, Liz, Becky, Chanel, and Mai, for their kind care, cheerful company and friendship. I would also like to express my appreciation to Mr Chuan Shi Zhang for the collection of my research data. I thank him for his patience and cooperation.

My ultimate thanks, as always, go to my parents, who have always believed in me and supported me and the love they give is far beyond what I deserve. This study is dedicated to them with respect and affection.

Chapter One

Introduction

1.1 Background of The Study

All Second Language Acquisition (SLA) theories presuppose that learners learn the target language largely from the spoken or written discourse to which they are exposed (Carroll 2001). The idea assumes that input influences L2 acquisition processes in some way. One of the most influential recent theories in SLA, Dynamic Systems Theory (DST), suggests that L2 learning is best viewed as a dynamic complex system in which a number of variables within the system continuously interact and this leads the system as a whole to change over time (De Bot et al 2005).

Normally, a change in the system results from a complex interaction between the environment and principles of self-organization. In other words, we could view learning as an outcome of the interaction between external input, such as speech signals or written texts, and internal cognitive processes, such as attention and awareness. Because of these interactions, only some input will become intake and will be accessible for further processing. It is difficult to determine what and how target L2 input will be digested and absorbed as intake. One way of helping to predict what might be learned is first to analyze how language knowledge is organized and structured in the mind of the learner and to attempt to understand how we learn language based on our physical experiences. This is the approach taken to language in Cognitive Linguistics.

Cognitive Linguistics is a recent linguistic theory which holds the belief that language is not only an instrument to organize, process, and convey the thoughts of human beings, but also a product of human cognition. In other words, both language itself, and language learning, use the same cognitive abilities that underlie all other types of information processing and learning (Ellis and Robinson 2008).

From the perspective of Cognitive Linguistics, the linguistic system that exists in learners' minds contains symbolic units (morphemes, words, or phrases) where each unit contains a conventional pairing of form and meaning/function (Langacker 1988a). The use of linguistic elements and structures is derived from the representation of the target linguistic system in the minds of speakers and it also influences their representation via the cognitive processes of routinization and entrenchment (Gries

2006). Put differently, a symbolic unit must have occurred frequently enough in the language to which a speaker or hearer has been exposed in order to become entrenched in their linguistic system.

Cognitive Linguists have also theorized about the way symbolic units are developed in the minds of learners via different types of frequency effects at several levels. A single word, such as *months,* can be stored as a symbolic unit, while multi-word units, such as *I don't know*, and *It's up to you* can also be stored as a single symbolic unit as they occur frequently. Building on this, Cognitive Linguistics and Corpus Linguistics can be considered complementary to each other. The latter is predominantly based on frequency information; it also analyses large collections of language, revealing how the recurring patterns of words, collocations, phrases, and constructions are exhibited in naturally occurring discourse. The former is a theoretical framework that in recent years has begun to make use of corpus-based methodology. One of the aims of this study is to use corpus methodology to investigate Cognitive Linguistic theory.

To gain a better understanding of the process of L2 acquisition, I will now discuss how learners learn a second language with regard to DST. In the following sections, I present the idea that learning a second language is a complex and dynamic process, involving interaction between external input and internal cognition. Two types of knowledge, namely explicit knowledge and implicit knowledge, are considered to be involved in the resulting categorization process.

1.1.1 How Learners Learn a Second Language

From the perspective of DST, learning a second language is a complex and dynamic process and the language system that exists in the mind of every learner changes and evolves through a series of stages and sub-stages. For individuals, the complexity of learning a language manifests itself in at least three different ways.

Firstly, the contexts are complex. For example, they might include the environments in which second languages are learned; the attitudes of the society to which one belongs towards learning a language and whether the institution places emphasis on learning a language. The ways in which individuals' families encourage and support them in learning a language, and affect their levels of motivation are also complex.

Secondly, what is being learned is complex. To know a language, one needs to know the linguistic elements such as syntax, lexis, pragmatics, phonology and the external and internal connections between them. Sometimes, it is even difficult for the native speakers of the language. In extreme cases, these linguistic elements are taught and learners are hardly aware of the internal connections between them.

Thirdly, the learning processes are considered complex. There are at least two sub-processes that contribute to the entire process. The first refers to the process whereby learners gain access to the L2. Learners learn a second language via linguistic data (both written and spoken) that surrounds them. The second refers to the process whereby learners create a linguistic system that contains a repeat perception allowing them to picture the linguistic data every time they incorporate and establish a link between the received data and the already existing information.

Learning a second language is also dynamic, and the processes involved vary according to proficiency levels. For example, learners may find themselves experiencing a period of learning a language very rapidly, and then going through a period of stagnation. Sometimes, they may backslide a little before improving again. Learners may go through several steps to acquire the correct form of the language. This could involve making correct use of one linguistic form and incorporating another linguistic form at the same time.

To conclude, learning a second language is complex and dynamic. During the second language acquisition process, the linguistic system that individual learner creates may evolve through sets of stages or sub-stages.

However, we know little about how knowledge is actually organized in the brain. There is a belief that the organization of L2 knowledge is more fixed for lower levels of proficiency, but more flexible for highly fluent L2 users (Saville-Troike 2006). For example, learners at lower levels rely largely on memorization, while those at higher levels have more creativity when constructing their sentences. In addition, the increasing proficiency involves a progression from controlled processing to automatic processing.

One way of seeing this difference is to view the controlled process as being rule-governed, whereas the automatic process is more intuitive. The distinction between a controlled process and an automatic process "relates to the degree to which the skills in question have been routinized and established in long-term memory" (McLaughlin 1990: 6). To some extent, we can say that language acquisition involves the development of both explicit knowledge and implicit knowledge. These two types of knowledge develop simultaneously and interact with each other in some way in the minds of the learners during the learning process (Saville-Troike 2006).

Language learning involves the development of both implicit and explicit knowledge

Learning a second language involves both implicit and explicit knowledge of language. Learners control the use of both types of knowledge during their learning processes. Explicit knowledge is generally considered to be "declarative knowledge" that can be brought into awareness and that is potentially available for verbal report (Roehr 2008:69). Such knowledge can facilitate language acquisition in the early stages of the process; later on controlled processes will become more automatic.

Playing a supporting and facilitative role, explicit learning refers to the circumstances where learners have "on-line awareness, formulating and testing conscious hypotheses" (Ellis 1996: 38-39). Accordingly, explicit knowledge might help learners to process input better because it makes them aware of how the target language is structured. For example, by using their explicit knowledge, learners may use examples provided by the teacher to work out how linguistic rules operate. Their explicit knowledge will focus their attention on certain aspects of the input whilst paying less attention to others. By manipulating a learner's explicit knowledge, a teacher can direct the learner's attention to certain things in the input that they might have missed and thus is potentially beneficial to the learner's entire linguistic knowledge.

In contrast, the implicit system is built up via "exposure to and processing of linguistic input and the subsequent accommodation of formal features that were attended to in that input" (Vanpatten 2002: 58-59). The implicit learning system incorporates new information according to its own method, which involves neither conscious inspection nor manipulation (De Bot et al 2005). Implicit learning refers to the situation when learning takes place without conscious cognitive processes. Building on this, implicit knowledge is defined as knowledge that cannot be brought into awareness. Such knowledge can be considered as a result of unconscious processes (Ellis 1996).

To summarise, the implicit system develops in parallel to the explicit system, and both systems are beneficial to the learning process, although it is not clear how the two systems influence each other. There are, however, two consensuses about the role of explicit and implicit knowledge in second language acquisition. Firstly, both of them provide ways of processing input, which allows learners to acquire the knowledge eventually. Secondly, based upon a recent proposal of the usage-based model, both types of knowledge are believed to be related to category structures.

Through the discussion of the idea that learning involves contributions from both implicit and explicit language systems, in the next section, I move on to discuss how implicit knowledge and explicit knowledge are characterized in terms of the way they structure categories.

The characteristics of implicit knowledge and explicit knowledge in terms of category structure

It is suggested that implicit knowledge is characterized by flexible and context-dependent categories with fuzzy boundaries, while explicit knowledge is classified in terms of stable, discrete and context-independent structures (Roehr 2008). To gain a better understanding of the concepts of these two types of knowledge, I shall briefly discuss how each type of knowledge contributes to L2 acquisition.

To begin with, both types of knowledge are processed and represented in the human mind via processing mechanisms. Explicit knowledge is considered to be a rule-governed process which is conscious and controlled. It is found particularly in form-focused instruction and textbooks as a source of linguistic input. A consensus regarding this type of knowledge is that attention is a necessary requirement for input to become intake (Roehr 2008).

In accordance with the views in cognitive psychology, implicit learning is considered to be exemplar-based. As learners experience a large number of examples, the repeated examples gradually shape the learners' mental representation. In other words, learners gradually abstract schemas by encountering a large number of examples.

It is believed that learners categorize and abstract the exemplars from the process of categorization; that is, learners understand the linguistic structures by schemas that derive from the best example of a category. In addition, during the process of categorization, learners not only remember a number of exemplars, but also tend to search for similarities between the new exemplar and ones that are already held in their memory.

With regard to the DST premise that the learning process is dynamic and developing, many would agree that learning can be understood as a matter of assimilation and accommodation (De Bot et al 2005) In other words, learning involves the repeated perception and noticing of links between new information and existing information (ibid).

Having discussed the two types of knowledge with reference to L2 learning, I now move on to discuss the next research area: explicit metalinguistic knowledge of classical categories and implicit knowledge with fuzzy categories.

Explicit metalinguistic knowledge of classical categories and implicit knowledge with fuzzy categories.

The discussion presented in the previous section was concerned with the differences between two types of knowledge in terms of category structures. In this section I discuss these two types of knowledge further.

It is acknowledged that a learner's explicit metalinguistic knowledge is derived from a bottom-up process of analysis of linguistic input, or built up by learning the grammatical rules that textbook writers have carefully selected and compiled (Ellis 2001, Roehr 2008). By the same token, metalinguistic knowledge has been found to rely on "Aristotelian, categorical, classical or scientific categorization" (Roehr 2008: 81). Because metalinguistic knowledge is derived from pedagogic grammar or textbooks, it appears to be characterised by stable, discrete, and context-independent categories with clear-cut boundaries. More specifically, it is used for monitoring and reasoning purposes in the L2 acquisition process, which is also classified as a problem-solving approach (Roehr 2008). In most circumstances, learners may consciously analyse the input in order to comprehend the utterances and in turn produce appropriate output.

Metalinguistic knowledge is based on yes/no distinctions, and prototype effects and frequent distribution are not taken into account. In fact, it is defined by means of a discrete fact or truth. For example, the metalinguistic category of "pronoun" is stable and clearly defined. Although some pronouns may occur less frequently than others in certain circumstances in a learner's metacognitive knowledge (for instance personal pronouns are rarer in academic writing than in everyday conversation), all pronouns may well have equal status as pronouns, and be equally valid exemplars of the category, regardless of context.

In contrast, implicit linguistic knowledge is represented in terms of flexible and context-dependent categories and is subject to exemplar-based categories. In addition, it is associated with unconscious cognitive processes. More specifically, linguistic knowledge is represented in a vast, dynamic, and associated network of form-meaning pairings. The form-meaning pairing can be more or less specific, as well as more or less complex (Roehr 2008).

By encountering a large number of examples, a schema "gradually emerges from distinct structures when one abstracts away from their points of differences by portraying them with lesser precision and specificity" (Langacker 2008: 8). In addition, linguistic structures are characterized as conventional units varying from specific to complex. In accordance with learners' conceptual and linguistic knowledge, implicit knowledge of the categories are flexible and context-dependent, sensitive to prototype effects and have fuzzy boundaries.

One's implicit knowledge of the category 'pronoun' would include knowledge of the fact that some words 'behave' more like pronouns than others. Although explicit metalinguistic knowledge and implicit knowledge are distinct from one other, it is suggested that these two types of knowledge can interact. It is hypothesized that an explicit metalinguistic understanding of linguistic knowledge may indirectly contribute to the development of implicit knowledge, and vice versa (Roehr 2008). I would argue that, when it comes to second language acquisition, both learners' explicit metalinguistic knowledge and implicit knowledge can be imprecise and inaccurate because of low language proficiency (see Roehr 2006, 2008). In addition, as these two types of knowledge interact during cognitive processing, it is difficult to clarify under what circumstances learners would use explicit metalinguistic knowledge or implicit knowledge. By and large, learners who are at higher levels and cognitively mature individuals may be more inclined to apply higher analytic metalinguistic and implicit knowledge (Roehr 2008). In addition, it should be borne in mind that there are many factors that affect the role of metalinguistic knowledge and implicit knowledge, such as target language exposure and internal cognitive processes. In the following section, I will proceed to the next research area: How external input and internal cognition contribute to the learning process.

<u>Learning is an outcome of the interaction of external input and internal cognition.</u>

L2 learning either happens as learners form memories of instances or examples they experience from external input or when input is made noticeable and salient and occurs with sufficient frequency (Schmidt 1990). This suggests that learning is an outcome of the interaction of external environment and internal cognition. Schmidt (1990) maintains that second language acquisition occurs under the condition of awareness. If this is the case, it might be interesting to look at how the internal cognitive systems possess certain constraints that can turn input to intake.

For most learners, L2 classroom input refers to the language "intentionally presented to the learners by the teacher or other learners in order to facilitate the process of L2 learning" (Nizegorodcew 2007: 13). EFL textbooks may serve as L2 linguistic input which can be considered an important form of input in the instructed classroom either as the essence of classroom activities, as the motivation for study, or as the guide or manual for learning the target language.

1.2 The Aims of This Study

We have discussed how learners learn or acquire a second language via interaction between external inputs, such as EFL textbooks, and their internal cognitive processes. This study also looks into 'External' (E) and 'Internal' (I) language, and explores how each of them relates to linguistic input in L2 language acquisition process. The notion of E and I is suggested by Taylor as follows: "E-language is the product of I-language of individual speakers, while I-language of individual speakers is the product of their exposure to E-language" (Taylor 2008: 29). In other words, in order to understand how learners learn or acquire a second language, we need to know what and how linguistic data they are exposed to (either written or spoken), and consider how it is processed in learners' minds.

However, by analysing learners' production, it can clearly be found that learners do not always produce the correct linguistic forms and structures which textbooks present. Therefore, the question arises as to how learners acquire the target forms or structures, which can be a difficult process. It is useful to begin by looking at how the language that learners are exposed to relates to what they produce. Most importantly, we can begin to understand the process of how learners' abstract schemas develop by looking at large numbers of exemplars of the language they produce. In this study we will look in particular the central wh-sentence type, and also the possibility that of the various interrogative constructions, some are more basic than others.

We have discussed the idea that the use of linguistic elements and structures is derived from the representation of the target linguistic system in the minds of speakers. The representation and processing of the target language can be considered to take place via general psychological mechanisms. One of the cognitive mechanisms, categorization, is considered the essential mechanism of human beings' conceptual understanding and linguistic knowledge (Dirven and Verspoor 2004, Roehr 2008, Gries 2008).

Categorization is influenced by the input with reference to the frequently encountered exemplars. In addition, many parameters such as "frequency, recency, and context interact, specific memory traces" may be more or less responsible for the process of categorization (Roehr 2008:7).

We may assume that learners' production can be considered as a product of both types of knowledge. In other words, with the help of form-focused instruction and the guidance of textbooks, learners gradually form the specific knowledge of how to use a particular form or structure. This kind of knowledge and the use of such knowledge are considered to be the metalinguistic knowledge of L2 learning. During this process, experiencing the incoming input and digesting the remaining information may gradually shape learners' mental representation of a specific form or structure. This process is considered to take place without much attention and awareness (Roehr 2008).

In brief, during the processing of both types of knowledge, many would agree that linguistic knowledge is regarded as the integral part of cognition. Categorization is a key mechanism in language representation and acquisition because it characterizes our linguistic knowledge, varying along the parameters of simplicity and complexity.

One category that has not been investigated but which occurs frequently is "wh" words. The "wh" category is frequently used and is important to analyze. It has consistently attracted the interest of researchers in the areas of SLA. Traditionally, studies (e.g. Groenendijk and Stokhof 1982; Berman 1991; Zanuttini and Portner 2003) of the acquisition of "wh" sentences have been focused on the characteristic use within syntactic categories. These studies provide examples of one way in which "wh" sentences can be analysed. The sentences that are produced illustrate the applications and constraints of the rules. However, the analysis does not reveal much about how language learners acquire these rules. In contrast, from the perspective of Cognitive Linguistics, language is learned from learners' language experience (Lieven and Tomasello 2003).

Factors in the environment, such as frequency, consistency, and complexity critically affect the process of learning a language. In addition, the process of sentence construction involves the use of knowledge that arises from interactions between language input and cognitive processing. A detailed analysis of "wh" sentences is likely to be useful for language teachers and syllabus writers. However, solely analysing sentences does not fully show how the sentences are acquired and produced by language learners. Rather, in order to investigate the knowledge learners have about "wh" sentences, it is important to focus on the characteristics of learners' production of "wh" sentences and identify the schemas that learners derive from a large number of exemplars and differences among these and a type of input (textbooks) and the target language.

1.3 Rationale for The Study

This study investigates how cognitive processes such as categorization can influence the way learners construct sentences. The main aim of the research project is to compare the substantial use of "wh" sentences by learners with the ways they appear in one type of language input (the student textbook), in elicited discourse and in authentic written learner discourse. The focus is on written input and output.

The reason why textbooks were chosen is that they constitute the type of written input that is most available to systematic study. Although textbooks do not contain *all* the language to which a learner is exposed, they do provide a good sample of the *type* of language to which they are exposed across the globe.

Elicited sentences contain the sort of language that language learners are often asked to produce in class in response to exercises set by the teacher. They can be seen as a reflection of a learner's explicit knowledge and mental representation of a target language structure. One of the aims of this study is to compare learners' explicit knowledge of their representations with that of native speakers. Therefore both native speakers and language learners were asked to produce elicited sentences.

Finally, written learner and native speaker corpora were searched for the presence of "wh" categories. All three data sources (textbooks, elicited written data and written corpus data) were compared to assess the impact of written input on explicit and implicit category knowledge for "wh" sentences.

The analysis focuses on the polysemous nature of each "wh" word, which is investigated on the basis of their usage (prototype interrogatives, extended declaratives, and extended subordinate clauses), together with the frequency of words occurring immediately after each "wh" word in terms of the three types of sentences.

The research question addressed in this study is as follows: What are the various constructions of "wh" sentences and how do their distributions differ across the following corpora:

- A corpus of English language textbooks used by Chinese learners of English
- A corpus of elicited sentences produced by native speakers of English
- A corpus of elicited sentences produced by non-native speakers of English

- A corpus of essays written by native speakers of English
- A corpus of essays written by non-native speakers of English

1.4 The Tools Used in The Study

In order to store and process the data in a reliable and systematic way, our analysis is based on corpus methodology. Corpus-based analysis is different from traditional paper-based analysis of language because computers can store and process large amounts of information.

In addition, a corpus can be planned and designed for any linguistic purpose. One of the main characteristics of corpus-based analysis is to focus on language use. From this usage-based perspective, we look at how "wh" sentences are exhibited in learners' written discourse and in learners' written elicited data.

Another theme of this study is to discover to what extent corpus linguistics can be used by cognitive linguists as a practical methodology. For instance, corpus findings can be objective and quantitative and it is important to identify any linguistic elements and structure, including the basic patterns and constructions and the frequency of constructions and patterns.

At this point the minimum points of similarity between Cognitive Linguistics and Corpus Linguistics are explicitly noted. Firstly, both discard the separation of syntax and lexis. From the cognitive perspective, lexis and grammar are essentially meaningful units of various degrees of specificity. For example, a construction can be any linguistic expression whose form and meaning cannot be partially derived. Corpus linguistics reveals that "words sharing the same patterns tend to fall into groups based on shared aspects… This in turn suggests that the patterns themselves can be said to have meanings" (Hunston and Francis 2000).

Secondly, both emphasize the frequency effect of linguistic elements and structures in the L2 acquisition processes. From the perspective of Cognitive Linguistics, symbolic units, either morphemes, words, or phrases, must have occurred frequently enough to be entrenched in the speaker or hearer's linguistic system (Gass 2006, Goldburg and Casenhiser 2005). On the other hand, the use of corpus linguistics methodology can help us to identify the status of frequency. Indeed, it is suggested that corpus linguistics is "the only reliable source of evidence for features such as frequency" (McEnery and Wilson 1996: 12).

Thirdly, both are usage-based. A cognitive view of sentence construction reflects a basic cognitive trait that human beings identify patterns and establish patterns from chaotic and unpredictable reality (Manzanares and López 2008). The language or languages that we learn arise from our linguistic experience that derives from our general experience of the world. This orientation guides and affects the ways in which we think and use the language, whether speaking or writing. More importantly, grammar patterns or constructions emerging from the repeat-co-occurrence of linguistic usage events, both in native speakers (e.g. Bybee 2008) and foreign language learners (Ellis 2008), emphasising the fact that knowledge of language emerges from language use. Corpus linguistics is also usage-based because a corpus can be planned and designed for any linguistic purpose. In addition, concordance lines may reveal important features of the linguistic elements or structures that we may not be consciously aware of. At a practical level, for example, word frequency, collocation, colligation, patterns and collostruction can be identified and analysed on the basis of corpus concordance lines.

The starting point for this study is to investigate the use of "wh" sentences by second language learners in both elicited and naturally-occurring written data. We aim to identify the schemas of the "wh" category with reference to the prototypical structure. Based upon this purpose, we need to look at a large number of "wh" sentences to derive their prototypical structure and extension structures. Corpus software here is used to store and process the data in a systematic way. The data was processed using Wordsmith Tools software. Each "wh" word is sorted in the centre and the sentences in which they occur are classified by clause type. The observation also focuses on the words frequently occurring after each "wh" word. Concordance lines allow information to be gathered on words occurring frequently after each "wh" word. For each type of sentence, the words following "wh" words will be manually scanned, and typed into a separate column.

To gain an idea of the prototypical effect amongst elicited data from EFL learners, native speakers, textbooks, and target language corpora, the study investigates the differences and similarities with which "wh" words are particularly likely to combine, therefore allowing researchers and language teachers to understand the choices that have been made with regard to each group. For this purpose, several target language corpora in terms of native speakers and non-native speakers' writing were consulted.

1.5 Outline of The Study

Chapter 2 contains a more detailed discussion of how the language system develops in the minds of the learners from the perspective of DST. I provide a framework for the developing language system in the mind of the learners. I use this theory to explain why the language that learners produce in essays is not the same as that which they produce in elicited data or that which they read in their textbooks. I also discuss the relationship between external input and an individual's cognitive process and look at how such learning works. Finally, two approaches i.e. categorization and prototype theory are discussed in this light.

In chapter 3, I present a detailed analysis of "wh" sentences, in particular the range of different constructions in which the "wh" words can occur. The analysis also focuses on the interrogatives as well as different kinds of subordinate clauses in which the words occur. Based on the analysis, we also look at the acquisition order of "wh" words and their structures, by both native speaker infants and second language learners.

Chapter 4 provides an overview of English language teaching and learning contexts in China. We look at in particularly the teaching approaches, and teaching materials to teaching "wh" sentences in Junior Middle school, Senior High school, and University in China.

In chapter 5 I investigate the central "wh" sentences type emerging from Chinese EFL textbooks together with the frequency of words occurring after each "wh" word.

Chapter 6 provides the investigation of elicited sentences from native speakers, and non-native speakers. The analysis is presented in the same format as chapter 5.

Chapter 7 contains the analysis of native speakers' and non-native speakers' written corpora, with reference to prototypical structures, words occurring frequently after each "wh" word.

In Chapter 8 the results are summarized and substantial differences are discussed between learner production, textbook language and natural language.

Chapter Two

The Developing Language System
in The Mind of The Learner

2.1 Introduction

Second language acquisition (SLA) has been distinctive as a field of study within applied linguistics since the late 1960s. Even though several important studies have been conducted to investigate how the acquisition of a second language occurs, we are still a long way from understanding the entire acquisition process. One of the main reasons for this is that acquiring a second language actually happens inside the mind and we cannot look inside people's minds (Vanpatten 2003). In order to understand how learners' minds respond to the linguistic data to which they are exposed, it is important to explore, as far as possible, what happens to a learner's mental representation of the system during the acquisition process.

Recent work in SLA suggests that learning a language is not a straightforward task; but a developmental dynamic one (Thelen and Smith 1994, Van Geert 1994). From this perspective, the learning process is viewed as a dynamic complex system; a number of variables within the system continuously interact which keeps changing the system as a whole over time. However, it is impossible to classify what exactly causes such changes. The language system is a complex system and its development normally results from a complex interaction between the environment and principles of self-organization (Verspoor et al 2007).

The word 'environment' here refers to external input which is organized by the human cognitive system (Van Geert, 2008). In the framework of a complex dynamic approach, external input and self-organization are by definition complex and develop over time because of a wide variety of variables.

External input is important for the entire acquisition process. It provides the information the learner needs in order to learn. Piaget (1968) and Vygotsky (1978) identify two levels of processing which operate via two different mechanisms: "assimilation" which is "the integration of external elements into evolving or completed structures of an organism", and "accommodation" which is "any modification of an assimilatory scheme or structure by the elements it assimilates" (De Bot et al 2005: 57). Simply put, the cognitive system encodes information and it is adopted only in the function of this encoding (Verspoor et al 2008: 214).

One of the consequences of looking at SLA as a dynamic complex system is that an individual's cognitive system is by definition a dynamic complex system, and development involves interaction between specific cognitive capacities in the learning process and the creation of an implicit system of L2 linguistic knowledge.

Cognition, perception, memory and forgetting, interconnect and self-organise to help the L2 language system develop. Such development may not neatly sequence and may even regress at times, especially in the early stages of learning (Siegler and Svetina 2002). This is because learning involves the adoption of new strategies and skills. Individuals use their cognitive capacities to seek their own techniques and strategies until they reach a regular sequence of activities. In addition, development is unstable and will vary according to the factors such as learners' age and intellectual level. There is some evidence to suggest that the older and the more mature learners are, the more quickly they will discover appropriate strategies to progress in the developing stage, although other characteristics such as motivation, personality, and aptitude are also very important (Lenneberg 1967).

On the other hand, even if learners are able to make use of the 'best' techniques and strategies, it does not necessarily follow that the knowledge will be stored implicitly in their linguistic system. Rather, what they are able to produce may be the result of their use of certain types of explicit knowledge and their ability to develop skills that make use of this explicit knowledge. Explicit knowledge does not always turn into implicit knowledge. Learners who have knowledge of two language systems (their L1 and L2) in their minds are different from those who have single language knowledge (L1) in mind (ibid). From the perspective of a complex systems approach the L1 of individual learners is a part of the system and interacts with other parts. Cook (1995) suggests that language teachers should focus on learners' own needs in terms of successful language use, rather than achieving 'native-like competence'.

This chapter provides the framework of the developing language system in the mind of the learners. It discusses the relationship between external input and an individual's cognitive process and looks at how such learning works.

To begin with, I shall introduce the concept of SLA as a complex and dynamic system and look at how language knowledge develops through interaction between many variables e.g., individual learners and the learning process. This wide range of variables exists in both the external input and the internal cognitive process. I then explore how one type of external input: textbooks, whether intuitively-based or corpus driven, can play an important role in language learning. I also explore how particular cognitive capacities (cognition, perception, memory and forgetting) play an important role in the development of an individual's cognitive system, and how they are involved in the development of an implicit linguistic system. I examine the ways in which learners use implicit and explicit knowledge to develop their language system.

2.2 SLA is a Complex, Dynamic and Developing System

The complex system that is used to describe the language knowledge of learners changes over time due to a number of factors and variations. In this section I discuss how SLA is a complex, dynamic and developing system. Where relevant, I relate the discussion to the acquisition of "wh" sentences.

2.2.1 SLA is Complex

SLA is a complex system which can be described in three main ways. The first refers to the context in which a second language is learned. Generally, the context of learning refers to the environment in which the language is spoken including a country where the learning is taking place or any institutional learning experience involved (Vanpatten 2003). This includes many contextual factors which affect one's learning of a second language. These include: the attitude of the society to which one belongs towards learning a language; whether the institution places emphasis on learning a language; how individuals' families encourage and support them to learn a language; the effect of an individual's cognition or motivation towards learning a language, and so on (ibid).

The second refers to the fact that what is being learned is also complex. To know a language, one should know, for example, the words and their meanings, the sound system, and the rules that govern what can be understood within sentences. Vanpatten (2003) lists ten possible types of knowledge that a person must acquire to learn a second language, e.g. the lexicon, the phonology, inflectional/derivational morphology, particles, syntax, pragmatics, sociolinguistics, and discourse competence. In addition, while learners may not master all of these aspects of language at any one time, they may nevertheless have the ability to speak, listen, read, and write. Though there is a reduction and simplification of what needs to be learned, we can still imagine how complex the learning process will be when learning those aspects at the same time. In spite of the fact that learning a second language happens in social contexts (such as a country, a company, or a classroom), the actual acquisition happens in the mind or brain. Indeed, the mind is the place that governs the behaviour of learners and how they act on the linguistic data to which they are exposed.

The third "given" is that the processes involved in SLA are also complex. At least three sets of processes are involved in language acquisition, all of them going on at the same time. The first process is "input processing", which refers to how learners make sense of the language around them and how they pick up linguistic data (Vanpatten 2003). The second process is "system change", in which learners have to create a repeat perception which allows them to picture the linguistic data (either a grammatical form or a lexical item) every time they incorporate and establish a link between the received data and the already existing information. For example, during the time elicited data was collected for this study, an interesting phenomenon was found among one of the groups of junior middle school students. One third of the students produced exactly the same sentence when asked to write five sentences containing the word "when":

What are you doing <u>when</u> the UFO landed? (JED)

The rest of the students in the group were found to use either the same grammatical structure, only changing the content words or using the same content words. However, the topic was also the same:

```
What are you doing when I watch TV? (JED)
I am walking down the street when the UFO landed. (JED)
When the UFO is landed, the boy is shopping. (JED)
```

In this case, when asked to explain their answers, the students replied that they had been taught the structure recently and that the above examples had been given. It makes sense that learners actually incorporate a particular form in a new context by noticing the link to this original context remains. In other words, their understanding of the particular linguistic form interacts with the context in which it was learned and acts as a signal which triggers information about the learning context.

The fact that these different processes are all involved in language learning at the same time explains why SLA is such a complex system. It is complex because the learner's brain or mind is interacting with and manipulating various things at once. This can cause a 'ripple effect' where the actual acquisition changes the acquisition system and its parts in a dynamic process over time (Vanpatten 2003).

2.2.2 SLA is Dynamic

One of the main characteristics of a dynamic system is that it consists of a number of interacting subsystems. For example, a single language will always consist of a variety of dialects spoken by groups of people, and within the language system, there are subsystems such as phonetic and grammar systems. One type of subsystem is the language system of an individual, which can also be considered as a dynamic system in its own right.

Learners may find themselves experiencing a period of learning a language very rapidly, and then going through a period of not really improving. Sometimes, they may backslide a bit before improving again. Such phenomena suggest that learning a second language is a dynamic process which evolves over a period of time (Vanpatten 2003).

In SLA, the evolution of the system is documented as developmental stages. There are at least two stages and several sub-stages in which certain linguistic forms are acquired. The first refers to the stage on the way to accomplishing native-like ability with one particular linguistic form. Learners may go through several steps to acquire the correct form. For example, in acquiring the interrogative form, learners produce sentences such as follows:

```
what you do?
What you doing?
What are you doing?
```

The second refers to the stage which involves the correct use of one linguistic form whilst incorporating another linguistic form at the same time, for instance:

```
What you do when I cook dinner?
What you doing when I cook dinner?
What are you doing when I cook dinner?
```

As can be seen, within each stage the correct use of form evolves through certain sub-stages. Vanpatten (2003: 16) suggests that learners may go through four stages to acquire negation: 1) in the first stage, learners may simply place *no* in front of what needs to be negated, e.g., *no drink beer, no bike, no have car*; 2) the second stage involves using the complete sentence structure, but the negation *no* is placed internally instead of in front, e.g., I no drink beer, He no has bike, we no have car; 3) the third stage is the incorporation of *don't* and sometimes *can't*, but simply replacing the negation *no* from the previous stage, e.g., *I don't drink beer, He don't/can't has bike*, etc; 4) the final stage involves the acquisition of auxiliaries (which means learners acquire the knowledge *do* as a functioning auxiliary), and the correct placement of negation, e.g., *I don't (do not) drink beer, He doesn't (does not) have a bike*.

Despite Vanpatten's claim that there are certain stages to complete the acquisition of the linguistic forms, it will not always be the case that acquisition is a straight and linear process. Stages are not neat and we should not expect learners to pass through the stages like walking through different doors. Rather, learners may go back and forth because one of the stages is not acquired accurately or learners on stage 3 of acquiring a linguistic structure will have vestiges of stage 2, and also show signs of stage 4 emerging (Vanpatten 2003).

So far we have considered that there is a language system in every individual learner which changes and evolves through sets of stages and sub-stages. Within each stage, the system and its components are chaotic and complex, but self-organised in their own way. The changes not only occur in L2 but also exist in L1. According to De Bot, Lowie and Verspoor (2007), if a language learner's knowledge is part of one dynamic system, then we would expect the two languages to interact. At the beginning of learning L2, changes in the L1 may hardly be noticed, but the changes of L2 can be dramatic. Later on, the learners' L2 may stabilise and the changes may be less noticeable. There will also be an effect on the L1.

Looking at SLA as a complex and dynamic system suggests that individual learners, the interlanguage which exists in each learner, and the learning process is part of the system, and that this system interacts with other systems to cause a consistent change over time. According to De Bot et al (2007), the change usually results from a complex interaction between internal and external factors.

2.2.3 SLA is Developing

Although there is a great deal of variation and change over time, the whole system and its subsystems vary in terms of their stability over time. Individuals and their language systems exhibit periods of stability which are called "attractor states" (De Bot et al 2007: 17). The relatively unstable periods which have profuse internal variation are normally a sign that the system is changing; while a period with little internal variation is a sign that the system is relatively stable (ibid). In such a case, only strong external factors will change the status of the system to any extent.

In SLA, external input refers to the language that a learner hears or reads. In other words, it is an intermediary environment that has some kind of communicative intent for learners (Vanpatten 2003). By communicative intent, we mean there is a message that learners are supposed to receive, comprehend, and give feedback on. Such a process occurs in learners' minds as learner is consciously trying to comprehend what they read and hear in the L2. In other words, the individual learner's cognitive system responds to the process of comprehension. The more thorough comprehension a learner experiences, the more efficient acquisition becomes. Thus, there seems to be a correlation between acquisition and how successfully learners comprehend the linguistic information around them.

Also, it is important to point out that second language development is dynamic through many variables, and that a wide range of variables exists in both external input and the internal cognitive system, which continuously affects language acquisition over time. Any types of variables in any context may have different effects. Thus, it is difficult to list all the variables which affect the acquisition process. In spite of the reservations, I will focus on three variables (individual learners, their interlanguage system, and the learning process) which also contain a number of sub-variables in themselves.

Individual learners can be understood as the main conductor in the language acquisition process. Without understanding their roles and behaviours in language acquisition, it is meaningless for researchers to study how a language is acquired. Individual learners, on the other hand, are a complex and dynamic system, with a number of interacting variables such as their wish to learn the language, their cognitive abilities and previous experience, interaction with teachers and other classmates, and so on.

In the following sections, I focus on the two variables (individual learners and the learning process) which interact with the second language acquisition as a whole, including coming to an understanding of how they are a complex and dynamic system in their own right, as well as how they contribute to the entire development of the language system.

2.3 Understanding The Language Learners: Start With The Problem

Research has shown that that the mental processing of the internal structure of sentences by learners is affected by many performance factors during real time production (Lyons 1996). Despite this finding, in most research on the development of language, the internal structure of processing events is ignored, which may be due to a belief that "comprehension is measured at the end of an utterance, rather than as it is being heard" (Tyler and Marslen-Wilson 1981: 400). However, it is important to focus on mental processing, as the ability to process the internal structure of sentences influences to a large extent the development of language use in learners' minds as their proficiency increases.

Usually, learners possess more language knowledge than they actually produce, so language production is not a perfect indicator for evaluating their language knowledge. Thus, we cannot know accurately how language is acquired or organised in the mind or brain. On the other hand, rather than being satisfied with the belief that learners' real knowledge is simply 'beyond their performance', we can at least investigate the ways in which the learners organise the L2 grammar structure and linguistic forms when they produce sentences in the target language.

This section focuses on studies that have explored learners' ability to process the internal structure of sentences involved in real-time production tasks. In the following sections three different levels of internal structure processing are discussed relating to my own research: 1) how learners organise linguistic forms (such as grammar and lexicon) during sentence production and comprehension; 2) in what way learners access the grammatical-lexical structure during sentence production and comprehension; 3) how knowledge of language is organised and represented in learners' minds.

2.3.1 How Learners Organise Linguistic Forms During Sentence Production

In this section, we consider how learners organise lexical information during sentence production. Generally, the production of sentences takes place in three distinct stages: conceptual build up, selection of sets of lexical items and grammatical structure encoding.

According to Levelt's (1993) model of speech production, the starting point of sentence production is to build up concepts which express a proposed message that learners intend to convey. These messages contain a number of conceptual units which can be developed by the selection of sets of lexical items. Such lexical items can be a single word (*bag*), a compound word (*school bag*), a fixed expression (*go to sleep*), or idiom (*where there is a will, there is a way*). Once these lexical items have been selected, the speaker organises them in an appropriate sequence to produce well-formed grammatical sentences.

In the study described in this study, one of the things that respondents are asked to do is produce sentences in response to a single word prompt. When they are asked to do this the language production process may be slightly different from what Levelt describes above. Learners may first think of the meaning and possible contexts in which they would use these lexical items. For instance, when learners are asked to write five sentences containing the word "*what*", they may think of the meaning of "*what*" as being simply that of a question word. Then, the context of using the word "what" may be considered to be a person's background (*name, like, dislike, character, career* etc.) or the desire to figure out something (*what happened*). When the context is considered, certain lexical items are likely to be selected in learners' minds and combined in well-formed sentences, for example:

```
What is your name?
What did you do last night?
What are you doing?
What happened?
```

It has been argued that concept development is most likely to be language-independent, referring to the fact that learners can have an almost universal concept framework in mind without knowing more than one language. Selection of lexical items is considered as semi language independent because it contains information about grammar. Hunston (1996) suggests that grammatical structure is heavily dependent on the organization of meaning as a whole. She explains that each lexical item associates with and forms its grammatical patterns, and that each grammatical pattern closely occurs within a restricted set of lexical items. Both are mutually dependent (Hunston 1996). There is a belief that learners attempt to progress their language by attending to contextual usage rather than by analysing the language word by word (Williams 2001). As we will see from my research data, learners not only produce many sentences containing fixed expressions and memorize them after several years.

So far we have considered how the three stages of sentence production, processing and lexicon selection play an essential role in the language production process. We have seen that both grammatical information and language-related information are involved. According to Cook (2002), though the sentence production processing model can be applied to both monolinguals (learners having one language knowledge) and multilinguals (learners having more than one language knowledge), the sentences that produced by multilingual learners may be complex and take longer because it develops its own distinctive way of accessing grammar structures and lexical items.

2.3.2 How Learners Access Lexico-Grammatical Knowledge During Sentence Production And Comprehension

In order to understand how learners gain access to lexico-grammatical knowledge during L2 production and comprehension it is important to look at how the bilingual mental lexicon is structured.

Research suggests a high degree of connection between the L1 and L2 mental lexicons. Cook (1997) recognizes the "intricate links between the two language systems in multicompetence" and notes that "total separation is impossible since both languages are in the same mind", although he does acknowledge, "total integration is impossible since L2 users can keep the languages apart". Singleton (1999), however, argues that Cook does not go far enough with regard to the degree and types of interconnection between the two languages. In fact, learners may even combine both languages in a single system. In recent brain–imaging research, the area called "cerebral cortex" has been found to help individuals make sense of processing lexical-semantic aspects whatever the language (ibid). This again suggests a very close connection between lexical operations relating to both the L1 and the L2, although the question remains whether both languages draw on a common system when individuals process lexical-semantic structures.

From the DST perspective, learners' L1 and L2 mental lexicons interact dynamically (Singleton 1999; Herdina and Jessner 2001) and co-exist in the same mind. Kirsner (1993: 228) suggests that "L2 vocabulary is represented and stored as variants of the L1 vocabulary at the formal level of integration". Recent research shows that people who are able to speak more than one language tend to have more advanced cognitive abilities than those who are able to speak only one language (Vanpanten 2003).

De Bot (1992, 2005: 42) describes three types of lexical representation in the mind by using the following metaphors: the spatial metaphor, in which each language has a separate lexicon and learners tend to build links between two or even more languages; the connectionist metaphor, in which words exist within the same network and are equally available to language learners; and the activation metaphor, in which the words activate knowledge by spreading through a network. He suggests that the third metaphor is probably the most appropriate way to represent lexicons in the mind. In addition, other research shows that the former two metaphors are associated with low proficiency and the third metaphor with higher proficiency (Jiang 2000).

Apart from the influence of the L1 lexicon, another important factor influencing the L2 lexical organisation is frequency of exposure. According to Ellis (2002), the recognition and production of words is a function of their frequency of occurrence in the language to which the learners are exposed.

When students are asked to read in the target language, high frequency words are reacted to faster and more accurately than low frequency words in a learner's working memory (Forster 1976, 1985, and Barry and Seymour 1988). It has also been suggested that there are significant word frequency effects on the speed and accuracy of the lexical recognition processes and the lexical production processes in children and adults, both in the L1 and the L2 (Kirsner 1994).

So far we have considered how learners access L2 lexis. In the following section I discuss how syntactic structures are organised during sentence production and comprehension.

First of all, learners organise the structure by clarifying the meanings from the lexicon. Consider you are given the word "where" and asked to write sentences containing it. Basically there are two choices: one is a question utterance which refers to finding a location and another is a subordinate clause which describes a location. For instance,

```
Where do you come from? (JED)
It is that shop where you can buy those beautiful flowers
for your mother. (UED)
Where you go? (UED)
```

When learners encounter a word, they must determine what kind of form will come next. Vanpatten (2003: 35) uses "parsing" to refer to the process where learners literally project the syntax structure of the sentence during the time of determination and hope the expectations are satisfied.

There are two different ways of parsing: The first is filling the gap. When you read the sentence *where you go/going*, you know what is missing after *where* is the verb *did* or *are*. Sometimes, English doesn't need a verb in that position and the verb can be omitted. You do not have to produce a sentence such as *where did you go? or where are you going?* The gap which refers to the omitted words is called an empty category. Vanpatten (2003: 35) points out that although language is full of empty categories, there might be fewer problems in sentence comprehension because parsers are built to handle them. In addition, learners process content words before grammatical forms if they carry the same semantic information, so when you see the word "where", you have the premessage in mind that it is about a place or location because the word itself contains such information. Then, during the processing, you may skip over the grammatical forms if they carry the same meaning. According to Ortega (2009), learners comprehend sentences without processing the complete sentence. Most of the time, learners comprehend sentences relying on the content words which provide knowledge of the world, "contextual clues, and guessing" (Ortega 2009: 62).

The second way of parsing is to figure out "who did what to whom" (Vanpatten 2003). This kind of parsing is dependent on word order. For certain aspects of language, the syntactic structures are universal, though they are expressed in a variety of ways. All languages have structures for making statements and asking questions and sentences in all languages consist of a subject and a predicate and predicates consist of a verb, or a verb and one or more objects, plus other possible phrases expressing something like time, place, frequency, manner, goal, source, or purpose (Saville-Troike 2006). The order and degree of flexibility of syntactic elements is different across languages. As shown below, S refers to subject, O refers to object, and V refers to verb (ibid). For example:

```
SVO: English, Chinese, French
SOV: Japanese, Finnish, Turkish
VSO: Irish, Welsh, Samoan
```

In general, languages have their own word order to express the same concept and L2 learners tend to use first-noun strategy in which they interpret the "first noun or noun phrase in the utterance as the subject of the sentence" (Vanpatten 2003: 36). For instance, when interpreting the sentence *It is that shop where you can buy those beautiful flowers for your mother,* learners tend to rely on the noun *shop* and then follow the order of subject (you)-verb (buy)-object (those beautiful flowers).

However, there are several problems with the first-noun strategy; for example, it delays the acquisition of case marking, pronouns, and structures which do not follow the expected order. Learners simply skip over those grammatical forms as they seem able to comprehend the sentences without knowing them. In many cases, learners tend to process the beginnings of sentences best, followed by the ends of sentences. The middle of a sentence is normally the most ambiguous place to process grammatical form. For example, let us look at the following sentence produced by a Chinese learner of English:

The hospital is at the next corner whose top is white. (UED)

Here the learner is talking about a hospital with a white roof, but what they end up saying is that that 'top of the corner' is white. Their problem lies in the fact that they are trying (unsuccessfully) to use a subordinate clause to add extra information.

The first-noun strategy can be understood as a consequence of self-organising in the cognition of learners. It suggests that the language system is chaotic and that it attempts to be self-organising to make things clear in the minds of the learners. Thus, the language system is developing from chaos towards a self-organising system. In the next section, I discuss how languages are organised and represented in learners' minds.

2.3.3 How Knowledge Of Language Is Organised And Represented In Learners' Minds

We know little about how the organization of knowledge in the brain might be related to the level of proficiency in a second language, but there is a belief that the organization of L2 knowledge is more diffuse for lower levels of proficiency and more compact for highly fluent L2 users (Saville-Troike 2006). In addition, the increasing proficiency of language knowledge involves a process from controlled processing to automatic processing.

Skehan (1998) argues that learners at the beginning level tend to produce prefabricated patterns in which they hear whole sentences as entire chunks. For example:

```
How do you do you? (JED)
How are you? (JED)
What time is it? (JED)
```

A multilingual learner at the beginning stage may use more memorization for their L2 and more direct meaning perception for their L1 (Skehan, 1998). Learners rely on meaning more than memory as their proficiency level increases. Learners at higher levels seem to pay attention to meaningful content or creative processing, for example:

```
Why do you always late to school? (SED)
when I realise that I'm wrong she was already gone. (UED)
```

Increasing proficiency of language knowledge also involves a process from controlled to automatic processing. Controlled processing refers to the activities of non-linguistic cognitive capacity. Learning a language initially demands considerable mental space and much attention and effort (Saville-Troike 2006). Ellis (2006) suggests that learning one's L1 involves rational contingency language processing, and that a learner's unconscious language representation systems are optimally prepared for comprehension and production. However, second language learning is less likely to involve rational contingency learning because it needs to be learned with great attention. Thus, the non-linguistic cognitive capacities play an important role during language acquisition. Tyler and Wilson (1981) point out that selection, inhibition, cognitive control, executive functions, resource allocation and memory are the main factors that influence language performance. Ellis (2006: 164) suggests seven factors: contingency, cue competition, salience, interference, overshadowing, blocking, and perceptual learning which affect second language acquisition, and many of these factors are shaped by the L1.

Such non-linguistic cognitive capacities seem to operate when we are beginning to learn a second language. For example, we consciously memorise lists of vocabulary or focus our attention on comprehending certain structures. This is because learning a new language involves learning different linguistic components. It is never easy for someone who has developed a linguistic knowledge beforehand. Most of the time, learners use control processing to select an appropriate way to understand either lexicon or structures and apply them.

It is almost impossible simultaneously to notice complex structure and create meaningful content. It is only after the basic vocabulary and syntactic structures have become automatic, that learners may acquire more complex and higher-order features and content through more practiced tasks need to involve attentional control to become automatic (Saville-Troike 2006: 74).

However, not all controlled processes can be changed to automatic processes. According to Saville Troike (2006), behaviour under attentional control is permeable, but once it becomes automatic, it is difficult to change. When learners store the memorised chunks of language automatically, high proficiency levels do not necessarily mean that they will always produce more complex sentences. In my research data, sentences such as *What's your name? How are you? What time is it? Where are you?* also occur in a large proportion for students at senior high school and university.

In fact, one of the explanations of L2 fossilization is that certain aspects of the L2 might become automatic before they reach the target level. In such cases, a combination of both external input and internal self-organisation is required to change the situation.

2.4 *Understanding The Learning Process*

As we have seen, learning a language involves moving from a controlled process to an automatic process. One way of seeing this distinction is to view the controlled process as being rule-governed, whereas the automatic process is more intuitive. In addition, according to McLaughlin (1990: 6), the distinction between a controlled process and an automatic process "relates to the degree to which the skills in question have been routinized and established in long-term memory". The skills involved in language acquisition contribute to both explicit knowledge and implicit knowledge.

2.4.1 Learning Involves Contributions From Both Implicit And Explicit Language Systems

Similar to learning a first language, learning a second language involves creating an implicit language system. By an implicit language system, we mean that the system exists outside of consciousness. When we use our first language, we can speak or hear it without thinking about it. This allows us, for example, to read newspapers or magazines while turning on the radio or TV. It is easy to understand what we read and hear without paying much attention. In addition, the whole process does not involve judgments about the structure, vocabulary and so forth. In the above cases, we are using an implicit linguistic system.

L2 learners construct similar implicit linguistic systems during their language acquisition process. However, this does not mean that they create the same implicit system as they do in their native language. In some cases, creating an implicit L2 system requires a great deal of time. In the early stages it is based heavily on explicit knowledge. This explicit knowledge is rule-based usage and is either taught explicitly in school or through textbooks. After repeated practice the rules start to become embedded in the learners' implicit systems that exist outside their awareness; they know them but they cannot always verbalize them. For example, when learners are asked "what are you up to?" they might respond immediately "nothing much" without knowing why they chose that particular structure.

In most L2 teaching situations, as we can imagine, many learners have experienced language learning under explicit conditions, where they are taught to learn grammatical rules, to memorize lists of words and to do intensive practice. These are the ways in which language learners gain access to linguistic knowledge, by responding to explicit learning. For instance, if individual learners want to learn some rules and are able to use these rules in appropriate contexts, then explicit learning of these rules may be unavoidable during their learning processes. Also, such learning can be seen as a type of controlled process of building knowledge and practicing skills. However, the connection between explicit and implicit knowledge is still not clear and researchers are unsure as to whether or how explicit knowledge can actually become implicit knowledge. According to recent neurolinguistic evidence, there is some kind of connection between implicit and explicit learning, although each of them has their own distinct roles (De Bot et al 2007). Explicit knowledge only plays a supporting or ancillary role in the fact that learners are aware of linguistic rules as a result of explicit learning, and such knowledge-driven instruction leads to understanding and producing language (VanPatten 2003).

We cannot automatically assume that explicit knowledge will always turn into implicit knowledge. However, due to the fact that both explicit and implicit knowledge exist in one mind, it is hard to say whether the sentences learners produce are based on explicit or implicit knowledge. This issue is heavily based on whether the learners have the ability to report their knowledge accurately or on their intent to use particular strategies (McLaughlin 1990). However, there is a major problem with such self-reporting in that it is based on "retrospect" (McLaughlin 1990: 629). Learners' reporting is more likely to derive from "what they think they have been doing than from what they actually were doing" (ibid). In addition, learners are the ones who control the use of both types of knowledge during their learning processes. Their access to such knowledge may vary according to their age, intellectual level, and their meta-cognitive abilities.

Hence, a less radical view can be proposed that with practice, explicit knowledge can facilitate language acquisition which helps the learning from the controlled processes become more automatic. Another consensus about the contribution of explicit knowledge and implicit knowledge to acquisition is that both of them help learners to manipulate the input which allows them to acquire the knowledge eventually.

Playing a supporting and facilitative role, explicit knowledge might help learners to process input better. Explicit teaching with examples may help learners to work out for themselves how the linguistic rules are organized and understood and learners may be more inclined to pay attention as they process input subsequently. Moreover, explicit knowledge may also direct learners' attention to certain things in the input that they have missed and thus is beneficial to learners' entire linguistic knowledge.

The implicit system, as we have seen earlier, is built up via "exposure to and processing of linguistic input and the subsequent accommodation of formal features that were attended to in that input" (Vanpatten 2003: 58-59). De Bot et al (2005) suggest that the implicit learning system incorporates new information according to its own method which is neither from inspection nor manipulation.

All in all, the implicit system develops in parallel to the explicit system, and both systems are beneficial to the learning process while linguistic input is needed, although it is not clear how the two systems influence each other. In the following sections, the role of input in SLA is discussed from both a historical and more updated viewpoint.

2.4.2 The Role Of Input In SLA

The central role of input in SLA has been long established, although the concept of input is still controversial (Ellis 1994, and Brown 1994). Gass (1997) defines input as raw primary L2 data that reaches the non-native audience's perceptual system, that is, the second language which is noticed by L2 learners. It is considered to be one of the crucial factors in the language acquisition process as it refers to the sample of the L2 that is decoded by non-native speakers of the meanings communicated by the native speakers (Nizegorodcew 2007). SLA theories assume the importance of input, considering L2 input as one of the crucial factors in language acquisition.

In the following section, four models of input in the L2 acquisition process are discussed with reference to both historical and more up-to-date perspectives. From a former historical perspective, input is much more strongly associated with comprehension as it is considered that comprehensible input is "necessary and sufficient". According to this perspective, the process of L2 comprehension can be understood as one in which learners simply 'decode' the language to which they are exposed (Schmidt 1983). According to more recent perspectives, the latter updated view, input is more concerned with interaction and negotiation and less narrowly focused on form-meaning acquisition.

Much discussion of the role of input in SLA took place in the early 1980s. Krashen (1985: 2) in his input hypostudy claimed that a second language is acquired "by understanding messages, or by receiving comprehensible input". He defined "comprehensible input" as language that is heard or read and that is slightly higher than a learner's recent proficiency level. Furthermore, the comprehensible input can be acquired accompanying the learners' positive attitude towards L2 learning. Thus, according to Krashen, L2 acquisition occurs automatically when "communication and comprehension are successful". However, McLaughlin (1987) argued that the input hypostudy is too vague due to, the fact that it is hard to define the levels of knowledge which allow learners to acquire it.

In addition, Krashen's idea that 'extralinguistic information' can help with the acquisition is also vague. Gregg (1984) questioned claims such as it may be possible for people to understand something beyond their grammatical knowledge, when how it can be translated into grammatical acquisition remains unclear. He found it difficult to imagine extra-linguistic information that would enable one to acquire "the third person singular-s or yes/no questions, or indirect object placement, or passivization" (Gregg 1984: 88).

Krashen's model attempted to show providing more comprehension brings about successful acquisition, although researchers had noted that comprehension and acquisition are two distinct processes (Doughty 1991, and Loschky 1994).

In the early 1980s, with the popularity of naturalistic learning, the discussion of the role of input had shifted its emphasis from comprehension to interaction and negotiation.

Long (1983) first proposed the Interaction Hypostudy (IH) which claims that input provided by a native speaker is adjusted in an interaction by non-native speakers in order to become comprehensible. He also identified several types of techniques that non-native speakers applied in their adjustment, such as "confirmation checks, clarification requests and comprehensible checks" (Long 1985: 388). Critics of Long's IH pointed out that the relationship between adjustment, comprehension, and acquisition is inaccurate. Ellis (1994) argues that if adjustment results in comprehension, and comprehension results in acquisition, then adjustment should result in acquisition. However, there is not enough evidence to support such a claim. Long (1996) modifies his claim to reflect that in certain aspects of L2 learning interaction, feedback or errors received from native speaker interlocutors during conversation contribute to L2 development.

However, in the mid-1980s, naturalistic exposure to the target language failed to result in successful acquisition, in particular grammar acquisition. Therefore, scholars began to take more of a bottom-up view. They began to appreciate that learners not only comprehend and negotiate the language input via interaction, but also in the process of producing the language, which is known as output.

Swain (1985) argued that large quantities of input alone hardly make non-native speakers achieve native-like competence in spoken language; rather, she emphasized that "comprehensible output" is an essential key for successful acquisition as learners tend to create accurate and appropriate messages while they speak (Swain 1985: 251). She proposed three functions of output in L2 learning: the noticing function, the hypostudy testing function and the metalinguistic function. She argued that L2 learners attempt to notice the gap in their knowledge between themselves and the native speakers, and then learners utilize the output as an input for their conscious learning, thus consequently contributing to their acquisition. However, Nizegorodcew (2007) points out that it is difficult to know when learners notice the gaps in their knowledge, and how they correct themselves during oral conversation. In addition, language production has little effect on accuracy (Vanpatten 2003).

Yet an emphasis on output has led to a reevaluation of the role of production in acquisition-related processes. More recent research has employed a combination of psycholinguistic and cognitive approaches focusing on the role of learners' internal abilities in language acquisition.

Gass (1997) in a more integrated model argues that the input available for learners does not automatically become integrated into their own language system. Rather, L2 input should be first interacted with so that it can be noticed by internal mechanisms which exist in each individual learner. According to Gass (1997: 6), the raw L2 data is filtered into the internal mechanism which is called "apperception" in order to become apperceived input. Therefore, the input for learners needs to be "comprehended rather than comprehensible" because the degree of noticing from learners is based on how much information they understand (ibid). More importantly, learners build some kind of connection between the remaining knowledge and the noticed input. Gass's model combines Universal Grammar with cognitive approaches to L2 learning.

Gass's model emphasized the attention of L2 input in immediate meaning communication, in the early 1990s. An attempt of understanding how input made sense for form-meaning acquisition had been made.

Ellis (1990) suggests two specific types of classroom input which attempt to integrate various aspects and stages of the process of L2 acquisition. He points to the importance of instructed input in the L2 classroom. Two kinds of instruction (meaning-focused and form-focused) have been considered as transformers of L2 input and as acceptable ways to acquisition processing. As he states, "meaning-focused instruction is likely to afford the learners an opportunity to listen to and to perform a greater range of linguistic functions than form-focused instruction and also with regard to the kind of response it typically evokes in the learners" (Ellis 1990: 188). Additionally, form-focused instruction encourages the learner to reflect on the formal features of the language, while meaning-focused instruction encourages semantic processing (ibid). The best way of absorbing instructed input is to combine both meaning-focused and form-focused instruction. Hence, language teachers should draw learners' attention to both complex natural meaning communications and to specific linguistic features as needed in a particular situation. Ellis's model emphasizes the role of learners in access to

L2 input. According to Ellis, learners explicitly and consciously learn about the language knowledge via form-focused instruction which can only "sensitize the learner to the existence of non-standard form in her interlanguage and thus facilitates the acquisition of target language forms" (Ellis 1990: 195). However, the implicit subconscious knowledge which is largely derived from meaning-focused instruction is responsible for spontaneous L2 use. This view seems less radical than Krashen's because Ellis acknowledges that form-focused teaching can somehow help L2 acquisition.

Although the role of input is emphasized in L2 acquisition, the available input is not always automatically processed and integrated into the learners' system. Instead, learners need to pay attention or be aware of the input in order for it to be turned into intake. Then the question of how the focus on meaning or focus on form input can be taken into account for its accessibility to learners should be considered (Nizegorodcew 2007). Schmidt (1990) proposes a Noticing Hypostudy according to which input can only be noticed if it is salient enough and if it occurs frequently enough. In the L2 classroom this can be done through both teaching approaches and textbooks. A more detailed discussion is provided in Chapter four.

2.4.3 Instructed Classroom Input: A Shift From Meaning-Focused And Form-Focused Input

According to Swain (1985: 249), meaning-focused processing emphasizes the fluency of spontaneous communication and learners always focus first on meaning. However, output "may force the learner to move from semantic processing to syntactic processing" (Vanpatten 2003). Moreover, it is pointed out that during the time that learners focus on meaning, their attention must also be simultaneously focused on relevant forms (Gass 1997). Thus, it is fairly safe to say that focusing only on meaning is generally not enough to serve the purpose of understanding the complex syntax of the language. For example, in the L2 classroom, learners may experience a large amount of comprehensible or comprehended input, though they may still not be able to reach native-like competence. Vanpatten (1996) also suggests that input processing for meaning precedes processing for form.

The above suggestion leads to a shift of interest from meaning-focused to form-focused instruction because L2 language forms as they are learned and /or acquired can be placed in communicative L2 classroom contexts (Doughty and Williams 1998).

As we saw above, Long (1991a) proposed two kinds of form-focused instruction: focus-on-forms (FonFs) and focus-on-form (FonF). The FonFs involves the pre-selection of specific features based on a linguistic syllabus and the intensive and systematic treatment of those features (Ellis, Basturkmen and Loewen 2002). Here, we can see the aim of FonFs is primarily focused on the target form and those forms are predetermined and present in the textbook. The principle of FonFs underlies approaches to language teaching that can be broadly defined as 'PPP' (presentation, practice and production) as this involves explicit grammar instruction.

On the other hand, FonF is focused on meaning and the attention of form arises out of meaning-centred activity driven by communicative tasks or activities (Long 1991 cited in Doughty 2001). The principle of Fonf can be applied to language teaching that is generally defined as 'Task-based learning'

(TBL) as learners may be asked to complete a task and during that time their attention is drawn to one or more linguistic forms which are needed to complete the task or perform the activity.

It should be mentioned that FonF is much commented on these days, especially some techniques (e.g. Consciousness-raising and input-enhancement) which aim to help learners to 'notice' the forms and integrate them into their own language system. In addition, focus on meaning and focus on form are not two distinct processes. Rather, such processes may continuously be changing as long as learners' needs and levels change, for example, from fully focused on meaning to fully focused on form or more or less focused on either meaning or on form (Nizegorodcew 2007).

Doughty (2001: 249) points out that classroom teachers could intervene by helping learners to focus on form while they are in the process of focusing on meaning. However, the question is when and how teachers can judge whether the time is right for each. Most of the time, teachers feel frustrated when trying to decide when to shift focus from meaning to form in the classroom because the textbooks have already made that decision for them (Nizegorodcew 2007).

2.4.4 Textbooks As A Form Of Input

According to Nizegorodcew (2007: 13), L2 classroom input refers to the language "intentionally presented to the learners by the teacher or other learners in order to facilitate the process of L2 learning". Textbooks, therefore, can be considered an important form of input in the instructed classroom either as they serve as the essence of classroom activities, as the motivation for study, or as the guide or manual for learning the target language. In the following section, we turn to the four ways in which textbooks operate as a form of input and contribute to L2 acquisition.

First of all, textbooks provide the L2 environment which at least makes the linguistic input accessible for learners. In most L2 classrooms, the linguistic environment for L2 learning is artificial. Some learners rarely use L2 communication outside the classroom. In addition, not every L2 classroom has foreign teachers and it is common to use the first language (L1) in the L2 classroom. Nevertheless, teachers and learners can still feel that they are in the atmosphere of learning the L2 because general functional social activities, e.g. travelling or shopping are provided in the textbook as well as the linguistic features, such as grammar and vocabulary. Thus, textbooks attempt to set up an environment for L2 learning and at least provide a solid foundation for the linguistic input.

Secondly, textbooks as a form of input provide convenient L2 resources for both teachers and students. Thus, textbooks contain direct information for both teachers and learners to process. According to Tomlinson (2001:66), textbooks are only one of the materials which can be used to facilitate the learning of a language; however, these are an essential resource specifically designed for language teaching and learning. In the L2 classroom, a lesson is organized based on the contents of textbooks, whether teachers want the learners to focus their attention on particular grammatical structures or communication activities. In addition, textbooks are generally organized to integrate with learners' acquisition processing. Although modern textbooks still mainly focus on grammatical items, other categories such as functional, situational, skills based, and topic based may also appear. For instance, a textbook may contain lists of grammatical structures as its main theme, with lessons organized around these structures, or a textbook may be organized by several topics which are selected articles from a local newspaper. Such variation provides abundant resources for L2 learners, not only by showing how language is taught in a particular context, namely the classroom, but also how language is actually used in authentic contexts.

Thirdly, textbooks as a form of input provide an opportunity for learners to self-adjust through their own strategies and consequently progress their language acquisition. According to Tomlinson (2001), language learning strategies are techniques that individuals use to help them to learn L2 material and improve their skill. Many L2 learners use textbooks for independent language learning outside the classroom which may have different effects on proficiency (ibid). For instance, some learners may prepare for the lesson before they actually learn it in the classroom and some prefer to revise the lesson after the class, both through textbooks. Such learning strategy helps to raise awareness of the contents learners will learn, as well as increasingly encouraging learners' own thinking about and understanding of the L2 learning process when they actually go through the contents. Thus, in this way textbooks may have great effectiveness in the development of learners' learning strategies and eventually contribute to the entire acquisition process.

Finally, textbooks help to build up the contextual knowledge which provides enough information to facilitate L2 processing. According to Nizegorodcew (2006), contextual knowledge refers to the learners' knowledge (both in L1 and L2) and their knowledge about the world, including their experiences of teaching and learning. Due to the fact that learning the L2 in most cases is less exposed to an authentic environment, learning in the classroom or through textbooks is an important channel for learners to acquire L2 knowledge. Such knowledge can be understood as general educational knowledge about the L2, as well as the linguistic level of lexico-grammatical knowledge and its usage.

While the function of textbooks is emphasized, there have been some criticisms of the types of the textbooks used. Some linguists (e.g. Carter 1998, Guariento and Morley 2001) note that textbooks should give precedence to the teaching of linguistic patterns and that the use of authentic materials causes frustration and confusion for low-level learners. On the other hand, Sutton and Cohen (1998: 37) claims that the sentences in textbooks are often isolated and have no context within authentic use and do not represent the way people use real language in real circumstances. Similar comments are made that "language is used for authentic communication" (Singelar 1992). In the following section, I discuss both the advantages and disadvantages of authentic and contrived textbooks.

2.4.5 Textbooks: Authentic Or Contrived?

With the acknowledgement that corpora can be used as source materials for L2 textbooks, corpus linguists argue that corpora can present lexical and grammatical patterns as they occur in real language and therefore allow learners to experience the authentic target language. Little (1997: 225) argues that "authentic texts have the capacity to draw language learners into the communicative world of the target language community and support the communicative purpose of language teaching". Biber et al (1994) note that the use of authentic language provides not only information concerning the frequency of occurrence of grammatical forms, but also reliable information of actual use.

However, problems also can be noted in that authentic language fails to give systematic precedence to teaching linguistic patterns, especially for low-level learners who may feel frustrated (Guariento and Morley 2001). Nation (2001:172) also emphasizes the importance of simplification, as he suggests that, "without the strands of meaning-focused input, meaning-focused output and fluency development become impossible for all except advanced learners".

Unlike authentic textbooks, language in contrived textbooks tends to be tidy and neat, or it aims to be more accessible for learners, more systematic and easier for teaching and learning. The language learners produce can often be traced back to the influence of textbooks. The contrived textbooks tend to be structured according to grammatical structures and contain a wide variation of multi-skills. In integrated grammatical syllabuses it is expected that learners will acquire the structure by systematic gradation which reduces the difficulties of language-learning by listing the target structure in understandable steps. In addition, such grading contrivance is considered as facilitating comprehension, especially for low level learners. However, there is an input question of how such formulated structures contained in textbooks can be processed by learners. According to Carroll (1999: 361), input for learning is a mental representation rather than "some part of the stimulus array" and feeds it into the learning mechanisms based on objective properties which make some aspects of the stimulus array salient". In other words, the acquisition processing of the sequenced grammatical structures is largely based on learners' cognitive mental representation and their comprehension, rather than the contrived structures shown in front of learners.

One of the failures of contrived textbooks is perhaps their failure to differentiate between written and spoken language. For example, from the way grammatical structures are organized in textbook dialogues, it is hard to see how spoken language uses features such as discourse markers. The following examples are chosen from textbooks and corpus which help to identify both benefits and shortcomings. Example 1 is taken from an EFL textbook, and Example 2 is taken from corpus data.

Example 1: Greeting (a dialogue in an English text book from an elementary school in China)

```
Jim: Good morning, Lei Liu.
Lei Liu: Good morning, Jim.
Jim: How are you?
Lei Liu: I am fine, thank you, and you?
Jim: I am fine too.
```

Example 2: Preparing for a party

```
C: Yean
[10 secs]
D: Didn't know you used boiling water
B: Pardon
D: Didn't know you used boiling water
B: Don't have to but it's erm…they reckon it's erm [inaudible]
… (Data of McCarthy and Carter 1995)
```

As can be seen from the above examples, it is clear that the interaction in example 1 is scripted without discourse markers (*well*, *you know*), and contains complete sentences. Although it is well-prepared for learners, there is an atmosphere of unreality. This is because in real life communication, people hardly ever produce sentences like this since conversation itself contains a great deal of overlap and interaction. In most cases (at least in the UK), people often say "morning" instead of "good morning", "you alright" instead of "how are you", and "cheers" or "Ta" instead of "thank you".

Learners in this situation may be confused about what constitutes 'correct' and 'standard' language. In addition, one popular concept about spoken language is that it is miswritten or it contains incorrect grammar forms. Their misapprehension may originate from people who 'study' their native language. In a native language teaching system, reading and writing always carry more weight than speaking. Nevertheless, it is still important to teach how people usually use the language. Otherwise, students might end up speaking like a book.

In the second example, one of the most important grammatical features is a "pervasive ellipsis", such as 'Didn't know you …' and 'Don't have to …' in which the subjects are omitted (McCarthy and Carter 1997). This phenomenon can be seen in real life communication. However, it may confuse the learners when they have only seen textbook English.

Given the differences between spoken and written grammar, it is reasonable to suggest that textbook writers should provide learners with varied choices of language use, which they can use freely both in real communication (both written and spoken) and in acquiring grammatical knowledge. In the following sections I discuss the differences between written and elicited data as well as the reasons for looking at each in this study.

2.4.6 Written and Elicited Language

Written language involves language production and involves 'productive skills'. An important aspect of building productive skills is the development of an awareness of "appropriacy". This involves a combination of the knowledge of the language system and knowledge of how to use language in the right circumstances (ibid: 13). For second language learners, the challenges here are enormous, the important thing being that written discourse, textbook language and elicited data are different, and each has its own underlying principles. Therefore in this study I will focus on these three types of language.

Written language

Written language refers to communication in its written form, more likely in the forms of reading and writing. It is the representation of a language by means of a writing system. Written Language requires specific rules and must be clearly taught. Many language teachers would agree that in terms of skills, producing a coherent, fluent, and thorough piece of writing is one of the most difficult tasks there is to do in language (Nunan, 1999).

There are two approaches involved in writing pedagogy, namely, product approach and process approach. The product-oriented approach focuses on the production of an entire piece of writing which is coherent and error free. It is often referred to as "reproductive language work" (Nunan 1991: 272). The focus is much more likely to be on the grammatical-lexical patterns. Learners may spend more time focusing on whether grammatical-lexical forms are used appropriately. It is important to focus on proficiency. A tenet of the product-oriented approach is that sentences are the building blocks of the discourse and that the discourse is created by fitting sentences together (ibid). This idea is not consistent with ideas in discourse analysis. Discourse analysis is a study of the relationship between language and the contexts in which it is used (McCarthy and Carter 2006). It is suggested that the choices of grammatical-lexical forms can often only be made after considering the discourse context within the sentence is to be placed (Nunan 1991, McCathy and Carter 2006). Sometimes the sentences that learners produce are grammatically-lexically error-free and yet it is difficult to understand the ideas that they are attempting to express.

In addition, it may be worth noting that writing involves a variety of skills ranging from physical skills, involving typing letters, to higher level skills such as knowledge of grammatical-lexical patterns. Existing writing systems fall into two groups: those that are based on meaning and those that are based on sounds (Cook 2001). Problems that arise in writing in a second language are more likely to occur because of the different writing system of the learners' first language, whether it is a meaning-based route, an alphabetic-based route, or a sound-based route. A study conducted by Chikamatsu (1996) shows that native speakers of English tend to use sound–based strategies during writing, while Chinese learners of English tend to use meaning-based strategies. This can lead to problems in the final 'product'.

The process-oriented approach to writing focuses on the steps involving in drafting and remoderating a piece of writing (Nunan 1991, Raimes 1993). This approach is evidenced by the study from White and Arndt (1991). They suggest that "writing is a complex cognitive process that requires sustained intellectual effort over a considerable period of time" (ibid: 273). They also suggest that a text involves six procedures, as Figure 2.1 indicates:

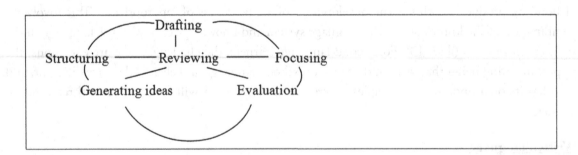

Figure 2.1 Procedures involved in producing a written text
White and Arndt (1991: 273)

Such a process-oriented approach is different in terms of the language teaching methods it involves and in terms of the teacher's role. In terms of language teaching methods, the above procedure can be elaborated by providing a sequence of activities, as White and Arndt (1991) outline:

1. Discussion
2. Brainstorming/making notes/asking questions
3. Fastwriting/selecting ideas/establishing a viewpoint
4. Rough draft
5. Preliminary self-evaluation
6. Arranging information/structuring the text
7. First draft
8. Group/peer evaluation and responding
9. Conference
10. Second draft
11. Self-evaluation/editing/proof-reading
12. Finished draft
13. Final responding to draft

(White and Arndt, 1991: 7)

Compared to the product-oriented approach, the process-oriented approach is designed to help learners to develop a particular set of skills. For example, learners can practise different types of structures in different modes of writing, particularly in areas of academic writing such as the writing of examination essays.

In this study, I look at how sentence types are used in learners' academic writing, with reference to three types of "wh" sentences: interrogative, declarative and subordinate clauses (which we refer to respectively as 'prototype', 'extension 1' and 'extension 2'). In addition, I investigate how learners manage to create the contexts with accordance to choose the correct linguistic forms. The focus is also on the functions performed by these different types of "wh" sentences within the paragraphs.

Elicited data

The study also involves elicited data. As we will see in subsequent chapters, informants are asked to produce five sentences containing each "wh" word. These sentences are then analysed, described, and explained. A description and analysis of elicited data that language learners produce is strongly associated with the two distinct and divergent styles of SLA research (Ellis 1990). One is the theory-then-research style and the other is the research-then-theory style (ibid). The former takes a strong theory as its starting point which is then tested by means of data collected from second language learners (Ellis 1990). Researchers applying this style have a specific hypostudy about learners' interlanguage constructions. Most of the time, research in this style is typically experimental and usually makes use of data elicited by means of tasks such as grammaticality judgement tests (ibid). In the latter style, the data sample is derived from naturally-occurring language use. The analysis mainly focuses on learners' production. Research in this style would provide more information than the theory-then-research style.

The purpose using elicited data in these two styles of research is reflected in different theories of language and different methodologies. The researchers in the different camps usually have very little to do with one other. Elicited data used in theory-then-research is normally designed to satisfy a particular aim. For example, in my study, I hypothesize that prototypes appear predominantly in learners' production of elicited data. Learners are then given tasks that are based on the hypostudy. On the other hand, elicited data used in research-then-theory addresses variation and contextual factors. For example, in my study, the written language from both native speakers and non-native speakers is analysed with reference to their variation and contextual features. Several issues are raised such as the fact that learners may have knowledge of how to construct sentences in accordance with the given tasks. Therefore, it might be difficult to identify whether a learner is using linguistic knowledge or pragmatic knowledge. Another concern in this study relates to whether the elicited data resembles written corpus data.

2.4.7 Learning Is An Outcome Of The Interaction Of External Input And Internal Cognition.

During the 1980s and 1990s, powerful cognitivist explanations of how L2 learning works were provided. According to Ellis (2009:103), L2 learning is built on "several nested assumptions that borrow from diverse contemporary schools in cognitive science". Larsen-Freeman (2006) also note as follows:

"Emergentists believe that simple learning mechanisms, operating in and across the human systems for perception, motor-action and cognition as they are exposed to language data as part of a communicatively-rich human social environment by an organism eager to exploit the functionality of language, suffice to drive the emergence of complex language representations."

(Ellis and Larsen-Freeman 2006: 577)

L2 learning either happens as learners form memories of instances or examples they experience from the external input (Ellis and Larsen-Freeman's associative learning), or when input is made noticeable, salient and also occurs frequently enough (Schmidt's noticing hypostudy). This all suggests that learning is an outcome of the interaction of external environment and internal cognition.

As discussed earlier, both the external input and textbooks as a form of input play an important part in L2 acquisition; however, only some input is accessible for further processing when particular perceptions such as attention or awareness are given attention. Schmidt (1990) maintains that second language learning occurs when learners are aware. This leads to a discussion of how the internal cognitive systems possess certain constraints that can change input to intake. In the following, the role of four cognitive capacities, perception, memory, attention and awareness, plus forgetting is addressed, with a discussion of how each processes and develops L2 language learning.

Perception

Perception, one of the mind's complex processes, can be understood as interpreting raw information according to its physical properties. According to Randall (2007), the brain receives information from different senses. People attempt to process input from the senses unconsciously and rapidly. Most of the time, we are unaware of actual physical properties of input. Perception is the result of an information processing system which is constantly interpreting incoming information according to previous experience, rather than simply making a photographic interpretation. It is a process whereby people receive physical information visually, and such information is sent back from "long term memory" which has built up through our previous experience. It is suggested that people perceive the world as meaningful concepts. In the L2 acquisition process, learners perceive linguistic data through certain sets of features which automatically appear to be supplied from long-time memory. In addition, such features are recalled more through conscious control, such as sentient noticing and awareness. For example, during the collection of elicited data, while I wrote the "wh" words on the blackboard, learners perceived the features from raw visual stimuli. Such stimulation allows learners to control and interpret the information which can be traced back to the previous knowledge of the "wh" words they have learnt.

Memory

According to cognitive psychologists and other researchers, memory plays an important role in SLA and a number of types of memory can be especially helpful to learners in L2 vocabulary knowledge.

There are three kinds of memory: working-memory, long-term, and permanent (see for example, Leaver et al (2005: 44). Working memory refers to the activity of "pulling together information stored for the purpose of processing information" (ibid). There are several ways that information can be transferred from working memory to long-term or permanent memory. One is through repetition and practice. It is a fact that most sentences are shown in a straight line from left to right, thus, people are more likely to repeat them from left to right and the words at the beginning attempt to stress as it can be sounded as natural as a string. Later on the study will look at the words immediately after "wh" words which are an important clue for learners recalling the information stored.

Terrell (1986) suggests that combining new information with old can be a short-cut from working memory to permanent memory. For example, cognates (words that are similar between two languages) are helpful for learners in learning a new language. English speakers may find it easier to remember French words than Chinese characters (*Student* in English, *Edudient* in French and 学生 *xuesheng* in Chinese). Similar sounds can build an association that can be made in order to improve memorization. For example, coffee in English is much more similar to café in French than ka fei in Chinese. For some languages, a collection of words with similar meanings also helps learners improve memory. For example, the words *show, indicate, demonstrate,* and *illustrate* share the same meaning in terms of action and facilitate understanding.

Long-term memory is about representation, with two different capacities being made: explicit-declarative memory and implicit-procedural memory (Ortega 2009). Much of knowledge encoded in long-term memory is explicit-declarative which is verbalizable and consciously recalled. In addition, such memory deals with the recognition of facts or events, such as what happened at a party one week ago (Randall 2007). On the other hand, unconscious knowledge is controlled by implicit-procedural memory. Such memory supports and develops skills or habit learning, e.g. learning to swim. There are two types of long-term memory: semantic and episodic memory. Semantic memory is considered to be an understanding of knowledge of facts, such as remembering content information or linguistic elements and their meanings, while episodic memory refers to knowledge of the events in which people are personally involved.

Permanent memory lasts forever, though it may become "latent and thus requires refreshing and activation when necessary" (Leaver et al 2005: 46). The knowledge stored in permanent memory may not be in use all the time, but it never really goes away. Generally, the more memory that is stored in permanent memory, the easier information can be recalled.

Working memory refers to a brain system that provides temporary storage and manipulation of the information necessary for the complex cognitive tasks as language comprehension, learning, and reasoning (Baddeley 1992). Working memory is important for L2 learning as Robinson describes it as a place "where skill development begins…and where the knowledge is encoded" (Robinson 1995: 304). Ortega (2009) notes that a good memory depends on memory strategies and body chemistry and both can be guided and improved by language learners. This may explain why some learners have a large capacity of vocabulary knowledge of L2 while some have not.

In most on-line production, we can trace the use of working memory. Leaver et al (2005: 47) believe that the use of working memory consists of up to four activities: recognition, recall, reconstruction or construction of information. For example, when learners are asked to write sentences containing the word *what*, the working memory may pull together the information they need, including the meaning of the word and the context of use. Most of the time learners produce sentences by recalling the information exactly as they experienced it previously, or by simple reconstruction of the new information with the information already stored in long-term memory. In such circumstances, learners may write the same sentences they learnt in previous studies or they may simply make up the new structures with the occasional addition of some new words.

Attention and awareness

According to Leaver et al (2005), attention and awareness are often referred to as sentient memory which is the first step in the process of storing information in memory and preparing it to be available for later use. Attention and awareness also play an essential role in information processing when input becomes intake. Schmidt (1990 cited in Saville Troike 2006: 75) lists six features that likely contribute to the degree of noticing or awareness, as shown below:

    a. Frequency of encounter with items
    b. Perceptual saliency of items
    c. Instructional strategies that can structure learner attention
    d. Individuals' processing ability (a component of aptitude)
    e. Readiness to notice particular items (related to hierarchies of complexity)
    f. Task demands, or the nature of the activity the learner is engaged in.

As Saville Troike (2006) points out, the above features or strategies highlight learners' attention and awareness of input. Attention has been a major thrust in instructed second or foreign language pedagogy which expects successful intake can occur. In addition, attention and awareness are an activation of stimulus which only lasts for a few seconds and then fades away. Here, attention and awareness, together with working memory, emphasize the activation level of input in working memory to allow them to stay long enough through repetition and practice and eventually make them available for further processing and become stored in permanent memory (Ortega 2009).

Research has shown that attention and awareness are important, but their roles are unclear. Schmidt (1995) suggests that traditionally attention and awareness refer to conscious learning. However, rather than "deliberate or intentional" learning, "incidental and unintended learning" can be very effective when some intended tasks are provided to focus attention on the target language (ibid). This raises the issue of unconscious language learning through conscious and well-prepared tasks.

Forgetting

Forgetting, as an essential component of cognition, has traditionally been ignored in research on SLA. In fact, forgetting is essential to good learning and the learning process. It is suggested that linguistic knowledge and language skills are not special if stored and retrieved in memory (De Bot et al 2007). In other words, information that is not retrieved regularly enough will become less accessible, which may ultimately cause it to disappear. According to DST, consistent change leads to development. The more frequently the language is used, the easier retrieval becomes. It also describes how people's L1 and L2 change over time, depending on the degree of exposure to those languages in different environments. When the target input learners receive is different from the environment they posses, learners tend to end up building mental representations about the language which has less target exposure, consequently causing forgetting. Forgetting is part of learning and a way of self-organizing. If we consider working-memory to have limited capacity, forgetting can thus be seen as a reconstruction process for a number of things that are redundant from the storage process.

We have considered several internal cognitive activities that play an important role during L2 acquisition process. These activities are involved in a wide variety of types of cognition, including language. This idea constitutes basic framework of Cognitive Linguistics (CL). In other words, CL is about the interrelationship between language, communication, and cognition.

In the following sections, I discuss one of the founding theories of CL, namely prototype theory. Some relevant issues such as where does prototype come from, traditional views and more up-to-date views of prototype, and the relationship between frequency and prototype are discussed separately.

2.5 Categorization and Prototype theory

It is well known that human beings are categorizing creatures and people categorize entities to reduce the complexity of the environment (Taylor 1995). Categorization is associated with many studies in the domains of philosophy, psychology, and linguistics. Cognitive Linguistics (CL) holds that human categorization is fundamental to language use and linguistic categorization. This belief tells us that the process of using language, along with their everyday experience of the world, makes humans categorize knowledge in different ways. It has been pointed out that the entities around human beings are complex and people hardly categorize them with clear cut-off points (Lakoff 1987). In other words, human categories vary between different people and for different concepts. For example, some people may think a *piano* is an instrument while others would prefer to regard it as a piece of furniture. Categorization is also important to language itself. Disregarding the fact that language itself is an object of categorization, linguistic terms can also be categorized into nouns, verbs, clauses, and so on.

Studies on categorization, particularly prototype theory, have primarily been concerned with how linguistic expressions are categorized, how they are acquired, and how they can be applied to language teaching and learning.

The best examples in the category are considered to be the prototypes. For example, the category 'fruit' has many members such as cherries, apples, watermelons and pears. If people are asked to write down three types of fruit, many would write apple, pear, and banana. This is not only because those fruits are the most frequently seen in daily life, but also because of their ordinary size and flavour, i.e. these fruits are not too big or too small and the taste is not too strong.

The early view of prototypicality: prototypes and the basic level

The theory of prototypes can be traced back to Aristotle, who developed the classical theory that suggested that all members of a category are equal, share a common essence, and exist within specific boundaries (Taylor 1995, 2002). An alternative theory was proposed by Wittgenstein which involves family resemblance. In this theory, he suggested that there are a number of overlapping and cross sets of similarities among members of a category. An object might also have features that cross over from one category to another. For example, piano belongs to the category musical instrument, also belongs to the category furniture.

The notion of prototypicality was proposed by Rosch on the basis of her work on categorization. She argued that categories have an internal structure in the sense that some members might be better or more representative examples of the category than other marginal members. For example, when people are asked to name a piece of furniture, many people will say *table, chair,* or *sofa,* as these three are the most representative members of the furniture category (Rosch, 1975, 1976, 1977). Such members are commonly known as prototypes. Both lexical and grammatical categories have prototypes. When people are asked to exemplify a lexical category such as noun, most people will answer with concrete nouns such as *book, chair,* but abstract nouns like *education* and *linguistics* rarely occur.

Prototypes often correspond to basic-level categories, and super-ordinate and subordinate categories both exist (see Figure 2.2). It was suggested that children tend to learn the basic level first, which is equivalent to the prototypical lexis, then the super-ordinate category level and finally, the subordinate extension level (Lakoff 1982). This organization is viewed as suitable for both our physical world and our social and intellectual life.

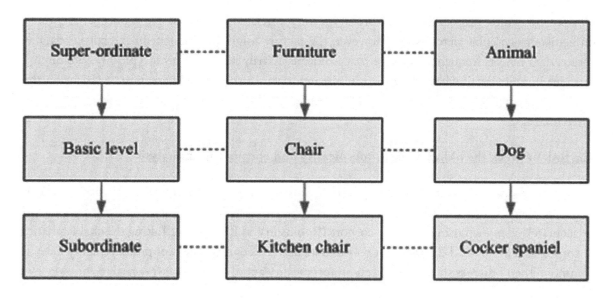

Figure 2.2 Levels of categorization

Where does prototypicality come from?

The notion of prototypicality is that a category comes to have more representative prototypical members, while others are marginal members. One may then ask the question: "Where do prototypes come from?" or "How do we define prototypicality?"

There are three possible answers to this question. First, Rosch (1975c) claims that prototypicality is "very plausibly a consequence of inherent properties of human perception". It is considered to be the human mental representation of physical objects which is pre-existent in human perception.

Another possible explanation based on Rosch proposes that prototypical members might possess more variable attributes of a category than any other members of the category. Certain attributes may result in salience and in turn such clusters of attributes form the status of prototypicality.

A further explanation is that members of a category achieve prototypical status because we encounter them more frequently than any other members of the category. It is a matter of relativity. For example, *table* and *chair* are considered as prototypical members of a category of FURNITURE while *piano* and *mirror* are less prototypical. The status of prototypicality is not a case of how frequently we encounter *table*, *chair*, *piano*, and *mirror* as single items. Instead, it might be the case that we encounter *table* and *chair* as a FURNITURE category more frequently than we encounter *piano* and *mirror* as a FURNITURE category. Frequency as a measurement of the status of prototypicality is used cautiously. Taylor (2003:56) emphasizes the idea that frequency might be a "symptom" of prototypicality rather than a "cause".

After considering the possible explanations of prototypicality, a question about the prototypicality status may rise. For example, prototypicality may be found predominantly in textbook data as prototypicality has a strong relation to textbook writers' intuition. Similar effects may be found in elicited data. Elicited data is based on informants' responses to a given task. Again, elicited data may largely exhibit prototypicality as prototypicality is related to less complex concepts and more immediately accessible perceptions. However, the picture might be different in the corpus data as corpus data reflects frequency of usage that is not necessarily related to prototypicality. We discuss this idea in more detail when analysing our research data. In the following section, we focus on the links between both the traditional view and the more up-to-date view of prototypicality and corpus-based analysis.

The link between the old view of prototypicality and corpus-based analysis

The use of corpus-based analysis is highly recommended in CL research. It is pointed out that several linguistic phenomena such as recurrent patterns of words, collocations, phrases, and constructions can be accurately identified using language corpora (Robinson and Ellis 2008). Taking the characteristics of corpus data as a start, I discuss what corpus data and the cognitive view of prototypicality have in common. Then I discuss the link between prototypicality and frequency with regard to the old view.

Cognitivists tend to consider the old view of prototype as "the cognitively most salient exemplar", while corpus linguists often equate it with "the most frequently corpus-attested item" (Gilquin 2004: 159).

The use of authentic data emphasises the messiness of language on the basis that large machine stored and processed linguistic data is somewhat fuzzy. Such a machine-readable collection of texts reveals the fuzziness of category membership in language (Gilaquin 2004). It is noted that compared to the traditional characteristics of texts as "comfortable discrete and of an entity-like quality", texts in corpora tend to be "scalar, obtainable in stepwise batches with hazy edges only" (Cermak 2002: 273).

The above views suggest that the description of linguistic features on the basis of corpus approach is no longer providing straightforward answers and absolute truths. Instead, the answers tend to be the type of "more of this and less of that" and "rather this than that" (Cermak 2002: 273). It points out that "if there is one lesson to be learnt from studying and analyzing corpus examples, it is the basic non-discreteness of categories" (Mair 1994: 128). Put together, corpus data reflects the notion of cognitive prototypicality as category-based lexis, with some elements being more representative of a linguistic category while others are more marginal.

Frequency in introspective data

The link between early views of prototypicality and frequency has been dominant for several decades. In general, people believe that frequency has a strong link with prototypicality. It is claimed that the quantitatively most prominent facts of language are the most salient kinds of usage (Geeraerts 1988). The strongest claim is made by Radden, as he claims that what is more frequent in language is claimed to be most salient and so most prototypical (Radden 1992). This view leads to a methodological shortcut whereby prototypical status can be established via frequency in linguistic usage.

A more recent view of prototypicality: polysemy

More recent views of prototypicality have focused on polysemy and it is here where cognitive and corpus linguists tend to part company. Polysemy is a particular application of the prototype notion. It states that a linguistic form (whether morpheme, words, or construction) typically yields a range of distinct meanings. In the examples of *a strong woman*, *a strong wine*, and *a strong argument* (Lee 2005: 72), the meaning of *strong* cannot be directly interpreted. Rather, the meaning of the word *strong* varies semantically from one example to another. The prototypicality in this case cannot be derived from the marginal members of concrete members because the word *strong* is polysemous and it has more than one meaning.

The various meanings of a polysemous item tend to have more or less prototypical or representative senses. It is derived from the interaction between the target items associated with the relevant words rather than with the meaning of their own (Taylor 2008). Therefore, polysemy is the phenomenon whereby a range of distinct, but related semantic senses are exhibited in a radial network (Evan 2007). Let us consider an example of the English proposition *over* (Lakoff 1987):

1. The picture is over the sofa.
2. The clouds are over the sun.
3. She has a strange power over me.

(Lakoff 1987)

The meaning of *over* varies in the three different examples and exhibits the most prototypical sense in example 1 and the least prototypical sense in example 3. In example 1, the meaning of *over* refers to the direction *above*, the meaning of over in example 2 is *covering*, while in example 3 is *control*.

As we have seen, the former view of prototypicality deals with lexical semantics as a surface extension from the single and more abstract lexical to the less abstract one. To contrast, the more recent view of prototypicality is concerned with lexical polysemy which reflects the way in which our conceptual systems are structured and organized (Lakoff 1987).

Two caveats need to be borne in mind here. First of all, the prototypicality of the polysemy senses of a word is different from the term that is used in Rosch's study. In the first case, we consider the conceptual understanding of different instances of one item. In the other, we deal with a category consisting of distinct senses. Second, the radial senses of polysemous words hardly constitute a concrete and reasonable category (Taylor 2008). Taking an example suggested by Jackendoff (2002: 340), the word *cardinal* contains the meaning of *principal* (retained in *cardinal sins*), through to *a church official* and to *the colour of his robes*, then to *a bird of that colour*. It has been claimed that although the links among different senses can be perceived, it hardly constitutes a coherent and useful category (Jackendoff 2002 cited in Taylor 2008).

The link between polysemy and corpus-based analysis

Corpus-based analysis, in particular frequency, can not identify polysemy because polysemy is considered to be a linguistic form typically yields a range of distinct meaning. Polysemy is derived from individual's conceptual understanding which can not be simply reflected from corpus data. Similarly, by investigating the concordance lines, "the most frequent meaning is not the one that first comes to mind" (Sinclair 1991: 36). Language users will have prototypes for certain aspects of language use, however they may find it difficult to discover what the most frequent forms are (ibid). A more recent study suggests that the same words distributed in different corpora have different rates of frequency (Gries 2008). The findings suggest that raw frequency can sometimes be a misleading indicator of the overall importance of a word. All in all, corpus-based frequency can rarely provide the evidence on prototypicality in the case of polysemy.

In addition, the frequency effects found in language users may not be the same as those in input data in which learners are absorbed, for example, textbooks. Instead, the frequency of certain aspects of language usage may be based on language learners' memory.

The argument has been put forward claiming that the theoretical-based linguistic analysis should not be expected to be clear-cut, particularly when the analysis is transferred from purely psychological to specifically linguistic domains of investigation (Tsohatzidis 1990).

Instead, the most appropriate method of examining a word with different senses is by establishing its usage patterns (Taylor 2008). This view may emphasize the new perspective of investigating the prototypicality in corpus-based analysis, in particular the frequency of linguistic usage as evidence in corpus data.

It is suggested that the most frequent statistics in corpus linguistics are frequencies of occurrence of two or more linguistic variables (Gries 2008). This being the case, it is useful to quantify the degree to which particular words are attracted to, or repelled by, syntactically defined slots in grammatical patterns or constructions (Stefanowitsch and Gries 2003).

In this study, the polysemous of each "wh" word is investigated on the basis of their usage, together with the frequency of words occurring after each "wh" word. A comparison between three sets of data (textbooks, elicited data, and corpus data) will be made.

Chapter Three

An Overview of The Analysis of "WH" Sentence Constructions

3.1 Introduction

The aim of this chapter is to investigate the constructions within which each "wh" word can occur. First, it will briefly review the main approaches to polysemy, namely the full-specification approach (Lakoff 1987), and the principled polysemy approach (Tyler and Evans 2001). Second, it will use the principled polysemy approach to identify the range of "wh" interrogative, declarative and subordinate constructions in which the "wh" words can occur. Finally, it discusses the order of acquisition for "wh" words and structures, by both native speaker infants and second language learners.

According to cognitive linguistic principles, language is intrinsically symbolic, and it is formed by a structured inventory of constructions (Langacker1987). Constructions are conventionalized as form–meaning pairings which operate at different levels of "complexity and abstraction" (Ellis 2010: 27). For example, they can comprise "concrete and particular items" (as in words and idioms), "more abstract classes of items" (as in word classes and abstract grammatical constructions), or "complex combinations of concrete and abstract pieces of language" (as in mixed constructions) (ibid: 27).

Constructions specify different forms of language with respect to morphology, syntax, and lexis. In this chapter we focus on an approach to constructions has been employed in lexical semantics, namely, cognitive semantics. Cognitive semantics holds the view that lexical items can constitute a type of complex category, namely the radial category (Lakoff 1987). Such categories are also conceptual categories in which a range of concepts is organised in relation to a central or prototypical sense (Lakaff 1987, Evans and Green 2006). The concept of the radial category is regarded as one of the most influential applications of the prototype theory.

In this chapter I will argue that the different senses of each "wh" word operate within a radial category. i.e they exist within a polysemy network organised with a central sense. The different senses within this category can be identified, to some extent, by focusing on the different constructions within which they occur. That is to say, each different sense will be largely characterized by a particular range of constructions.

3.2 Previous approaches to polysemy networks

This section briefly reviews two main approaches to polysemy networks, focusing on the main criteria of each approach and looking at how the primary sense can be identified.

3.1.1 The full-specification approach

The full-specification approach is based on the analysis of the English preposition *over* by Lakoff in 1987. According to this approach, the senses of *over* can be derived from humans' spatial experience, and are structured with reference to image schemas (Evans and Green 2007). The prototypical sense of *over* is considered to combine with the image of ABOVE and ACROSS, as shown in Figure 3.1.

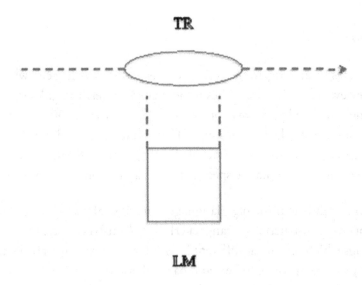

Figure 2.1 The central schema for *over* (Lakoff 1987: 419)

To understand Lakoff's image schema better, two concepts, TR and LM, are introduced. TR refers to trajector and is described as the entity in the scene that is smaller but capable of motion (Evans and Green 2007). LM stands for landmark and relates to the entity with respect to which the TR moves (ibid). As we can see from figure 3.1, the LM is unspecified, while the oval represents TR, and the arrow represents its direction of motion. The TR and its path motion are located above the LM (ibid). Lakoff's image schema of *over* is considered lack detail as well as not specifying the contact between the TR (Trajector) and the LM (Landmark). The consideration simply turns the TR and the LM into its physical position so that a smaller entity is horizontally above the LM. Such an explanation underlies an example such as *The plane flew over.* (Evans and Green 2007).

Lakoff proposed a number of image schemas related to this central schema. These image schemas are considered to show the possibilities of the position between the LM and the TR. Let us consider the following examples:

(1) The bird flew over the yard.

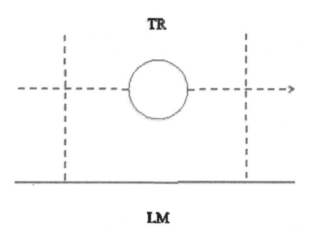

Figure 2.2 The central schema for *over*. (Lakoff 1987: 421)

According to Lakoff, the bird is the TR, and the yard is the LM. Similar to Figure 3.1, the moving entity shown in Figure 3.2 is considered as TR; however this image schema describes a distinct sense from the central schema, as we can see that TR and LM represent a typical horizontal and vertical extension. Furthermore, Lakoff discovered the possibility that the LM can be vertically extended with V. He then uses the symbol X to refer to fact that the entity is "horizontally eXtended" (Evans and Green 2007: 334). In addition, he uses NC (no contact) to refer to there being no contact between TR and LM, as in the example shown as follows:

(2) The plane flew over the hill.

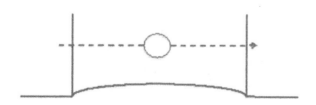

Figure 2.3 The plane flew over the hill. (Lakoff 1987: 421)

According to Lakoff, Figure 3.3 displays a distinct sense for the word *over*, which can be abbreviated as the symbol VX.NC. This can be understood as meaning that the LM is both vertically and horizontally extended and there is no contact between the LM and the TR.

Lakoff also gives examples where the TR and the LM are not horizontally extended but are vertically extended. The image schema is shown in the following example in Figure 3.4.

(3) The bird flew over the wall.

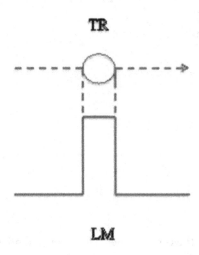

Figure 2.4 The bird flew over the wall. (Lakoff 1987: 421)

Figure 3.4 shows that the LM is vertically extended, but the TR is not horizontally extended. This is considered to be a distinct sense of the word *over*.

The above examples both involve situations where the LM and the TR have no contact. Lakoff also proposed several image schemas where the LM and the TR are in contact. He then uses the symbol C to refer to the concept contact. Let us consider the following examples:

(4) John walked over the bridge.

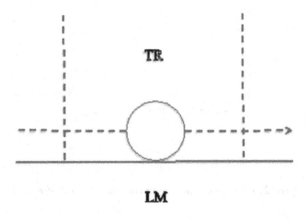

Figure 2.5 John walked over the bridge. (Lakoff 1987: 422)

According to Figure 3.5, John refers to the TR, and the bridge stands for the LM. This image schema shows that the LM and the TR are horizontally and vertically extended, as well as there being contact between the LM and the TR. This image schema can be considered to be one of the distinct senses of the word over, and can be abbreviated as VX.C.

From the above examples, we can see there are a number of image schemas that derive from the central image. Lakoff identified six distinct but closely related variations (see Figure 3.6). Table 3.1 illustrated these six senses of over in addition to the ABOVE-ACROSS sense. It is suggested that each individual lexical item can be illustrated in a number of distinct but related senses that are stored in semantic memory (Evans and Green 2007).

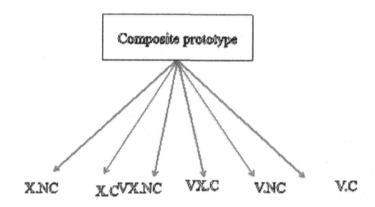

Figure 2.6 Instances of schema 1, the central image schema (Lakoff 1987:423)

Table 2.1 Schemas proposed by Lakoff (1987) for *over* in addition to the central schema

Schema type	Basic meaning	Example
ABOVE schema	The TR is located above the LM.	The helicopter is hovering over the hill.
COVERING schema	The TR is covering the LM.	The board is over the hold.
RELEXIVE schema	The TR is reflexive: the TR is simultaneously the TR and the LM. The final location of the TR is understood with respect to its starting position.	The fence fell over.

EXCESS schema	When over is employed as a prefix it can indicate 'excess' of TR relative to LM	The bath overflowed.
REPETITION schema	Over is used as an adverb to indicate a process that is repeated.	After receiving a poor grade, the student started the assignment over (again)

Problems with the full-specification approach

While Lakoff's full-specification approach has been hugely influential in the notions of cognitive lexical semantics, there are several major problems with this approach (Evans and Green 2007). The first problem is that the approach fails to take account of the role of context. In other words, Lakoff's approach fails to take into account the fact that contexts can help readers or speakers to predict the meanings of texts. In addition, the lexical structures identified from the word *over* exhibit several distinct but related senses. These senses can be analysed from a bottom-up view. In other words, the senses are derived from highly abstract image schemas. However, human being process simple and direct information before they process complex and indirect information. For example, let us consider the following examples:

a. The picture is over the sofa. [ABOVE]
b. The clouds are over the sun. [COVERING]
c. She has a strange power over me. [CONTROL]

(Evans, Bengen, and Zinken 2007)

As we can see from the above examples, the word *over* in example a has a less abstract image schema than in examples b and c. While the word *over* exhibits different senses, it is possible to argue that human beings rely more on contextual knowledge in highly abstract image schemas in order to understand meaning.

The second problem is that the full-specification approach lacks methodology constraints (Evans and Green 2006). It has been suggested that Lakoff's approach does not provide principled criteria for determining what counts as a distinct sense (ibid). In other words, the analysis is based on purely intuitive knowledge of semantics rather than presenting the way a particular category is represented in the speakers' minds" (Evans and Green 2006). Sandra (1998) argues that while the different usage of a particular lexical item may yield the phenomenon of polysemy, it does not follow the idea that many distinct senses associated with a lexical item are instances of polysemy (Sandra 1998 cited in Evans and Green 2007).

Based on the Lakoff's work and taking Sandra's suggestion, a new approach called principled polysemy has been proposed by Vyvyan Evans and Andrea Tyler. This approach is considered to analyse the semantic network more objectively by achieving two goals. The following section will discuss the principled polysemy approach and how it will help to identify "wh" sentence constructions.

3.2.1 *The principled polysemy approach*

The principled polysemy approach is proposed in order to achieve two goals. First, the principles should provide clear criteria for what counts as a distinct sense, and in turn distinguish senses stored in semantic memory as the polysemy and context-dependent of on-line meaning construction (Evans and Tyler 2003). Second, the principles should establish the basic and central sense, namely the prototypical sense that is associated with a particular radial category (Evans and Green 2006).

Taking the preposition *over* as an example, Tyler and Evans provide two criteria for distinguishing between senses as follows:

1. for a sense to count as distinct, it must involve a meaning that is not purely spatial in nature, and/or a spatial configuration between the TR and LM that is distinct from the other senses conventionally associated with that preposition; and
2. there must also be instances of the sense that are context-independent: instances in which the distinct sense could not be inferred from another sense and the context in which it occurs.

(Tyler and Evans 2003 cited in Evans and Green 2007: 343)

To understand how the above two criteria can be applied, let us consider the following examples:

(5). The hummingbird is hovering over the flower.
(6). The helicopter is hovering over the city.

(Tyler and Evans 2004: 189)

As we can see from the above examples, the word *over* in examples 5 and 6 indicates a spatial relationship where the TR (i.e. the hummingbird, and the helicopter) is located higher than the LM (i.e. the flower and the city). In both cases, the TR is located higher than the LM. Therefore, based on the first criterion, neither of the above examples indicates a non-spatial relationship, and consequently there are no context-dependent meanings. Hence, the word *over* in the above examples cannot be treated as two distinct senses.

To contrast with this, let us consider another example.

(7). Joan nailed a board over the hole in the ceiling.
(8). Joan nailed a board over the hole in the wall.

(Tyler and Evans 2004: 194)

In examples 7 and 8, the word *over* contains a distinct sense, as here it does not contain the purely spatial ABOVE meaning. Instead, an additional meaning arises here suggesting that the word *over* can be interpreted as the COVERING meaning. In addition, the position of the LM in examples 7 and 8 is obscured from the position of the TR. This is clearly different from examples 5 and 6 where the TR and the LM have a purely spatial configuration.

For the second criterion, we need to discover whether the additional meaning can be derived from the context. If it can be, then the distinct sense fails by measuring the second criterion. For example:

(9). The tablecloth is over the table.

In example 9, the TR, the tablecloth is located higher than the LM, the table. But as the fact is that the tablecloth is usually larger than the table, the additional meaning of "covering" can be derived from the context. Therefore, the interpretation of *over* combines the spatial configuration "higher" as well as the additional meaning "covering" from the context.

On the other hand, we have considered that the primary sense of the word *over* involves the spatial configuration between the TR and the LM, and this configuration contains the fact that the TR is located higher than the LM. Clearly, the "covering" meaning cannot be identified from the context in examples 7 and 8 because the spatial configuration in these two examples is coded by the meaning of *below* rather than *over*.

Methodology for determining the primary sense

Having discussed how to distinguish the distinct senses, this section looks at the criteria that Tyler and Evans provide for establishing the primary sense of a polysemy semantic network. They identified four types of linguistic evidence that can be narrowed to the "arbitrariness of the selection of a primary sense" (Tyler and Evans 2003: 196):

1. earliest attested meaning;
2. predominance in the semantic network;
3. relations to other prepositions;
4. ease of predicting sense extensions.

To clearly understand the criteria, they are briefly examined and discussed with the example proposed by Tyler and Evans (2003). The semantic network for *over* is shown in Figure 3.7.

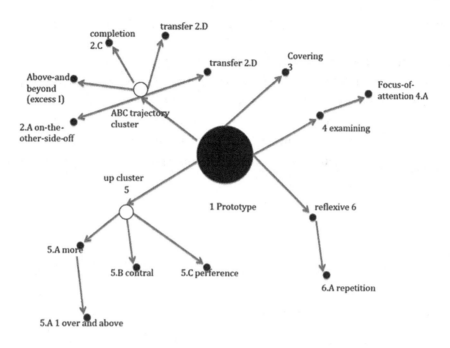

Figure 2.7 The semantic network for 'over'

To begin with, the earliest attested meaning is related to the historically earliest sense (Evans and Green 2006). In other words, taking the word *over* as an example, the earliest sense should provide the basic spatial interpretation in many different languages. For example, the word *over* is related to the meaning of "higher", and "above" in the Chinese language.

The second criterion, predominance in the semantic network, suggests that the primary sense will be the most frequently involved in or related to the other distinct senses (Evans and Green 2006). For example, Tyler and Evans (2003) identified fifteen distinct senses associated with the word *over*. Among these senses, there are eight senses directly related to the fact that TR is located higher than the LM, which becomes the most frequently involved sense (Evans and Green 2006). Therefore, the meaning of "above" is considered as the primary sense for *over*.

The third criterion suggests that the central sense will be related to other prepositions. It is pointed out that among English prepositions, several appear as a "contrast set that divide up various spatial dimensions" (Evans and Green 2006: 345). For example, *above, over, under,* and *below* tend to form "a compositional set that divides the vertical dimension into four related subspaces" (Tyler and Evans 2003: 197). *Over* and *under* appear to refer to the TR being physically closer to the LM, while *above* and *below* tend to form a location where TR is further away from the LM (Evans and Green 2006).

The fourth criterion concerns the degree of predicting sense extensions. In general, the central sense has the greatest ease of prediction, and the other distinct senses should be distinguished on the basis of the central sense.

3.3 Application of the principled polysemy approach to "wh" words

In this section, we apply Tyler and Evans' principled polsemy approach, which was described above, to the word *what*. *What* is different from the previously studied preposition as it can appear as more than one word class. For example, *what* can be considered as belonging to the pronoun group as well as the determiner group. This presents a problem for the analyst in that the senses that derive from the words may not always share the same sentence construction. In contrast, previous studies show that the lexical item that has been analysed shares the same sentence construction. To illustrate this point clearly, consider the following example:

(10). What time is it?
(11). What a lovely view.

As the above example shows, *what* in example 10 is used as pronoun and is used to ask for information about people or things. This might be regarded as one of the senses, most likely the central sense. The word *what* in example 11 is used as a predeterminer and used to introduce the point of view. Although we have not analysed the senses of *what*, the usage of *what* in example 11 is different from that in example 10, and the two sentence types are also different.

Taking things a step further, in theory, the principled polysemy approach can be used to identify a network of senses for any word, regardless of its word class. If this is the case, then the mental lexicon would be a vast, complicated and inter-related network. In order to reduce this complexity, researchers in the usage-based framework have hypostudied that a speaker's knowledge about individual lexical items develops from relatively specific, low level templates. In other words, speakers are able to establish correspondences between different senses of a lexical item and the relevant sentence constructions. To be able to do this, for words that have more than one lexical class, it might be a good idea to analyse the senses relating to each lexical class separately.

On the other hand, from the perspective of cognitive linguistics, grammar cannot be separated from lexis, form from function, meaning from context, nor structure from usage (Ellis 2010). Thus the various senses relating to a word are likely to correspond to an equivalent number of usage and sentence constructions. This may indicate that each usage of each lexical item can be considered as one of the senses under certain circumstances. However, in some ways this is too fine-grained an approach and it is useful for the analyst to attempt to group together a number of constructions under an umbrella sense. This is what we attempt to do below for the word *what*.

As we saw in Chapter 2, the focus of this study will be on "wh" words more generally. "Wh" words have a relatively wide variety in their linguistic terms as well as their usage. Such words are interesting because they exhibit a wide range of sentence structures and vary from simple to complex ones. A further reason for looking at the "wh" words is that these words have more than one lexical class. The analysis should be a useful way of examining the principles of the principled polysemy network.

Our analysis in this chapter will focus mainly on the distinct senses of the word *what* along with corpus examples. Under each sense of the word *what*, the possible sentence constructions are reviewed.

In addition, a summary table of the senses of other "wh" words will be provided. It should be noted that not all the senses that emerged in the word *what* will also occur in the other "wh" words.

Figure 3.8 shows a semantic network for the word *what*. The analysis is based on the study of BNC (The British National Corpus) and The Bank of English. A total of 200 lines were abstracted: 100 lines are from the BNC and another 100 from the Bank of English. The diagram shows three distinct senses, including the central and prototypical sense. The numbers of occurrences for each particular sense are shown in brackets.

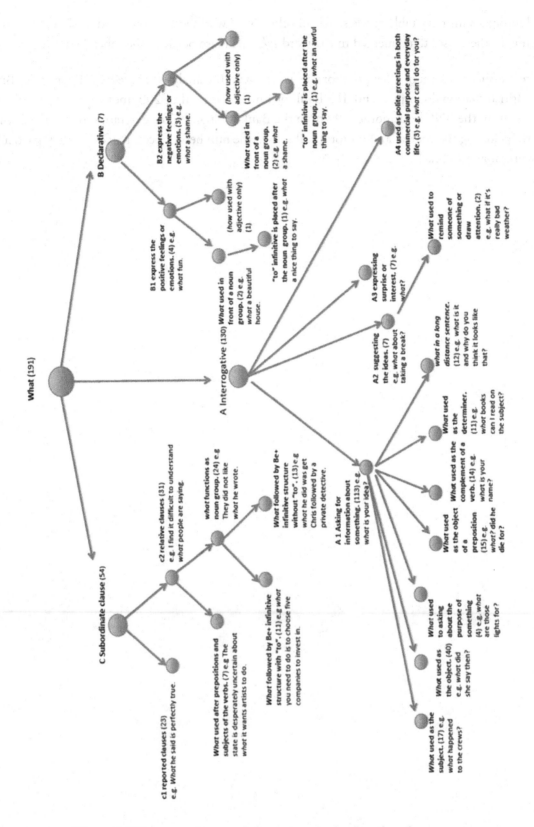

Figure 2.8 The semantic network for the word *what (number of occurrences in 200-word sample shown in brackets)*

Figure 3.8 shows the three main senses for *what*, namely interrogative, declarative, and subordinate clauses respectively. Because the interrogative is the most productive of these three senses it can in some ways be considered to be the most central or prototypical sense (Evans and Greeen, 2006). The figure then shows several distinct and conventionalized senses arising from the three main senses, indicating a large variety of sentence constructions. The sentence constructions for each conventionalized sense also show the different grammatical functions that *what* can serve. For example, the central sense of *what* in Figure 3.8 is considered as interrogative, representing the form of a sentence that is used for asking a question. In addition, there are four distinct senses (i.e., A1, A2, A3, and A4) arising from this central sense. There are seven different sentence constructions arising from one of the distinct senses (A1).

One weakness of this analysis is that it has relied on a limited number of concordance lines (200). In other words, a large number of corpus concordance lines need to be studied in the future, and such an analysis may give rise to more distinct senses. A detailed study of the three main senses of *what*, together with their distinct senses and sentence constructions, will be provided in the following sections.

3.3.1 *The interrogative*

The four distinct senses (A1, A2, A3, and A4) all derive from the central sense, i.e. the interrogative. These four distinct senses involve the fact that *what* is used to inquire about information or to make suggestions. In addition, the conceptual configurations involved in the four senses vary along with their sentence constructions in which the conceptual configurations may result from how frequently people use them in authentic contexts. In the following sections, I discuss the individual senses together with corpus examples.

A1 Asking for information about something

One of the most common and frequent usages of *what* is to ask for information about something. Three criteria are used to identify this usage. First, the sentences contain *what*; second, the sentences are used in the question forms; third, the sentence will not give rise to any polarity information or additional information. Consider the following examples:

```
What's going on? (BNC)
What about taking a break? (BNC)
```

Notice in the first example, *what* is used to ask for information, and there is no additional information suggested. The second sentence is not asking for information, rather, the information is suggested by *taking a break*. Hence, the answer to the second sentence is more or less agreement or disagreement.

What particularly belongs to a group of words starting with "wh" (plus the word *how*), such as "when" and "who", which are used in questions in most cases. In addition, it has more than one grammatical class, including noun, pronoun, determiner, and predeterminer. I hypothesized that there would be a vast variety of sentences constructions emerging as a result of its complex grammatical nature. According to the 200 concordance lines that were taken from the BNC and the Bank of English

(BoE), I found that there are about seven main sentence constructions under the distinct sense A1. Examples are shown as follows:

a. *What* used as the subject.
    What happened to the crew? (BoE)
b. *What* used as the object.
    What did she say then? What do you drive? (BNC)
c. *What* used to ask for the purpose of something.
    What for? (BNC)
d. *What* used as the object of a preposition.
    What did he die for? (BoE)
e. *What* used as a complement of the verb.
    What is your name? (BoE)
f. *What* used as a determiner.
    What books can I read on the subject? (BoE)
    What role should librarians and information scientists play in this process of information transfer? (BNC)
g. *What* used in a long-distance question.
    What is it and why do you think it looks like that? (BNC)

A2 Suggesting ideas

In the following examples, *what* is used to suggest ideas rather than asking for information. Thus, the information has already been given, and in most cases agreement is expected. This usage tends to be strongly associated with the collocations or fixed expressions of *what*. For example:

```
What about professional aromatherapy treatment? (BNC)
What about the other dimension? (BNC)
What about taking a break? (BoE)
What if it's really bad weather? (BNC)
```

The last sentence in the above example indicates an additional possibility. The sentence is formed with a possibility that it might or might not happen. In most cases, the question tends to predict negative future situations. Notice the use of present tense in the sentence *what about the other dimension?* can be indicated.

A3 Expressing surprise or interest

In sense A3, *what* is used to express surprise or interest. In extreme cases, the sentences express a strong point view according to the contexts. In addition, there is no answer to be expected in such cases. For example,

```
What? (BNC)
So what? (BoE)
```

A4 used as polite greetings in both commercial and everyday contexts

In this usage, *what* is used in greetings and usually occurs in fixed expressions. An answer may or may not be expected. For example, when a shop assistant says "What can I do for you?", the customer may respond by referring to a particular item that he or she is looking for, or the answer might be "Thanks, I am just looking". In most cases, we store this sentence construction as a whole in our memory (Wray, 2008).

3.3.2 *The declarative*

As noted earlier, the interrogative is considered to be the central and prototypical sense of *what*, indicating that unknown information has been requested. The declarative, one of the three main senses of *what*, requires a different conceptualization. In particular, the scene associated with the sentence is no longer in a question form, asking for the unknown information; rather, it describes the degree of one's feelings or emotions. It is interesting to note that only two "wh" words have this usage, namely, *what* and *how* (see Chapter five). The feelings and emotions can be classified into positive and negative groups. In the following sections, we look at the particular sentence constructions of *what*.

B1 expressing positive feelings

What is used in front of the noun group (sometimes, the to infinitive is placed after the noun group) to express positive feelings. For example:

```
What a good idea! (BNC)
What a good gift! (BNC)
What a beautiful house! (BNC)
How bright his eyes were! (BNC)
How marvelously quaint. (BNC)
```

B2 expressing negative feelings

The same sentence construction can be applied when expressing native feelings. For example:

```
What a lovely view (BoE)
What an awful play! (BNC)
What a horrible thing to say! (BoE)
How aggressively you play! (BNC)
```

3.3.3 *The subordinate clause*

Unlike the previous two senses, *what* in subordinate clauses is used either to clarify the information or to add extra information. The sentence is focussed on the descriptive details.

C1 Clarifying the information, and evaluating the situation.

In C1, *what* subordinate clauses are closely related to the degree of simplicity and evaluation. In this case, the information that is derived from the main clauses is emphasized and narrowed. For example:

```
That's what you really need. (BNC)
That's what I want. (BoE)
```

Notice from the above sentences, that *what* is used neither as a question word nor as an exclamation marker. Rather, *what* is used as a link that combines the main clause and the information that clarifies the main clause.

C2 Adding information, and providing possible solutions.

What subordinate clauses can also be used to add extra information as well as to provide possible solutions to contribute to our conventional conceptualizations. There are two sentence constructions that derive from this usage. First of all, *what* used after a preposition or the subjects of the verbs. For example:

```
The state is desperately uncertain about what it wants artists to do.
(BNC)
I find it difficult to understand what people are saying. (BoE)
… and sensed already that what he might achieve in months… (BNC)
Second, what itself functions as a noun group. For example,
They did not like what he wrote. (BoE)
What he said is perfectly true. (BNC)
```

There are also two different sentence constructions under this condition: first, *what* followed by be + infinitive structure with to, for example:

```
What you need to do is to choose five companies to invest in. (BoE)
What I am saying to myself is ok. (BNC)
Second, what is followed by be + infinite structure without to, for
example:
What he did was get Chris followed by a private detective. (BoE)
What hits home is if Batty wanted to leave… (BNC)
```

In this section, we have provided an analysis of the semantic network of *what*. The features and different kinds of sentence structures in which *what* occurs have been identified and discussed. In the next section, we provide a summary table that shows the structures that the other "wh" words appear in, apart from *whom*. Having noticed that *whom* occurs less frequently in both corpora, it might be interesting to provide a short analysis of the *whom* structure separately. Table 3.2 illustrates the features and sentence structures that the eight "wh" words appear in. I will put a tick by the features and sentence structures that appear in these eight "wh" words. In addition, it is worth discussing some of the features and sentence structures that do not seem appear in *what*, but exist in the other "wh" words.

Table 2.2 The features and sentence structures that the eight "wh" words appear in

	Interrogatives — A1 Asking for information about something							A2 suggesting the ideas. ("wh" words used to remind someone of something or draw attention.)	A3 expressing surprise or interest.	A4 used as polite greetings in both commercial and everyday life.	Declarative — B1 expressing positive feelings or emotions.		Declarative — B2 expressing negative feelings or emotions.		Subordinate clauses — c1 reported clauses	Subordinate clauses — c2 relative clauses		
	"wh" words used as the subject.	"wh" words used as the object.	"wh" words used to ask about the purpose of something.	"wh" words used as the object of a preposition	"wh" words used as the complement of a verb.	"wh" words used as the determiner.	"wh" words in a long distance sentence.				"wh" words used in front of a noun group. / "to" infinitive is placed after the noun group.	(how used with adjective only)	"wh" words used in front of a noun group. / "to" infinitive is placed after the noun group.	(how used with adjective only)	(how used with adjective only)			
how		✓					✓	✓	✓	✓		✓		✓	✓			
where		✓					✓								✓	✓		
when		✓					✓		✓						✓	✓	✓	
who	✓	✓		✓	✓		✓	✓							✓	✓	✓	✓
why	✓	✓	✓		✓		✓	✓	✓						✓	✓	✓	✓
which	✓	✓		✓	✓	✓	✓								✓	✓	✓	✓
whose	✓	✓			✓	✓									✓	✓	✓	✓

How

As we can see in Table 3.2, the behaviour of *how* appears to be different from that of *what* in section A1 'asking for information about something'. In this section, *how* only shares two patterns with *what*. In the first pattern, both *how* and *what* can be used as an object. Within this pattern, *how* can operate as an adverb, and is used to express the means of doing something, such as in what way or by what methods, for example:

```
How did you hear about the concert? (BoE)
How do you get rid of a nasty smell? (BoE)
```

Also within this first pattern, *how* can be used to mean in what condition, especially of physical or emotional health, for example:

```
How is your father? (BoE)
How are you feeling this morning? (BoE)
```

And again, still within this first pattern, *how* can be used to ask what an experience or event was like, for example:

```
How was your trip? (BoE)
How was the smoked trout? (BoE)
```

How and *what* share a second pattern in that they can both be used in long-distance questions, for example:

```
And how do you think you'd spell classical like do you like classical
music? (BNC)
```

As we can see in Section A2 in the table, *how*, like *what*, can both be used to make a suggestion. In most cases, it is used with its collocates or fixed expressions, for example:

```
How about the cinema tonight? (BoE)
How about fish? (BoE)
```

How also shares a similar pattern with *what* in Section A3 in that both of them can be used to emphasize that something is surprising, for example:

```
Sales are up by thirty-six percent. How about that? (BoE)
How come. (BoE)
```

As we can see in Section A4 in the table *How* is used for greetings, such as How are you? or How do you do?

How shares a similar pattern with *what* in declaratives in sections B1 and B2. Both of them are used to emphasize that something is positive or negative, for example:

```
How beautiful. (BNC)
How strange. (BNC)
```

In terms of subordinate clauses, *How* shares the same pattern as *what* in section C1 in the table. *How* subordinate clauses are used in reported clauses to clarify information. In most cases, it is used to emphasise the degree of a feeling or emotion, for example:

```
I can't tell you how pleased I am. (BoE)
```

When

As seen in Table 3.2, *when* and *what* share two similar patterns in Section A. First, *when* is used as an object to ask about the time that something happened or will happen, for example:

```
When did you arrive? (BoE)
When are you getting married? (BoE)
```

Second, *when* also occurs in long–distance questions. In some cases, *when* can be used to ask someone why they believe a situation to be different from how it really is. It also forms part of the construction *Since when did you…?*, to express anger, for example:

```
Why is she training to be a teacher when she doesn't even like children?
(BoE)
Since when did you have the right to tell me what to do? (BoE)
```

When and *what* share the two main usages (reported clauses and relative clauses) in Sections C1 and C2; however, the sentence structures appear differently in *when* subordinate clauses. The reason for this might be that *when* serves particular grammatical functions in subordinate clauses. First of all, *when* is used as a conjunction when comparing two apparently conflicting situations, for example:

```
How can you say you don't like something when you've never even tried
it! (BoE)
I don't understand how he can say that everything's fine when it's so
obvious that it's not. (BoE)
```

Second, *when* is used in relative clauses to indicate that something happened, happens, or will happen at a particular time. Again, the clauses can be classified into the same usage as *what*.

```
He left school when he was seven. (BoE)
When I have free time, I always spend it fishing. (BoE)
```

Another way in which the sentence structures of *when* and *what* subordinate clauses contrast quite dramatically is that *when* is used in non-finite clauses, in other words, clauses that contain an infinitive or participle rather than a finite verb, for example:

```
We are now being told much more specifically when not to enter a horse
for a race. (BoE)
```

```
Adults sometimes do not realize their own strength when dealing with
children. (BoE)
```

Where

As can be seen from Table 3.2, *where* and *what* share two usages in Section A1. First, *where* is used as object and it is used to ask questions about place or position, for example:

```
Where is Jane? (BoE)
Where does she live? (BoE)
Where does all this energy come from? (BoE)
```

Second, *where* also occurs in longdistance questions, for example:

```
How did you know where to find me? (BoE)
```

In terms of subordinate clauses, *where* shares the same pattern in the Section of C1 and C2. Generally, *where* can be used in both reported clauses and relative clauses. For C1, it is used in non-finite clauses containing a 'to'-infinitive, for example:

```
I have no idea where to go (BoE)
```

In addition, *where* can be used in relative clauses when talking about the place or position in which someone or something is. *Where* can be used in both defining and non-defining relative clauses, for example:

```
He came from Herne Bay, where Lally had once spent a holiday. (BoE)
...the room where they work. (BoE)
...the room where I did my homework. (BoE)
...the street where my grandmother had lived. (BoE)
```

Unlike *what*, it is interesting to note that *where* is also used in front of adjectives (such as *possible*, *necessary*) as collocations or fixed expressions. When it is used like this, *where* shares a similar meaning with *when* or *whenever*, for example:

```
Where possible, prisoners with long sentences were put in the same blocks.
(BoE)
Help must be given where necessary. (BoE)
```

Who

As we can see in Table 3.2, the behaviour of *who* appears to be different from that of *what* in section A1 'asking information about something'. *Who* is used when asking about someone's identity. *Who* can be the subject, object, or complement of a verb. It can also be the object of a preposition, and is used in long-distance questions, for example:

```
Who invited you? (BoE)
Who are you going to invite? (BoE)
```

```
Who are you? (BoE)
Who did you dance with? (BoE)
Do you know who will be invited to the party? (BoE)
```

Who and *what* share a similar pattern in sections C1 and C2 in terms of subordinate clauses. Both of these words can be used in reported clauses as well as relative clauses to add information about a person just mentioned, for example:

```
She didn't know who I was. (BoE)
```

However, *who* can be used in both defining and non-defining relative clauses, while *what* is used in nominal relative clauses in section C2, for example:

```
He's the man who I saw last night. (BoE)
Joe, who was always early, was there already. (BoE)
```

Why

Why and *what* share two usages in section A1; first, *why* is used as the object in questions asking about the reason for something, for example:

```
Why did you do it, Martin? (BoE)
```

Second, *why* can be used in long-distance questions in section A1, for example:

```
Why do you think it is that there wasn't that motivation? (BNC)
```

In addition, *why* and *what* share a similar pattern in section A2 when the use of negative form *why* (e.g. don't) is used to make a suggestion, for example:

```
Why don't we all go? (BoE)
Why don't you write to her yourself? (BoE)
```

Also, *why* and *what* share a similar pattern in section A3 in that *why* can be used in a question that emphasises that there is no reason for something to be done by using the collocation 'why should'. On the other hand, we can also use the collocation 'why shouldn't' to emphasise that there is no reason for something not be done, for example:

```
Why should I be angry with you? (BoE)
Why shouldn't he go to college? (BoE)
```

Similarly to *what*, *why* is used in reported clauses (section C1) as well as relative clauses (section C2). For reported clauses in section C1, *why* is used with a noun phrase to explain the reason for something, for example:

```
I knew why Solly had been killed. (BoE)
He wondered why she had come. (BoE)
```

Unlike *what, why* can be used on its own instead of in reported clauses when the meaning is clear to both informants, for example:

```
They don't call me David - I don't know why. (BoE)
```

For relative clauses in section C2 in the table, *why* is used after the word "reason", for example:

```
That's a major reason why they were such poor countries. (BoE)
```

Which

As we can see in Table 3.2, the behaviour of *which* appears to be different from that of *what* in section A1 'asking information about something'. In this section, *which* shares six patterns with *what*. *Which* is used when we ask for information about one of a limited number of things or people. It can be the subject, object, or complement of a verb. It can also be the object of a preposition, determiner, and in long-distance questions, for example:

```
Which came first? (BoE)
Which do you fancy? (BoE)
Which is her room? (BoE)
Which did you take it from? (BoE)
Which areas were run by Trusthouse Forte and which by Granada? (BNC)
Which problems do you think that Jane believes that Bill claims that
Mary solved? (BNC)
```

Which and *what* share a similar pattern in terms of subordinate clauses in sections C1 and C2. *Which* is usually used for things, rather than people, it shows what thing or things we are referring to. In reported clauses C1, *which* is also used to add information about the thing just mentioned, for example:

```
I don't know which to believe. (BoE)
```

Unlike *what*, used in section C2 as a nominal relative pronoun, *which* is used as a relative pronoun, and can be used in both defining and non-defining relative clauses, for example:

```
Last week we heard about the awful conditions which exist in British
prisons. (BoE)
I'm teaching at the Selly Oak Centre, which is just over the road. (BoE)
```

Whose

As we can see in Table 3.2, the behaviour of *whose* appears to be different from that of *what* in section A1 'asking information about something'. In this section, *whose* can be used as subject, object, the complement of a verb, and a determiner, for example:

```
Whose fault is it? (BoE)
Whose babies do you think they were? (BoE)
```

```
Whose is this? (BoE)
```

In terms of subordinate clauses, *whose* and *what* are used in both reported clauses and relative clauses in sections C1 and section C2 to add information about a person or thing just mentioned, for example:

```
It would be interesting to know whose idea it was. (BoE)
```

Unlike *what*, which is used as nominal relative clause, *whose* is usually used within a noun group containing *whose* at the beginning of a relative clause, for example:

```
...a woman whose husband had deserted her. (BoE)
```

Notice that when *whose* is used as the object of a preposition in section C2, the preposition can come at the beginning or end of the clause, for example:

```
...the governments in whose territories they operate. (BoE)
...some strange fragment of thought whose origin I have no idea of. (BoE)
```

Whom

In the corpora studied, *whom* is the least frequently occurring "wh" word. It is therefore worth considering it on its own. Figure 3.9 illustrates the different usages and sentence structures of *whom*.

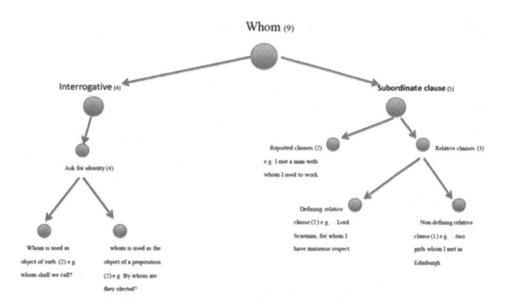

Figure 2.9 The semantic network for the word *whom*

As we can see in Figure 3.9, the behaviour of *whom* appears to be different from that of *what* in section A1 'asking information about something'. In this section, *whom* is used instead of *who* on formal occasions. It is used as the object of a verb or preposition, for example:

```
To whom do you wish to speak? (BNC)
Whom shall we call? (BoE)
```

Although *whom* should be used after a preposition, most people avoid it by putting the preposition towards the end of the sentence and using *who* instead. Notice that *whom* has the fewest occurrences in the two corpora compared to the other "wh" words. The reason might be that the usage of *whom* is very similar to that of *who*, but it is used in old-fashioned English or formal language such as in the Bible.

Whom and *what* share the same pattern in sections C1 and C2 in terms of subordinate clauses. *Whom* can be used in reported clauses, for example:

```
As we have seen, Home thought Macmillan, whom he liked and admired... (BNC)
```

Unlike *what,* which is used as nominal relative clause, *whom* is used in both defining and non-defining relative clauses, for example:

```
...perfectly clear to the man at the National Westminster Bank with whom
he was dealing ... (BNC)
At present the scheme only applies to those buyers to whom reports are
addressed... (BNC)
```

3.4 *The acquisition order of "wh" words and structures by both native speaker infants and second language learners.*

Because in this study we will be looking at the acquisition of "wh" words by Chinese learners of English, it is useful to look briefly at the work that has been done on the order of acquisition of these words by both native and non-native speakers. Most research studies have focused on "wh" questions, so the discussion will follow that trend here. However there will be a short discussion of the findings that have been made with respect to the acquisition of "wh" subordinate clauses and declaratives.

Research findings have suggested that semantic and syntactic complexity have both served as the primary determinants of the order in which children acquire particular words or grammatical constructions (Rowland, *et al.* 2003). The literature shows that semantically and syntactically simple structures are acquired first and that this is true for "wh" questions (ibid). "Wh" questions in particular have been found to exhibit a very robust order of acquisition in which "wh" words that encode syntactically simple relationships are acquired before other "wh" words that refer to more complex concepts (ibid). At the same time, studies have also taken account of semantic verbs that have been influential on "wh" question acquisition. These studies suggest that early "wh" questions tend to occur primarily with semantically general verbs, regardless of the fact that more complex verbs are introduced at the same time in other structures (Bloom 1991). General verbs refer to those that tend to be more easily acquired than other descriptive verbs as they carry less information. They therefore involve fewer restrictions from a syntactic perspective, and can be used in a wider variety of contexts (Bloom 1991, Bloom et al 1992).

Bloom and her colleagues proposed one of the best-specified accounts of "wh" question acquisition with reference to complexity. The key concept in their work is that the acquisition of "wh" questions is determined by the syntactic and semantic complexity of the concepts encoded by the "wh" words and the verbs to be acquired (ibid). Their findings suggest that the first "wh" questions to appear are questions that ask for the identities of things and places. In other words, *what* and *where* are acquired first, followed by *who*. These three "wh" pronominals tended to combine with a wider variety of general or light verbs. After the acquisition of the "wh" pronominals, the "wh" sententials *when, how* and *why* appear in the children's data (Bloom et al 1982). Finally, the "wh" adjectival forms *which* and *whose* occur last (ibid). This finding reflects the degree of the "wh" words' syntactic complexity. In other words, the "wh" sententials are considered to be more complex than the "wh" pronominals because "the answers…specify a reason, a manner or a time that the entire event encoded in the sentence occurs" (Bloom et al 1982: 1086). The "wh" adjectivals occur last; this appears to be because they are "more complex still, since they require the answer to specify something about the object constituent" (ibid).

In terms of the verbs that occur in the "wh" sentences, both "wh" pronominals occur primarily with general verbs, while the "wh" sententials are acquired with descriptive verbs. Very little data is available for the acquisition of "wh" adjectivals and this data is insufficient to draw any conclusions about whether they occur with general or descriptive verbs.

The data from Bloom et al's studies of English children on the acquisition of "wh" questions seems to indicate remarkable consistency in the acquisition order predicted from the interlocking influences of the syntactic complexity of the "wh" words and the semantic generality of the verb (Rowland et al 2003). However, Rowland et al point out that previous studies and analysis did not consider the role of frequency, in particular the language input (such as the caregivers using particular "wh" words and verbs) surrounding the children (ibid). Therefore the analysis from Bloom et al's data would show a different picture if the frequency of the input is considered. A later study carried out by Clancy (1989) suggests that children acquire high frequency "wh" words and verbs earlier than lower frequency lexemes. Again, we see that complexity and input frequency are highly connected and both of them play an important role in the acquisition process.

Another study that combined both parameters was Rowland et al (2003). They set out to establish "the extent to which "wh" complexity, verb semantic generality and input frequency predict the order of acquisition of "wh" questions in children's early speech" (Rowland et al 2003: 613). The focus of their study was at the level of the individual "wh" word + verb combination (what+are). The findings from this study reveal the acquisition order that was suggested by Bloom et al. They also reveal the relationship between complexity and input frequency, suggesting that of the two, input frequency is likely to be the more powerful predictor of order of acquisition (Rowland et al 2003: 628). However, the researchers also point out that "wh" complexity and verb semantic generality hardly affect the acquisition once input frequency is taken into account. In most cases, "the early-acquired, low frequency" "wh" words were indeed more complex than those that were "late-acquired but high frequency" (ibid). The same phenomenon can be found for verbs.

Although previous studies have emphasized that input frequency is a more important predictor than complexity, input frequency itself is too broad to be measured. For example, it is almost impossible to take into account the frequency of each interrogative, declarative, noun, verb or different form of verbs, etc. In addition, for the "wh" pronominals (*what* and *where*) and the "wh" sententials (*when, how*, and *why*), it is important to consider the frequency of verbs during acquisition; however, different types of noun may also need to be considered for the "wh" adjectivals (*which* and *whose*).

In my research, the frequency of the words occurring immediately after each "wh" word is investigated. The reason for doing this is that the words occurring immediately after the "wh" pronominals and "wh" sententials are more likely grammatical words that are relatively a small amount. In addition, the collocations of the "wh" adjectivals can also be revealed (for example: which ball? whose dinner?). Another reason is that L2 learners, in particular beginners, tend to memorise the sentences that they read or hear. Following Hoey's (1991) lexical priming theory, one or two words can trigger a whole sentence via a process that is similar to remembering a telephone number.

For L2 learners, English questions presumably occur frequently in the input, in particular in the classroom context. On the syntactical level, the "wh" questions are formed via inversion, using the auxiliary *do* in some cases, with "wh" phrases in initial positions (White et al 1991). Such a formation is difficult for learners whose first languages do not have such structures, for example French and Chinese. Therefore, apart from the syntactic complexity and the verb generality, and the relationship between the learner's first language and input frequency needs to be considered in the L2 acquisition process, as differences between the first language and second language might be an obstruction for the acquisition of "wh" sentences. To address this problem, it has been suggested that "input enhancement" may serve to draw learners' attention to a feature that is otherwise difficult to perceive (White et al 1991: 420). The input enhancement can be either sentence examples that are shown in the textbooks or the examples provided by language teachers. A discussion of the types of input enhancement that are offered in English language teaching settings in China is provided in the next chapter where typical approaches to teaching English in China at different levels will be discussed.

Chapter Four

An Overview of English Language Teaching In China

4.1 Introduction

In recent years, China has seen an explosion in the demand for English as a result of its rapid social, economic and political development (Jin and Cortazzi 1996). This indicates impressive commitment but also brings a challenge to both teachers and language learners. It is no exaggeration to say that China is among the pioneering countries within the framework of globalization. There are more teachers and learners of English as a foreign language in China than in any other country. On the other hand, it brings challenges such as how to design a syllabus that meets the students' needs with regard to their proficiency levels, or how to adopt modern language teaching methodologies in an authentic Chinese classroom context.

In this chapter, I discuss the situation of English language teaching and learning in China with regard to the three different age groups (junior, senior and university) of Chinese speakers of English. The chapter attempts to provide a general picture of the current situation of English language teaching and learning in China. Issues such as the general description of the students from the three different age groups, the purpose of their English language study, the syllabus and selected examples, and language teaching methodology are discussed.

4.2 Junior Middle School

Students from junior middle school are basically defined as Chinese national adolescents living within mainland China who fall inside the 12-15 age bracket. Most of the students have been introduced to basic English language at their primary school (where tens of millions of pupils out of a total of 130 million are now learning English) before they enter junior middle school (Jin and Cortazzi 2006). With a total of 63 million students attending junior middle school, English language is one of the main compulsory subjects that has been developing for years within the education system. At this level the main purpose of English language study is no longer to pass examinations; rather, many students have a high motivation to learn English starting at junior middle school.

English at the junior middle school level adopts communicative approaches and focuses exclusively on everyday conversation. Activities such as role-play, pair work, games, pictures and objects are involved in daily classes. Teachers often use cassettes or CD-ROMs to introduce the target language input. Chinese language is occasionally introduced to support comprehension of unknown words or phrases. Students at this level show an obvious enthusiasm because English is considered to be one of the fundamental courses in the junior education system, carrying the same weight as other subjects such as Chinese language and Mathematics. In addition, their parents play a positive role in supporting their children's learning of English, since they consider it as a way of reflecting their social and economic status.

Textbooks at junior middle school level are national. They are designed and published jointly with the "international publisher Longman through a United Nations Development Programme" (Jin and Cortazzi 2006: 55). As mentioned earlier, communicative skills are emphasized in both textbooks and teaching methodologies at this level.

As can be seen from the above lesson, the content is based on everyday conversation, and textbook writers tend to place the topic (introducing yourself) in authentic contexts. Rather than simply listing dozens of dialogues, a variety of activities such as role-play, pair work, games, and listening to cassette tapes are included in the lesson. This is believed to help students to develop the four aspects of language skills, namely, listening, speaking, reading comprehension and writing.

However, for a 50 minute class and an average class size of 55, there are clear constraints on such communicative-based language teaching, resulting in an unsurprising tendency for the structure of the lesson to incline towards a "book-based or teacher-centred" format (Ross 1993, Jin and Cortazzi 2006: 56). First, there are fewer practice opportunities for individual students, particularly in speaking. Second, teachers often use the Chinese language to explain the grammar rules of English to save more time. This goes against most communicative teaching approaches. In addition, we can see that the Chinese translated instructions are provided in the textbook together with the English version.

In contrast, grammar rules are explained in the Chinese language and are listed at the end of the textbook. For each grammar point, a few examples are listed with an explanation of their usage.

4.3 Senior High School

As the students from junior middle school pass the entrance examinations, they enter senior high school. The students are aged between 15-18. Students at this level will have to study hard to prepare for the national examinations for university entrance. Like the textbooks at junior middle school, textbooks at this level are based on communicative skills, and put more weight on speaking skills. The content of textbooks combines both domestic and international culture, particularly in the selection of the textbook topics. However, because of the pressure of the university entrance examination, reading comprehension and vocabulary are heavily emphasised. Tailor-made examination preparation exercises are used to evaluate the students' progress. Classroom teaching concentrates on explicitly explaining grammar rules and reviewing the use of vocabulary. After class, students spend long hours memorising the rules of grammar and vocabulary usage. An extract from the English paper of a university entrance examination is shown as follows:

Example 1.

I wasn't sure if he was really interested or if he _____ polite.

A. was just being   B. will just be
C. had just been   D. would just be

Example 2.

It is generally considered unwise to give a child_____ he or she wants.

A. however   B. whatever
C. whichever   D. whenever

Example 3.

---We could invite John and Barbara to the Friday night part.

--- Yes, ____? I'll give them a call right now.

A. why not   B. what for
C. why   D. what

As can be seen from the above examples, the examination has a relatively broad focus. The correct use of certain grammatical rules such as example 1, the correct use of collocation and fixed expressions such as example 2, and the correct use of phrases or words in different contexts such as example 3 are all assessed. In this way, it is ensured that the examination covers most aspects of the target language system; however, it is easy to predict of the content of these examinations. This might be the reason why both teachers and students tend to focus on practising exam papers, rather than on teaching the different aspects of the target language system explicitly.

4.4 University

We have discussed the idea that it is vital for students at senior high school level to pass the national examination to enter university. In the national university entrance examination, the weighting of English as an academic subject increased significantly from 100 to 120 in the early 1990s and then peaked at 150 in recent years (Jin and Cortazzi 2006). Unlike the textbooks in junior middle school and senior high school, apart from the national syllabus used in the majority of the cities of mainland China, a selection of locally developed syllabus and materials are used (ibid).

Textbooks at this level focus largely on authentic texts selected from newspapers or magazines from English-speaking countries. Grammar is no longer the key aspect that occupies the most classroom teaching; rather, different usages of vocabulary are explicitly taught. However, the content of English language teaching is mainly determined by the final examination. In order to graduate, students who study non-English majors need to pass at least the Band 4 national college and university English test. For better employment prospects, students are often encouraged to take the Band 6 national examination. Band 6 is more difficult than Band 4: students need to acquire more vocabulary and more grammatical rules to achieve Band 6. In addition, Band 4 is compulsory for students at colleges or universities, while Band 6 is optional and the decision to take it is entirely up to students themselves. Students who are studying for an English major, however, need to pass a special exam, also named Band 4 but considered to be equivalent to or even more difficult than Band 6 for non-major students. Let us consider the following examples from Band 4 and Band 6 (non-English major) and Band 4 (English major).

Examples from Band 4 (non-English major):

45. The other day, Mum and I went to St. James's Hospital, and they did lots and lots of tests on me, most of them _____ and frightening.

A) cheerful   B) horrible
C) hostile   D) friendly

46. In the Mediterranean seaweed is so abundant and so easily harvested that it is never of great _____.

A) fare   B) payment
C) worth   D) expense

47. The writer was so _____ in her work that she didn't notice him enter the room.

A) absorbed   B) abandoned
C) focused   D) centered

Examples from Band 6 (non-English major):

41. If you want this painkiller, you'll have to ask the doctor for a _____.

A) transaction B) permit
C) settlement   D) prescription

42. The _____ from childhood to adulthood is always a critical time for everybody.

A) conversion   B) transition
C) turnover   D) transformation

43. It is hard to tell whether we are going to have a boom in the economy or a _____

A) concession   B) recession
C) submission   D) transmission

Examples from Band 4 (English major):

76. When invited to talk about his achievements, he refused to blow his own _____ and declined to speak at the meeting.

A. trumpet   B. whistle
C. bugle   D. flute

77. In spite of the treatment, the pain in his leg grew in_____.

A. gravity   B. extent
C. intensity   D. amount

78. Bus services between Town Centre and Newton Housing Estate will be _____ until the motorway is repaired.

A. discontinued   B. suspended
C. halted   D. ceased

As we can see from the above examples, the three different examinations focus on students' ability to distinguish between different vocabulary usages in the correct contexts. Students are required to understand the meanings of the words as well as the meanings of the sentences. Furthermore, such examinations are highly predictable, allowing both teachers and students to spend long hours reviewing these test papers. On the other hand, the examinations of colleges and universities seem to focus on meaning and its context, as opposed to some perhaps more interesting aspects of linguistic structures such as fixed expressions and collocations, which are tested less frequently. In this they differ from the examination that students from senior high school need to take in order to enter university.

In this chapter, we have discussed the current situation of English language teaching in mainland China. We have seen that L2 language teaching and learning in mainland China are developing and also face challenges, including pedagogic settings, changing aims in teaching and learning, and language teaching methodologies. Because the curriculum and teaching materials as well as the teaching methodologies are mainly determined by a number of national examinations, to some extent students' reading and writing skills have been strongly emphasised. At the same time, students' communicative skills have been left far behind. To improve the current situation in English language teaching and learning in mainland China, general educational decision-makers, classroom teachers and individual students need to be encouraged to tackle the existing factors (such as the national examinations) that constrain the successful English language teaching and learning.

Chapter Five

A Corpus-based Analysis of Wh-sentences from EFL Textbooks

5.1 Introduction

In this chapter, we investigate whether any prototypical structures for "wh" sentences emerge in three sets of Chinese EFL textbooks. A total of 40 Chinese EFL textbooks that are used in Junior Middle School, Senior High School and Universities in China were analysed; the school textbooks are prescribed by the Ministry of Education. The investigation sets out to see whether, as was hypothesized in Chapter 1, more prototype structures occur in junior textbooks than in senior textbooks and university textbooks. Differences in the frequencies of the words occurring after the "wh" words were also discussed in order to establish whether and how such patterns develop across the three sets of corpora.

5.2 Textbooks Selected

The school textbooks, such as the *People's Education Press* series by DaoYi Liu and David Nunan, run from beginner level through intermediate level and are used in junior middle schools and senior high schools respectively. For both junior middle schools and senior high schools, six series with a total of 24 EFL textbooks were analysed. These textbooks change little annually. Advanced level textbooks are chosen by the universities themselves. Four series with 16 textbooks are currently used by universities in China, namely, New Horizon College English (NHCE)", "College English-Integrated Course (CEIC)", "21Century College English Reading and Writing (21CCERW)" and "College English Extensive Reading (CEER)" respectively. The textbooks analysed here are the complete sets of textbooks available for use in junior, senior high, and universities in China. Table 5.1 shows the publication dates and numbers of textbooks analysed:

Target	No. of Textbooks analysed	Publication Dates	Level
Junior	12	2003	beginner
Senior	12	2001	intermediate
University	16	1998, 2002	advanced

Table 5.1 Selected Chinese EFL Textbooks

I have labeled these textbooks "beginner", "intermediate" and "advanced" based on the descriptions of the contents and proficiency levels.

5.3 Hypotheses

The hypotheses addressed are as follows:

1). The textbook data will be largely prototypical as it relies on the intuition of textbook writers.
2). Textbook patterns incline more towards non-prototypical structures according to proficiency level. For example, textbooks for university will be more non-prototypical than those for junior and senior schools.

5.4 Data Processing Procedure

Textbook data for Junior Middle schools, Senior High schools and Universities were obtained from the internet. In Junior Middle School textbooks, occurrences of "wh" words were selected manually from www.pep.cn. Textbooks for Senior High Schools and Universities were downloaded from www.ebigear.com/res-665-7777700016115.htm

and http://jpkc.ecust.edu.cn:8080/dxyy/jiaoan/bkzl/jiaoan_new.htm respectively. Although these websites only exist for a short period of time, they are easy to search for in Google and free to download.

5.4.1 Data Processing of Prototypical Senses

In my MA study 'Distribution of the word *what* in Chinese Learner Data, EFL Textbooks and a Natural Language Corpus', the word "what" was analysed. A set of features for 'what', with the interrogative and main clause being the prototype were identified (Zhang 2007). The prototype and extensions were illustrated as follows:

What:

Prototype: + interrogative, + main clause (interrogative) What the hell is he building in there?

Extension 1: - interrogative, + main clause (declarative) What a summer. What a beginning.

Extension 2: - interrogative, - main clause (subordinate clause) I understand what he says.

Taking the analysis from my MA as a starting point, we now move on to analyse and exemplify the other "wh" words). It is notable that Extension 1 does not occur at all for many of these "wh" words in any of the textbooks. The examples of the other "wh" words can be seen from appendix.

Wordsmith Tools' (Version 4) suite of analytical programs (Scott 2006) was used to create and compile the concordance lines from the textbooks. The three textbook sets were saved as Wordsmith Tools files. Through out the chapter, I use JTD to refer to textbooks from Junior Middle Schools, STD for textbooks for Senior High Schools, and UTD indicates the textbooks for University.

A total of 5826 "wh" lines were extracted from JTD. STD amounted to 4020 "wh" lines. 4473 lines of "wh" words were extracted from UTD. Table 5.2 shows the number of occurrences of "wh" words across the three sets of textbooks.

Data set	No. of concordance lines
JTD	5826
STD	4020
UTD	4473
All books	14319

Table 5.2 Sizes of concordance lines across the three sets of textbooks

5.4.2 *Data Processing of Word Frequencies*

The three sets of data were processed (i.e. analysed, grouped, selected, and compared) to investigate the words occurring immediately after these "wh" words.

First, the three sets of data were converted into three Excel documents. Second, each sentence in the Excel document was analysed into one of three categories, i.e. interrogatives, declaratives and subordinate clauses as follows:

Interrogative:	they occur.	What	are the main differences between
Declarative:	thinks,	What	a fascinating man. I hope he asks me
Clause:	'If we knew	What	the limits of his (Mr Bates's)

In the third stage, the words occurring after each "wh" word are chosen from the concordance lines of the three sets of data:

UTD (what)		
Word	No.	%
Is	217	41.41%
Do	67	12.79%
Are	56	10.69%
Can	49	9.35%
Does	25	4.77%
About	16	3.05%
Did	15	2.86%
Should	14	2.67%
Color	12	2.29%
You	8	1.53%
Time	7	1.34%
Will	6	1.15%
If	5	0.95%
kind of	5	0.95%
The	5	0.95%
Would	5	0.95%
happened	4	0.76%
Have	4	0.76%
I	4	0.76%

Table 5.3 Words occurring immediately after 'what' in UTD in interrogatives

The most frequent words occurring immediately after the "wh" words in the three sets of textbooks are shown later in the results section.

5.5 Results and Discussion

In the following section, the results are presented and discussed. First, the prototypes and extension structures of the different sentence types across the three corpora are presented. Second, the frequencies of the words occurring immediately after "wh" words will be discussed.

5.5.1 Prototypes and Extensions across the Three Datasets

In following sections, we look at the prototypes and extension structures across the three datasets. Table 5.4 and Table 5.5 show the number and proportion of concordance lines for each "wh" word. Figure 5.1 and Figure 5.2 show these results in graphical form.

Feifei Zhang

	Total size of the data	What	how	where	when	why	who	whom	whose	which	Total
JTD	11463	1630(142)	858(75)	340(30)	440(38)	203(18)	302(26)	12(1)	34(3)	207(18)	5826(508)
STD	273105	876(3)	509(2)	339(1)	647(2)	265(1)	806(3)	27(0)	43(0)	518(2)	4020(15)
UTD	452541	468(1)	519(1)	258(1)	1065(2)	206(0)	1132(3)	49(0)	72(0)	704(2)	4473(10)
Total	737109	2974(4)	1886(3)	937(1)	2152(3)	674(1)	2240(3)	88(0)	149(0)	1429(2)	14319(19)

Table 5.4 Number of concordance lines of "wh" words across the three dataset (frequencies per 1000 words are shown in brackets)

	What	how	where	when	why	who	whom	whose	which
JTD	55%	45%	36%	20%	30%	13%	14%	23%	14%
STD	29%	27%	36%	30%	39%	36%	31%	29%	36%
UTD	16%	28%	28%	49%	31%	51%	56%	48%	49%

Table 5.5 Proportion of concordance lines of "wh" words across three datasets

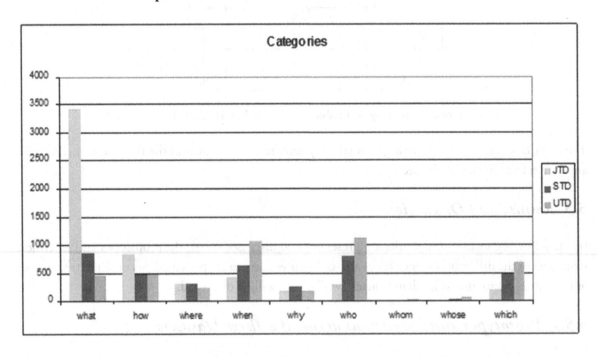

Figure 5.1 A comparison of the number of "wh" words across three datasets

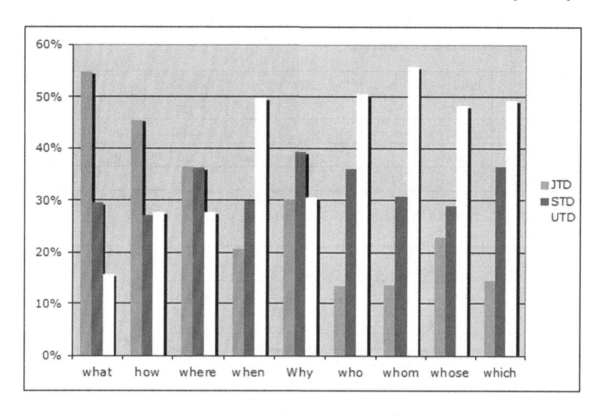

Figure 5.2 A comparison of the proportion of "wh" words across three datasets

Table 5.4 gives the results for "wh" words that are taught across the three datasets across the three levels of proficiency. Clearly, the distribution of some "wh" words such as "what" and "where" decreases steadily, so it seems that the basic prototypical forms of "wh" are taught at lower levels of proficiency. On the other hand, the proportion of the words "when" and "who" increases steadily. This might mean that those words occur more frequently at complex clause levels and so are more likely to occur at higher proficiency university levels. For example, the word *who*, occurs at 13% in JTD (302 out of 2240), but in STD rises to 36% (806 out of 2240), and then increases to 51% (1132 out of 2240) for UTD.

The word *how* occurs at 45% (858 lines) in JTD, but reduces to 27% (509 lines) in STD, and increases to 28% (519 lines) in UTD. UTD contains higher occurrence rates of non-prototypical words such as *who, when* and *which*. This may suggest that the more prototypical "wh" words are generally taught at lower levels of proficiency. Within the "wh" category, the words "what" and "how" appear to be more prototypical than the other "wh" words. Let us now look at the ways in which these "wh" words are used. For each word, we examine the distribution of prototype, Extension 1 and Extension 2 sentences across the three corpora.

Distribution of "what" sentences across the three corpora

We now look at the distribution of "what" sentences across the three corpora. As seen from the above discussions, the word "what" can be considered to be one of the most prototypical words among the "wh" category. It is predominately taught at beginner level. Table 5.6 and Figure 5.3 show the different types of "what" sentences in each data set.

	Prototype	%	Extension 1	%	Extension 2	%	total
JTD	1482	90.9	20	1.2	128	7.9	1630
STD	407	46.4	25	2.9	444	50.7	876
UTD	245	52	11	2.4	212	45	468
All books	2134	71.8	56	1.9	84	26.4	2974

Table 5.6 Different types of "what" sentences across three datasets

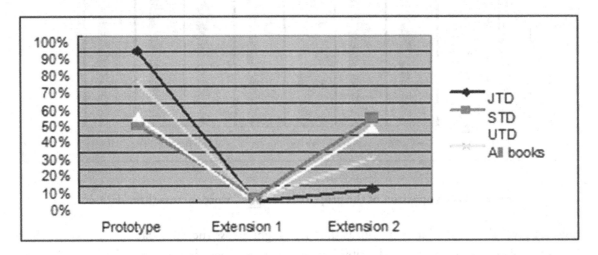

Figure 5.3 "what" sentence types across three sets of data

As Table 5.6 and Figure 5.3 show, prototypes (+ interrogative, + main clause) predominate in both JTD and UTD at 90.9% and 52% respectively. However, STD has fewer prototypes with around 47%, of those occurring in JTD. JTD and STD have almost the same distribution for Extension 1: JTD at 1.2% and 2.9% at STD. UTD has the lowest percentage for Extension 1 at only 2.4%. Table 5.6 shows that STD and UTD have almost the same proportion of Extension 2 at 50.7% and 45% respectively, while for JTD, Extension 2 only occurs at 7.9%.

Examples of prototypes from each set of data are shown below.

```
What is her telephone number? (JTD)
What was the nicest part of your holiday? (STD)
What was the main cause of the problem discussed in the listening aural
section? (UTD)
```

Extension 1 declaratives (- Interrogative, + main clause) had the lowest numbers in all data sets: 1.2% for JTD, 2.9% for STD, and 0.24% for UTD, for example:

```
What a fine day! (JTD)
```

```
What a coincidence! (STD)
What a dumb idea! (UTD)
```

Extension 2 clauses (- interrogative, - main clause) accounted for 50.7% of STD concordances, with much lower figures for UTD (45%) and JTD (7.9%), for example:

```
We never know what will happen in the future. (JTD)
Now John Jacob illustrated what can be done anywhere. (STD)
The person does not refer to what the previous speaker has said. (UTD)
```

Thus, as we seen from the above discussions, the prototypical "what" predominates in the lower level textbooks. As we move up to the higher level, extension 2 is the most frequent sentence type. A possible explanation for this might be that textbooks increasingly focus on complex grammatical structures as the proficiency level increases. This pattern is slightly different from the "how" sentences.

Distribution of "how" sentences across the three corpora

The pattern of the distribution of "how" sentences is similar to the "what" sentence pattern, as prototypes largely occur in lower level textbooks. However, as we move up to the higher level, extension 2 is observed to occur slightly more frequently in STD, and predominates for UTD.

Table 5.7 and Figure 5.4 show the different types of "how" sentences in each data set.

	Prototype	%	Extension 1	%	Extension 2	%	total
JTD	773	90.1	25	2.9	60	7.0	858
STD	260	51.1	33	6.5	216	42.4	509
UTD	123	23.7	27	5.2	369	71.1	519
All books	1156	61.3	85	4.6	645	34.2	1886

Table 5.7 "how" sentence across the three datasets

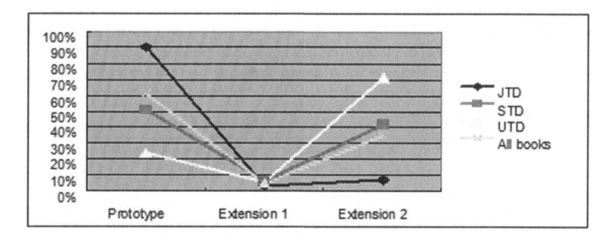

Figure 5.4 "how" sentence across the three sets of data

Similar to the situation in relation to the word "what", Table 5.7 and Figure 5.4 show that the prototypes are very strong at beginning and intermediate level, at 90.1% for JTD, 51.1% for STD. However, for UTD, only 23.7% of prototypes occurred. This indicates that the higher the level of the textbook, the fewer prototypes are taught. Extension 1 has a small proportion across the datasets with 2.9% for JTD, 6.5% for STD, and 5.2% for UTD. In the case of Extension 2, the distribution increases significantly at 7.0% for JTD, 42.4% for STD, and 71.1% for UTD. The data shows that prototypes of the word "how" are predominant at the beginning level (JTD) while Extension 2 occurs most frequently at the higher level (UTD).

Examples of the different sentence patterns are shown below:

```
How much are these socks? (JTD)
How are you getting to the airport? (STD)
How was the school different? (UTD)
```

STD and UTD have relatively similar frequencies for Extension 1, with 6.5% for STD and 5.2% for UTD:

```
How funny they are! (JTD)
How lucky you are! (STD)
How little I have ever really done! (UTD)
```

For the advanced textbooks, Extension 2 predominates. However, the sample for JTD is quite small, with only 60 concordance lines:

```
This is how the SOS children's village started. (JTD)
...dark and dreary nights wondering how this thing is going to come out.
(STD)
...practical applications everywhere for how companies should decide whom
to (UTD)...
```

Distribution of "where" sentences across the three corpora

Now we shall look at the distribution of "where" sentences across the three corpora. The pattern of the distribution was similar to that found in relation to the words "what" and "how". In relation to "where" sentences, however, the pattern was even more marked, as more non-prototypical sentences occur as the proficiency level increases. Table 5.8 and Figure 5.5 show the different types of "where" sentences across the three datasets.

	Prototype	%	Extension 1	%	Extension 2	%	total
JTD	281	82.6	0	0	59	17.4	340
STD	74	21.8	0	0	265	78.2	339
UTD	21	8.1	0	0	237	91.9	258
All books	376	40.1	0	0	561	59.9	937

Table 5.8 "where" sentences across each datasets

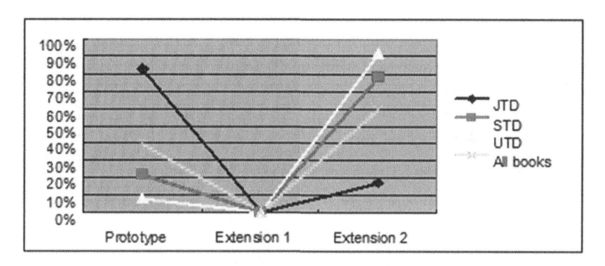

Figure 5.5 "where" sentences types across three sets of data

According to Table 5.8 and Figure 5.5, prototypes predominate at almost 83% in JTD. For STD and UTD, prototypes (+ interrogative, + clause) are relatively rare at only 21.8% (STD) and 8.1% (UTD). Below are examples of prototypes across the three datasets:

```
Where did you go in the U.S.? (JTD)
Where is the best place to meet? (STD)
Where, then, does your happiness lie? (UTD)
```

The most frequent sentence pattern in STD and UTD is Extension 2 (- interrogative, - subordinate clause), at 78.2% and 91.9% respectively, for example:

```
I followed it to see where it was going, and I was very… (JTD)
…the last year of his life in Switzerland, where he was buried in 1977.
(STD)
It is put where it will lie flat. (UTD)
```

Distribution of "when" sentences across the three corpora

The distribution of "when" sentences can be seen to be different from those for previous words. In this case, the prototype is not found to occur predominately in lower level textbooks. A possible explanation might be that it is considered more important to teach "when" extension 2 at the lower levels.

Table 5.9 and Figure 5.6 show the different types of "when" sentences across the three datasets.

	Prototype	%	Extension 1	%	Extension 2	%	total
JTD	108	24.5	0	0	332	75.5	440
STD	21	3.2	0	0	626	96.8	647
UTD	11	0.1	0	0	1054	99.9	1065
All books	140	6.5	0	0	2012	93.5	2152

Table 5.9 "when" sentences across the three datasets

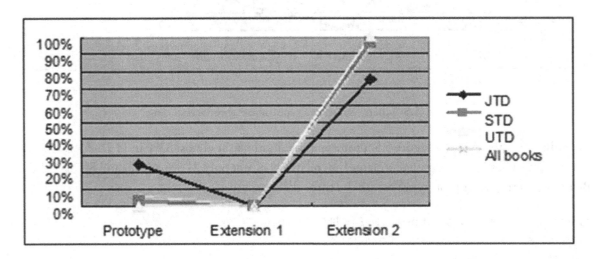

Figure 5.6 "when" sentences across the three datasets

As Table 5.9 and Figure 5.6 show, prototypes occur at 24.5% for JTD, 3.2 % for STD, and 0.1 % for UTD respectively. Extension 2 occurs at 75.5% for JTD, 96.8% for STD, and 99.9% for UTD. Extension 1 is not found in any of the three datasets; again, this form does not seem to exist. Examples from each set of data are shown below.

```
When do you want to go? (JTD)
When are you going off to Guangzhou? (STD)
After all, when all is said or done (UTD)
```

STD and UTD have a relatively similar distribution for Extension 2. Both are over 95%, while JTD is just under 80%:

```
…there were growing trees, when that sufferer was put to death. (JTD)
They are better when you are hot. (STD)
"We don't know when he'll be out of danger," the doctor said. (UTD)
```

Distribution of "why" sentences across the three corpora

"Why" sentences are revealed as one of the most prototypical sentences among the "wh" category, as prototypes occur more at JTD, STD and UTD than extension 2. We may assume that the "why" interrogative form is the most frequent pattern, as well as one of the most prototypical "wh" words.

Table 5.10 and Figure 5.7 show the different types of "why" sentences across three datasets.

	Prototype	%	Extension 1	%	Extension 2	%	total
JTD	167	82.3	0	0	36	17.7	203
STD	189	71.3	0	0	76	28.7	265
UTD	109	52.9	0	0	97	47.1	206
All tbooks	465	69	0	0	209	31.0	674

Table 5.10 "why" sentences across the three datasets

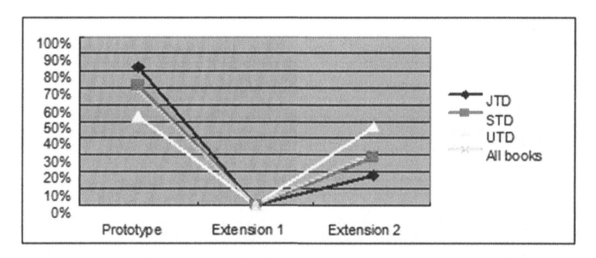

Figure 5.7 "why" sentences types across the three datasets

Table 5.10 and Figure 5.7 show that prototypes are predominant among the three sets of textbooks, with 82.3% for JTD, 71.3% for STD, and 52.9 for UTD:

Examples are shown below:

```
Why do you like koalas? (JTD)
Why don't you do the experiments? (STD)
Why are these statistics amazing? (UTD)
```

Extension 2 subordinate clauses (- interrogative, - main clause) accounted for 47.1% of UTD, with much lower figures for JTD (17.7%) and STD (28.7%):

```
That is the reason why it is so important to protect every… (JTD)
That is why we are getting anxious about you. (STD)
```

```
Then we wonder why our children refuse to take their… (UTD)
```

Extension 1 is absent from the three sets of data, suggesting again that this form does not exist.

Distribution of "who" sentences across the three corpora

We now move on to discuss the distribution of "who" sentences across the three corpora. "Who" sentences follow a similar pattern to "where" sentences, as prototypes occur more in lower level textbook (JTD), while extension 2 predominates in higher level textbooks (STD and UTD).

Table 5.11 and Figure 5.8 show the different types of "who" sentences across three datasets.

	Prototype	%	Extension 1	%	Extension 2	%	total
JTD	166	55.07	0	0	136	45.03	302
STD	45	5.6	0	0	761	94.4	806
UTD	12	1.1	0	0	1120	98.9	1132
All books	223	10.0	0	0	2017	90.0	2240

Table 5.11 "who" sentences across the three datasets

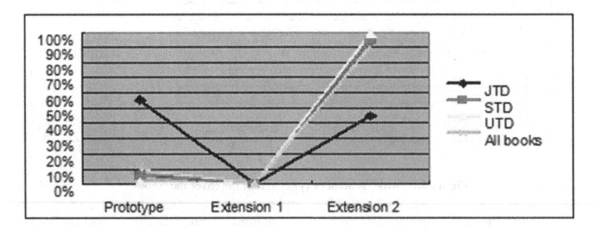

Figure 5.8 "who" sentences types across the three datasets

Table 5.11 and Figure 5.8 clearly show that JTD has almost the same distribution for prototypes and Extension 2: 55.07% for prototypes and 45.03% for Extension 2. Prototypes are rarely present in STD and UTD, at only 5.6% (STD) and 1.1% (UTD). Extension 2 in UTD has almost double the number of JTD, with 98.9% for UTD and 45.03% for JTD. Examples of the three sentence patterns are shown below:

Prototypes:

```
Who is not on duty today? (JTD)
Who is the boy over there? (STD)
```

```
Who makes history and why? (UTD)
```

There is an increase in the frequency of Extension 2, from 45.3% (JTD) to 94.4% (STD), and 98.9% (UTD):

```
If there is someone in your class who has a big problem, make a plan to…
(JTD)
It is also about the man who wanted to end slavery. (STD)
…the first paragraph quickly and find out who the author is. (UTD)
```

Distribution of "whom" sentences across the three corpora

"Whom" sentences are different from the other "wh" words as they have the lowest number of occurrences across the three corpora among "wh" words. However, "whom" sentences follow a similar pattern to "when" sentences, as extension 2 predominates across the three corpora. We will find in the next two chapters that "whom" sentences were barely found in the elicited data and written corpora. One possible reason might be that such patterns rarely occur in textbook data, and learners therefore have fewer examples stored in their long-term memory.

Table 5.12 and Figure 5.9 show the different types of "whom" sentences across three datasets.

	Prototype	%	Extension 1	%	Extension 2	%	total
JTD	1	8.3	0	0	11	92.7	12
STD	3	11.1	0	0	24	88.9	27
UTD	0	0	0	0	49	100	49
All books	4	4.5	0	0	84	95.5	88

Table 5.12 "whom" sentences across the three data sets

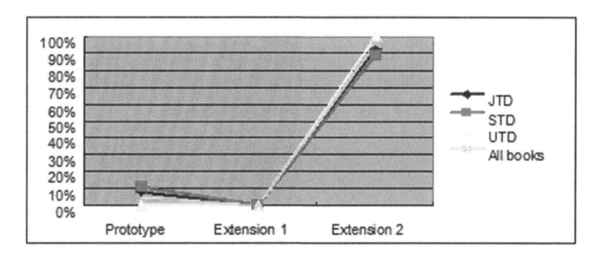

Figure 5.9 "whom" sentences types across the three data sets

As Table 5.12 and Figure 5.9 show, in terms of prototypes, JTD has only 8.3% (one occurrence), while STD has only 11.3% (three occurrences). Both are very small numbers. Prototypes are absent from UTD. Extension 2 has a relatively high frequency, with 100% for UTD, 92.7% for JTD, and 88.9% for STD.

Examples of the sentence patterns are shown below:

Prototypes:

```
Whom did he travel with? (JTD)
For whom have you prepared this feast? (STD)
```

Extension 2:

```
She should ever see the prince, for whom she had forsaken her kindred
and …(JTD)
…man relaxed with the others, some of whom would owe their lives to him.
(STD)
…for companies should decide whom to hire, how couples can increase…(UTD)
```

Distribution of "whose" sentences across the three corpora

We now look at the distribution of "whose" sentences across the three corpora. "Whose" sentences follow a similar pattern to "who" and "where", as prototypes primarily occur in JTD while non-prototypical structures predominate in STD and UTD.

Table 5.13 and Figure 5.10 show the different types of "whose" sentences across three datasets.

	Prototype	%	Extension 1	%	Extension 2	%	total
JTD	29	85.3	0	0	5	14.7	34
STD	6	14.0	0	0	37	86.0	43
UTD	3	4.2	0	0	69	95.8	72
All books	38	25.5	0	0	111	74.5	149

Table 5.13 "whose" sentences across the three data sets

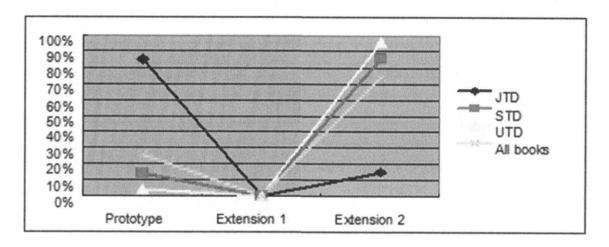

Figure 5.10 "whose" sentences across the three data sets

As Table 5.13 and Figure 5.10 illustrate, prototypes only predominate in JTD at 85.3%, while STD and UTD have a relatively small percentage, with only 14.0% (STD) and 4.2% (UTD). These are examples:

```
Whose schoolbags are these? (JTD)
Whose is this? (STD)
Whose opinion do you agree more with? (UTD)
```

Extension 2 predominates in both STD and UTD, at 86% (STD) and 95.8% (UTD) respectively. For JTD, Extension 2, with a percentage of 14.7%, has a much lower frequency in the data, for example:

```
To be able to wander about with those whose world seems to be so much…
(JTD)
While the whole house moved, Flora, whose beautiful hair and dress were
all…(STD)
I am luckier than some of my friends, whose father died while they were
still young. (UTD)
```

Extension 1 is again absent across the three datasets.

Distribution of "which" sentences across the three corpora

We now discuss the distribution of "which" sentences across the three corpora. "Which" sentences are similar in terms of distribution to the findings for the previous words "who", "where", and "whose" as the prototype largely occurs at JTD, while extension 2 is identified more in higher level textbooks (STD and UTD).

Table 5.14 and Figure 5.11 show the different types of "which" sentences across three datasets.

	Prototype	%	Extension 1	%	Extension 2	%	total
JTD	112	54.1	0	0	95	45.9	207
STD	20	3.9	0	0	498	96.1	518
UTD	35	5.0	0	0	669	95.0	704
All books	167	11.7	0	0	1262	88.3	1429

Table 5.14 "which" sentences across the three data sets

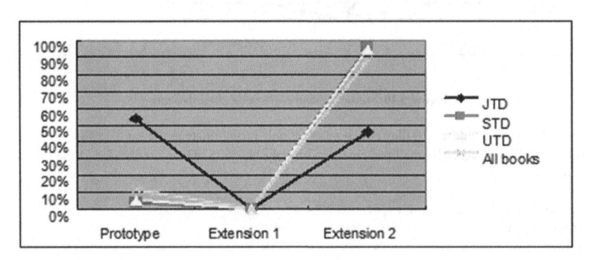

Figure 5.11 "which" sentences types across three data sets

According to Table 5.14 and Figure 5.11, prototypes only predominate in JTD, at 54.1%, while they occur at only 3.9% for STD and 5.0% for UTD only. Examples are shown below:

```
Which sports do you like most? (JTD)
Which places did you go to? (STD)
Which of the following best describes…(UTD)
```

Extension 2 occurs frequently in STD and UTD, at 96.1% and 96.5% respectively. On the other hand, JTD has a relatively small amount of Extension 2, at only 45.9%. This again suggests that at the beginning level, textbooks writers tend to provide more prototypes than Extension structures. Examples are as follows:

```
She said I was lazy, which is not true. (JTD)
…of smokers die because of illnesses which are caused by smoking tobacco.
(STD)
…of British subjects in America: which strange to relate, have proved…
(UTD)
```

Again, Extension 1 is not found in any of the datasets.

In this section, we have looked at the prototype and extension structures in three sets of textbooks. As may be seen from the data, at least five patterns can be identified: 1) prototypes largely occur in JTD and UTD, while extension 2 largely occurs in STD, for example, "what" sentences; 2) prototypes largely occur in JTD and STD, while extension 2 largely occurs in UTD, for example, "what" sentences; 3) prototypes largely occur in JTD, while extension 2 largely occurs in STD and UTD, for example, "where", "who", "whose", and "which" sentences; 4) extension 2 largely occurs across the three corpora, for example, "when" and "whom" sentences; 5) prototypes largely occur across the three corpora, for example, as "why" sentences.

Generally, prototypes predominate in lower level textbooks such as JTD and STD, as opposed to the fact that higher level textbooks, UTD, display more extension 2 subordinate clauses. This may suggest that prototypes are involved in early learning and textbook writers tend to provide prototypes at the fundamental learning stage because this arrangement is more appropriate for human mental processing. In the next section, we look at the frequency of words occurring immediately after "wh" words in three types of sentences. The focus is on the ways in which grammatical-lexical words occur in three types of sentences across the three sets of textbooks.

5.5.2 Frequency of the Words Occurring Immediately after "Wh" Words in Interrogatives, Declaratives, and Subordinate Clauses across the three Datasets

In this section, we look at the words that occur immediately after the "wh" words. This is therefore an investigation of collocation and colligation. We have chosen to look at the words immediately following the "wh" words as this often gives us a clear picture of the grammatical and lexical words that the "wh" words are particularly likely to combine with. The reason for choosing the word immediately following the "wh" word is that it provides the key to the subsequent sentence structures. For example, if the first word following *what* is the indefinite article *a*, the likely pattern is what+a+adjective+noun in sentences like *what a beautiful day*. Similarly, if the first word after *what* is the definite article, *the*, the pattern might be what+the+expletive (+VP) as in *what the hell (are you doing?)*.

Frequency of the words after "what" in interrogatives across the three sets of data

We now turn to look at words immediately following the word 'what'. We will see the findings with respect to the behaviours of such words, as well as the similarities and differences across three sets of data.

Feifei Zhang

Table 5.15 shows the frequencies of the words occurring after "what" in interrogatives across the three sets of data.

JTD			STD			UTD		
word	**No.**	**%**	**word**	**No.**	**%**	**word**	**No.**	**%**
is	273	25.68%	do	66	18.97%	is	33	18.97%
are	142	13.36%	about	42	12.07%	do	26	14.94%
do	106	9.97%	is	33	9.48%	about	12	6.90%
does	59	5.55%	was	29	8.33%	are	12	6.90%
did	48	4.52%	are	25	7.18%	does	10	5.75%
about	44	4.14%	happened	18	5.17%	was	9	5.17%
time	44	4.14%	does	17	4.89%	kind	5	2.87%
color	39	3.67%	kind	14	4.02%	can	5	2.87%
can	37	3.48%	did	14	4.02%	happened	4	2.30%
kind	29	2.73%	should	12	3.45%	makes	3	1.72%
was	26	2.45%	can	10	2.87%	have	3	1.72%
were	21	1.98%	will	8	2.30%	other	3	1.72%
day	18	1.69%	time	6	1.72%	would	3	1.72%
else	17	1.60%	would	5	1.44%	will	3	1.72%
would	15	1.41%	sort	5	1.44%	problem	2	1.15%
will	15	1.41%	difference	4	1.15%	else	2	1.15%
does	12	1.13%	have	3	0.86%	others	2	1.15%
should	10	0.94%	happens	3	0.86%	did	2	1.15%
kinds	8	0.75%	the	3	0.86%	am	2	1.15%
have	7	0.66%	shall	2	0.57%	sort	2	1.15%
happened	6	0.56%	were	2	0.57%			

Table 5.15 Comparison of the frequencies and percentage of different words occurring after "what" in interrogatives

The most frequent words to follow the word "what" in interrogatives are be-verb auxiliaries across the three sets of data. This suggests that the basic usage of grammatical words in "what" interrogatives is provided more frequently at the lower level. It is clear from Table 5.15 that JTD focuses almost exclusively on be verbs *is* and *are*: 25.68% and 13.36%. For example:

```
What is this in English? (JTD)
What's that in your hand? (STD)
What was the main cause of the … (UTD)
What does he eat for breakfast? (JTD)
What do we have today to show for it? (STD)
What do you know about his background? (UTD)
```

Lexical items occur gradually in accordance with the increase in proficiency levels. In lower level textbooks, more fixed expressions such as *what time... what color... what kind... what happened...* are provided. For example:

```
What colour is it? (JTD)
What kind of movies do you think... (JTD)
What happened? (JTD)
```

In higher level textbooks STD and UTD, both adjectives and nouns occur frequently, suggesting the word "what" has a wider range of fixed expressions and collocation. For example:

```
What interesting things did you do? (STD)
What happened next? (STD)
What time does the performance start? (STD)
What happened? (UTD)
What kind of technological innovations ... (UTD)
What makes consumers buy one brand... (UTD)
```

Frequency of the words after "what" in declaratives across the three sets of data

Table 5.16 shows the frequencies of the words occurring after "what" declaratives across the three sets of data.

JTD			STD			UTD		
word	**No.**	**%**	**word**	**No.**	**%**	**word**	**No.**	**%**
a	10	71.43%	a	19	100.00%	a	3	75.00%
beautiful	1	7.14%				fun	1	25.00%
an	1	7.14%						
horrible	1	7.14%						
lovely	1	7.14%						

Table 5.16 Comparison of the frequencies and percentage of
different words occurring after "what" interrogatives

The most frequent word across the three sets of data is *a* at 71.43% for JTD, 100% for STD, and 75% for UTD, indicating a high frequency of exclamatory expressions:

```
What a big house! (JTD)
What a delicious supper! (STD)
What a dumb idea! (UTD)
```

It is interesting that JTD has a wider range of adjectives such as *beautiful, horrible,* and *lovely*:

```
What beautiful flowers!
What horrible weather!
What lovely flowers!
```

Frequency of the words after "what" in subordinate clauses across the three sets of data

Table 5.17 shows the frequencies of the words occurring after "what" in subordinate clauses across the three sets of data.

JTD			STD			UTD		
word	No.	%	word	No.	%	word	No.	%
you	27	16.67%	they	45	9.39%	is	81	12.11%
they	24	14.81%	we	44	9.19%	you	79	11.81%
I	18	11.11%	you	39	8.14%	we	51	7.62%
the	15	9.26%	it	38	7.93%	I	50	7.47%
to	11	6.79%	I	36	7.52%	they	32	4.78%
she	10	6.17%	he	35	7.31%	the	31	4.63%
time	8	4.94%	the	32	6.68%	it	27	4.04%
will	5	3.09%	is	30	6.26%	he	24	3.59%
he	5	3.09%	to	21	4.38%	one	21	3.14%
it	4	2.47%	was	13	2.71%	she	17	2.54%
is	4	2.47%	has	11	2.30%	was	14	2.09%
happened	3	1.85%	this	8	1.67%	to	12	1.79%
we	3	1.85%	she	6	1.25%	has	9	1.35%
your	2	1.23%	a	6	1.25%	happened	9	1.35%
would	2	1.23%	had	6	1.25%	they	8	1.20%
if	2	1.23%	kind	6	1.25%	a	7	1.05%
life	2	1.23%	that	5	1.04%	would	6	0.90%
other	2	1.23%	happened	5	1.04%	someone	6	0.90%
people	1	0.62%	their	5	1.04%	your	6	0.90%
movie	1	0.62%	your	5	1.04%	can	5	0.75%

Table 5.17 Comparison of the frequencies and percentage of different words occurring after "what" in subordinate clauses

As Table 5.17 shows, pronouns occur the most frequently across three sets of data. This is interesting as it is the opposite of what was found with the interrogatives. For "what" interrogatives, be verbs and auxiliaries occur frequently, as opposed to a few pronoun occurring across the three sets of data. For "what" subordinate clauses, only pronouns predominate across three sets of data. The reason might be that there are strong conventions with pronouns tending to follow 'what' in subordinate clauses. It therefore appears to be a relatively restricted construction in English. For example:

```
The other students guess what it is. (JTD)
...but I didn't find what I was looking for. (STD)
...and let them guess what you decided to do. (UTD)
```

Lexical items occur more frequently in JTD than those in STD and UTD. This contrasts with what we found for "what" interrogatives. There, lexical items were found to occur increasingly frequently according to proficiency level. Here lexical items occur frequently at the beginner level. For example:

```
Write a story reporting what happened. (JTD)
...for a special dinner and explained what food she was planning to cook.
(STD)
We don't always recognize that what looks like failure may, in the long...
(UTD)
```

It was found that the word '*to*' collocates *what* in subordinate clauses in three sets of data, for example:

```
She doesn't know what to do. (JTD)
I wonder if you know what to do now. (STD)
It is important to show a child what to do, and that we certainly did
not... (UTD)
```

Frequency of the words after "how" in interrogatives across the three sets of data

In the following sections, we look at the frequencies of words occurring immediately after "how" in interrogatives, declaratives, and subordinate clauses. The analysis focuses on the patterns with types of words that tend to be provided.

Table 5.18 shows the frequencies of the words occurring after "how" in interrogatives across the three sets of data.

JTD			STD			UTD		
word	**No.**	**%**	**word**	**No.**	**%**	**word**	**No.**	**%**
long	92	14.58%	many	43	19.11%	do	25	18.38%
do	88	13.95%	about	35	15.56%	can	23	16.91%
many	82	13.00%	do	25	11.11%	did	18	13.24%
much	71	11.25%	long	22	9.78%	much	13	9.56%
are	66	10.46%	did	16	7.11%	many	8	5.88%
about	50	7.92%	can	16	7.11%	will	4	2.94%
is	31	4.91%	much	16	7.11%	could	4	2.94%
often	30	4.75%	to	10	4.44%	the	3	2.21%
far	20	3.17%	is	6	2.67%	would	3	2.21%
old	15	2.38%	well	6	2.67%	long	3	2.21%
was	13	2.06%	could	5	2.22%	does	3	2.21%
can	12	1.90%	are	4	1.78%	is	2	1.47%
did	12	1.90%	will	3	1.33%	come	2	1.47%
does	12	1.90%	tall	3	1.33%	you	2	1.47%
would	6	0.95%	come	3	1.33%	should	2	1.47%
to	5	0.79%	far	2	0.89%	important	2	1.47%
could	4	0.63%	high	2	0.89%	often	2	1.47%
you	2	0.32%	does	1	0.44%	honest	2	1.47%
well	2	0.32%	large	1	0.44%	are	1	0.74%
she	2	0.32%	and	1	0.44%	was	1	0.74%
we	2	0.32%	has	1	0.44%	serious	1	0.74%

Table 5.18 Comparison of the frequencies and percentage of different
words occurring after "how" in interrogatives

As expected, Table 5.18 shows that there are frequent occurrences of quantifying words across three sets of the data, such as *much, many, long, far,* and *old*. This might be one of the main features of "how" interrogatives. Textbook writers tend to provide the same proportion of qualifying words so we can assume this is definitely something they believe language learners need to learn. Examples are shown as follows:

```
How much have you learnt so far? (JTD)
How long are you staying in Xi'an? (STD)
How long does Gates expect it to go on? (UTD)
```

Be-verbs, auxiliaries and modals are also provided in the same proportion, although UTD contains more variation as it is expected to be in accordance with higher proficiency. For example:

```
How are you? (JTD)
How is it going? (STD)
In China, how are the most hardworking and … (UTD)
How do people live in places far away? (JTD)
How do you pronounce this word? (STD)
How did their new white neighbours treat…(UTD)
How would it help? (JTD)
How could you do that? (STD)
How would it effect your life? (UTD)
```

It is interesting to note that STD contains more lexical items than JTD and UTD. The reason for this might be that at intermediate level, it reflects a wider variety of word choices, particular in adjectives. For example:

```
How important is this research? (STD)
How honest are we? (STD)
How serious a threat do you consider... (UTD)
How important is it to you?(UTD)
```

Pronouns occur frequently at JTD as grammatical words are considered to be useful for learners at the beginner level, for example:

```
How does she get to school? (JTD)
Can you see how your way of looking actually does? (UTD)
```

As seen from above, grammatical words such as be verbs, auxiliaries, and modals tend to occur in the three sets of textbooks in the same proportion. This contrasts with the fact that lexical items occur more in higher level textbooks (STD and UTD). This might well because a wider variety of word choices are provided as proficiency level increases.

Feifei Zhang

Frequency of the words after "how" in declaratives across the three sets of data

Table 5.19 shows the frequencies of the words occurring after "how" in declaratives across the three sets of data.

JTD			STD			UTD		
word	**No.**	**%**	**word**	**No.**	**%**	**word**	**No.**	**%**
funny	1	7.14%	nice	12	35.29%	creative	3	13.64%
interesting	1	7.14%	unlucky	5	14.71%	lucky	2	9.09%
dare	1	7.14%	odd	3	8.82%	unworthy	2	9.09%
good	1	7.14%	simple	2	5.88%	productive	2	9.09%
peaceful	1	7.14%	little	2	5.88%	fascinating	1	4.55%
well	1	7.14%	lucky	2	5.88%	sorry	1	4.55%
gladly	1	7.14%	beautiful	2	5.88%	lovely	1	4.55%
handsome	1	7.14%	difficult	1	2.94%	little	1	4.55%
heartily	1	7.14%	important	1	2.94%	foolish	1	4.55%
clever	1	7.14%	rich	1	2.94%	wonderful	1	4.55%
stupid	1	7.14%	fortunate	1	2.94%	inconsiderate	1	4.55%
happy	1	7.14%	central	1	2.94%	mysterious	1	4.55%
silly	1	7.14%	lonely	1	2.94%	infinitely	1	4.55%
embarrassing	1	7.14%				big	1	4.55%
						happy	1	4.55%
						silky	1	4.55%
						unbelievable	1	4.55%

Table 5.19 Comparison of the frequencies and percentage of different words occurring after "how" in declaratives

According to Table 5.19, UTD has a wider range of adjectives than those in JTD and STD. In addition, adjectives with a positive meaning occur more than those with negative meanings across the three sets of data. This might explain the fact that declaratives predominate in elicited data and non-native speakers' written discourse (as we will see in chapter 6 and 7). This suggests that textbooks, to some extent, are one type of input that influences learners' production.

The most frequent word across the three sets of data is *nice* in STD at 35.29%, indicating different exclamatory expressions:

```
How nice!
How nice the classroom is!
How nice the desks are!
```

UTD contains a wider range of lexical words. The adjectives *romantic, unbelievable, silky,* and *happy* are associated with the word "how".

```
How romantic!
```

```
How unbelievably boring life would be!
How silky your skin has become.
How happy they are!
```

Frequency of the words after "how" in subordinate clauses across the three sets of data

Table 5.20 shows the frequencies of the words occurring after "how" in subordinate clauses across the three sets of data.

JTD			STD			UTD		
word	**No.**	**%**	**word**	**No.**	**%**	**word**	**No.**	**%**
to	78	32.91%	to	15	21.43%	to	76	25.08%
we	21	8.86%	much	9	12.86%	much	22	7.26%
much	15	6.33%	you	6	8.57%	the	20	6.60%
the	12	5.06%	long	5	7.14%	many	18	5.94%
I	12	5.06%	they	4	5.71%	they	17	5.61%
it	7	2.95%	the	3	4.29%	it	11	3.63%
many	7	2.95%	we	2	2.86%	we	10	3.30%
they	6	2.53%	many	2	2.86%	I	8	2.64%
long	5	2.11%	well	2	2.86%	people	8	2.64%
your	5	2.11%	people	2	2.86%	he	7	2.31%
a	4	1.69%	far	2	2.86%	you	6	1.98%
our	4	1.69%	old	2	2.86%	long	5	1.65%
this	4	1.69%	do	1	1.43%	one	4	1.32%
he	4	1.69%	fast	1	1.43%	well	4	1.32%
difficult	3	1.27%	wide	1	1.43%	your	3	0.99%
important	2	0.84%	glad	1	1.43%	useful	3	0.99%
can	2	0.84%	she	1	1.43%	hard	3	0.99%
big	2	0.84%	happy	1	1.43%	very	2	0.66%
did	2	0.84%	dirty	1	1.43%	schools	2	0.66%
well	2	0.84%	excited	1	1.43%	this	2	0.66%

Table 5.20 Comparison of the frequencies and percentage of different words occurring after "how" in subordinate clauses

As with the interrogatives, Table 5.20 shows that there are frequent occurrences of quantifying words like *much, many, long, far,* and *old.* This may suggest that quantifying words are the most important grammatical-lexical features that the word "how" is particularly likely to combine with, for example:

```
Today men even know how far it is for the earth to go round…(JTD)
No matter how long it may take us to overcome… (STD)
…between two amounts, which show how many times one contains the other…
(UTD)
```

JTD and UTD have a wider range and variety of pronouns, suggesting that pronouns are likely to be used to link the main clauses. This contrasts with what we found for "how" interrogatives. For example:

```
Talk about how you have been doing things. (JTD)
I'd like to ask how your career in theatre started. (STD)
That was how they saw things, at least. (UTD)
```

Lexical items occur frequently across the three sets of data, with adjectives only occurring at JTD. This may suggest that the basic sentence structure *main clause+ declaratives* is provided at the beginner level. For higher level textbooks, both nouns and adjectives occur at STD and UTD. The meaning is completed when a main clause is attached. For example:

```
Have you thought of how people make a book? (JTD)
He makes new friends and learns how important and difficult it is to be
a… (STD)
…there is considerable debate over how severe the greenhouse effect
will… (UTD)
```

Frequency of the words after "where" in interrogatives across the three sets of data

We now turn to the behavior of the word "where" in interrogatives and subordinate clauses. The identifiable patterns of the word "where" allow us to investigate the behavior of "where" across the three sets of data.

Table 5.21 shows the frequencies of the words occurring after "where" in interrogatives across the three sets of data.

JTD			STD			UTD		
word	**No.**	**%**	**word**	**No.**	**%**	**word**	**No.**	**%**
is	94	42.15%	are	15	27.27%	did	4	36.36%
are	50	22.42%	is	10	18.18%	do	1	9.09%
do	19	8.52%	did	7	12.73%	does	1	9.09%
did	18	8.07%	would	6	10.91%	could	1	9.09%
were	11	4.93%	shall	5	9.09%	am	1	9.09%
does	9	4.04%	was	3	5.45%	on	1	9.09%
was	5	2.24%	have	2	3.64%	are	1	9.09%
have	5	2.24%	were	2	3.64%	have	1	9.09%
can	5	2.24%	can	1	1.82%			
the	2	0.90%	to	1	1.82%			
shall	2	0.90%	does	1	1.82%			
will	1	0.45%	had	1	1.82%			
am	1	0.45%	on	1	1.82%			
would	1	0.45%						

Table 5.21 Comparison of the frequencies and percentage of
different words occurring after "where" interrogatives

Again, the main words to follow "where" are only grammatical words: be-verb, auxiliaries, and modals. Similar to the word "when", the word "where" has a restricted collocation with grammatical words. JTD and STD share three words in the top five (*am, is, did*), and share two words with STD (*did* and *do*), for example:

```
Where are my books? (JTD)
Where am I going? (UTD)
Where is the chimney? (STD)
Where does your sister work? (STD)
Where did you go last Sunday? (STD)
Where did you get that thing? (UTD)
Where would you keep them? (STD)
```

```
Where will you be next year at this ... (STD)
Where could I have lost it? (UTD)
```

Frequency of the words after "where" in subordinate clauses across the three sets of data

Table 5.22 shows the frequencies of the words occurring after "where" in subordinate clauses across the three sets of data.

JTD			STD			UTD		
word	**No.**	**%**	**word**	**No.**	**%**	**word**	**No.**	**%**
the	12	18.18%	the	36	16.29%	the	20	10.05%
she	8	12.12%	we	25	11.31%	they	17	8.54%
he	7	10.61%	it	18	8.14%	she	13	6.53%
you	6	9.09%	they	16	7.24%	there	10	5.03%
we	6	9.09%	he	14	6.33%	to	8	4.02%
they	4	6.06%	I	14	6.33%	he	8	4.02%
it	4	6.06%	you	11	4.98%	we	8	4.02%
to	4	6.06%	to	7	3.17%	people	7	3.52%
there	2	3.03%	a	6	2.71%	I	7	3.52%
I	2	3.03%	there	6	2.71%	a	6	3.02%
English	1	1.52%	she	6	2.71%	one	5	2.51%
his	1	1.52%	people	5	2.26%	it	5	2.51%
large	1	1.52%	no	5	2.26%	you	5	2.51%
several	1	1.52%	your	4	1.81%	two	3	1.51%
people	1	1.52%	those	3	1.36%	they	2	1.01%
rumors	1	1.52%	many	2	0.90%	hear	2	1.01%
next	1	1.52%	religious	2	0.90%	ten	2	1.01%
many	1	1.52%	all	2	0.90%	milk	2	1.01%
your	1	1.52%	every	2	0.90%	something	2	1.01%
all	1	1.52%	some	2	0.90%	nothing	2	1.01%

Table 5.22 Comparison of the frequencies and percentage of different
words occurring after "where" in subordinate clauses

Table 5.22 shows that the word *the* is the most frequent word found in JTD, STD and UTD, with 18.18%, 16.29%, and 10.05% respectively. The only reason to explain this is that definite article is restricted collocation of the word "where" in subordinate clauses, where it is predominately provided, for example:

```
...she told them where the prince came from... (JTD)
Say where the fire is. (STD)
It is because that's where the problem is. (UTD)
```

Personal pronouns have a high frequency across the three sets of data. This is similar to what we found in "when" subordinate clauses. The word "where" introduces the main clauses to classify the actions. Examples are shown as follows:

```
...easy for a child to wake up and know where they are. (JTD)
Tell someone where you are going. (STD)
I kept everything just where I could get my hands on it. (UTD)
```

In terms of lexical items, the word "where" occurs primarily with the noun *people:*

```
...a big building where people wait to get onto planes... (UTD)
...these are usually office jobs where people work with organizations...
(UTD)
```

Some abstract nouns are found across the datasets, for example:

```
I don't know where rumors of my disagreement.... (JTD)
Finally, I believe in an America where religious intolerance will... (STD)
He pointed to one recent study where college students were given a... (UTD)
```

Frequency of the words after "when" in interrogatives across the three sets of data

Table 5.23 shows the frequencies of the words occurring after "when" in interrogatives across the three sets of data.

JTD			STD			UTD		
word	**No.**	**%**	**word**	**No.**	**%**	**word**	**No.**	**%**
did	25	30.49%	will	4	26.67%	did	2	50.00%
was	20	24.39%	did	3	20.00%	does	1	25.00%
is	14	17.07%	was	3	20.00%	you	1	25.00%
do	9	10.98%	are	2	13.33%			
are	5	6.10%	asked	1	6.67%			
can	3	3.66%	does	1	6.67%			
were	2	2.44%	can	1	6.67%			
will	2	2.44%						
you	1	1.22%						
shall	1	1.22%						

Table 5.23 Comparison of the frequencies and percentage of different
words occurring after "when" in interrogatives

The only words which follow "when" are be-verb, auxiliaries, and modals. It is interesting that JTD has a wider range of grammatical words. This may be because JTD has more prototypes and tends to list the possible auxiliaries that come after interrogatives. The interrogative construction may be a bigger category than Extension 1 and Extension 2. Examples are shown as follows:

```
When is your birthday? (JTD)
When are you going off to Guangzhou? (STD)
When do you want to go? (JTD)
When do you take your next exams? (STD)
When does it reach its highest point? (UTD)
When shall we meet? (JTD)
When will you be satisfied? (STD)
```

Frequency of the words after "when" in subordinate clauses across the three sets of data

We now turn to look at words immediately following the word 'when'. We will see the findings with respect to the behaviours of such words as well as the similarities and differences across the three sets of data.

Table 5.24 shows the frequencies of the words occurring after "when" in subordinate clauses across the three sets of data.

JTD			STD			UTD		
word	**No.**	**%**	**word**	**No.**	**%**	**word**	**No.**	**%**
you	61	21.11%	he	84	14.84%	I	126	13.21%
he	49	16.96%	I	72	12.72%	you	116	12.16%
the	37	12.80%	the	66	11.66%	he	90	9.43%
she	30	10.38%	you	60	10.60%	the	90	9.43%
I	30	10.38%	we	54	9.54%	they	69	7.23%
they	28	9.69%	they	46	8.13%	we	61	6.39%
we	18	6.23%	it	24	4.24%	she	46	4.82%
it	8	2.77%	a	15	2.65%	a	41	4.30%
people	4	1.38%	she	11	1.94%	it	30	3.14%
a	2	0.69%	there	10	1.77%	one	19	1.99%
to	2	0.69%	our	10	1.77%	your	11	1.15%
someone	2	0.69%	all	8	1.41%	people	10	1.05%
her	2	0.69%	that	8	1.41%	his	9	0.94%
once	2	0.69%	this	6	1.06%	there	9	0.94%
was	1	0.35%	suddenly	4	0.71%	someone	8	0.84%
man	1	0.35%	one	4	0.71%	our	8	0.84%
there	1	0.35%	terrorists	4	0.71%	that	7	0.73%
summer	1	0.35%	her	3	0.53%	my	7	0.73%
their	1	0.35%	his	3	0.53%	to	7	0.73%
first	1	0.35%	my	3	0.53%	their	7	0.73%

Table 5.24 Comparison of the frequencies and percentage of different words occurring after "when" in subordinate clauses

All books have relatively higher frequencies of pronouns. JTD and STD share the 4 pronouns (*you*, *he*, *I*, and *they*), and three (*you*, *he*, and *they*) pronouns with UTD in top of six words. For example:

```
I saw her play when I was eight. (JTD)
When he makes friends with Wilson, he… (STD)
When I began to read, I had a sense of… (UTD)
```

It is interesting that that the word "when" in Extension 2 is particularly likely to occur with human nouns such as *people, someone, man*:

```
When someone else says that his... (JTD)
When smokers who are used to... (STD)
A time when people thought in terms of settling... (UTD)
```

The word *to* occurs across the three sets of data, where it is used as a type of conjunction, for example:

```
They didn't know when to go. (JTD)
…past long before a set of gears told us when to go to bed. (STD)
Knowing when to ask for help may help you… (UTD)
```

Frequency of the words after "why" in interrogatives across the three sets of data

In the following sections, we will look at the behavior of "why" interrogative and subordinate clauses. We will also look at the similarities and differences of the three sets of data, as well as the behaviours compare with the previous words.

Table 5.25 shows the frequencies of the words occurring after "why" in interrogatives across the three sets of data.

JTD			STD			UTD		
word	**No.**	**%**	**word**	**No.**	**%**	**word**	**No.**	**%**
do	24	24.24%	do	21	18.75%	do	10	13.70%
don't	24	24.24%	don't	21	18.75%	are	10	13.70%
is	10	10.10%	is	13	11.61%	did	8	10.96%
does	9	9.09%	are	12	10.71%	don't	8	10.96%
did	7	7.07%	not	11	9.82%	should	6	8.22%
are	6	6.06%	can't	5	4.46%	not	5	6.85%
didn't	5	5.05%	did	5	4.46%	does	4	5.48%
was	4	4.04%	does	5	4.46%	shouldn't	4	5.48%
haven't	2	2.02%	should	4	3.57%	is	3	4.11%
or	1	1.01%	didn't	3	2.68%	am	2	2.74%
could	1	1.01%	did	2	1.79%	would	2	2.74%
can't	1	1.01%	was	2	1.79%	has	1	1.37%
were	1	1.01%	doesn't	2	1.79%	doesn't	1	1.37%
on	1	1.01%	this	1	0.89%	women	1	1.37%
isn't	1	1.01%	were	1	0.89%	indeed	1	1.37%
aren't	1	1.01%	isn't	1	0.89%	build	1	1.37%
not	1	1.01%	will	1	0.89%	get	1	1.37%
			school	1	0.89%	the	1	1.37%
			a	1	0.89%	didn't	1	1.37%
						torture	1	1.37%
						ban	1	1.37%
						was	1	1.37%

Table 5.25 Comparison of the frequencies and percentage of different words occurring after "why" in interrogatives

The most frequent word in the JTD, STD, and UTD is *do*, at 24.24%, 18.75%, and 13.70% respectively. This may suggest that auxiliary *do* is the most frequently used word in these question forms. For example:

```
Why do you want to join the club? (JTD)
Why do you like maths? (STD)
why do you always stay in the water? (UTD)
```

Compared to the fact that only grammatical words are found in JTD, lexical items are only found in STD and UTD. For example:

```
Why is she turning off the light? (JTD)
Why are you making this journey? (STD)
Why are these statistics amazing? (UTD)
```

The negative form also has a relatively high occurrence across three sets of data. This may have something to do with the negative polarity of the word "why". Examples are shown as follows:

```
Why don't you come over and see us sometime? (JTD)
Why shouldn't we believe that? (STD)
Why didn't you tell her to use her own? (UTD)
```

Frequency of the words after "why" in subordinate clauses across the three sets of data

Table 5.26 shows the frequencies of the words occurring after "why" in subordinate clauses across the three sets of data.

JTD			STD			UTD		
word	No.	%	word	No.	%	Word	No.	%
I	5	18.52%	I	11	18.03%	the	8	11.76%
they	5	18.52%	the	10	16.39%	they	7	10.29%
you	3	11.11%	we	9	14.75%	we	6	8.82%
it	3	11.11%	they	8	13.11%	he	5	7.35%
people	2	7.41%	he	5	8.20%	some	5	7.35%
he	2	7.41%	you	3	4.92%	you	4	5.88%
we	2	7.41%	people	2	3.28%	she	4	5.88%
she	1	3.70%	more	1	1.64%	I	4	5.88%
did	1	3.70%	whether	1	1.64%	her	3	4.41%
not	1	3.70%	oceans	1	1.64%	our	2	2.94%
ambition	1	3.70%	lions	1	1.64%	certain	2	2.94%
things	1	3.70%	plants	1	1.64%	there	2	2.94%
			our	1	1.64%	this	2	2.94%
			can't	1	1.64%	my	1	1.47%
			in	1	1.64%	America	1	1.47%
			it	1	1.64%	Americans	1	1.47%
			for	1	1.64%	EQ	1	1.47%
			many	1	1.64%	something	1	1.47%
			bother	1	1.64%	people	1	1.47%

Table 5.26 Comparison of the frequencies and percentage of different words occurring after "why" in subordinate clauses

As table 5.26 shows, pronouns are the most frequent words across the three sets of data. The personal pronoun *I* predominates at 18.52% for JTD, 18.03% for STD, followed by the word *the* at 11.76% for UTD. For example:

```
That's why I've come to see you. (JTD)
Now it is the Western rule to begin at the head of the horse, that is
why I was surprised. (STD)
That's why I like it. (UTD)
```

Apart from pronouns frequently occurring across three sets of data and, as expected, lexical words increasing based on textbooks levels: 3 for JTD and 9 and 10 for STD and UTD respectively, there is also a relatively higher frequency of nouns across the three sets of data, for example:

```
That's why ambitions need to be realistic. (JTD)
So we'd very much like to understand why plants are doing this now.(STD)
Yet there are other reasons why people travel. (STD)
To explain why EQ is more important in life than… (UTD)
```

Frequency of the words after "who" in interrogatives across the three sets of data

In the following sections, we look at the behavior of the words following "who" and how it appeared across the three sets of data. We also compare such behaviour with the previous words.

Table 5.27 shows the frequencies of the words occurring after "who" in interrogatives across the three sets of data.

JTD			STD			UTD		
word	**No.**	**%**	**word**	**No.**	**%**	**Word**	**No.**	**%**
is	49	42.24%	said	9	21.95%	dies	4	11.11%
are	18	15.52%	is	6	14.63%	pays	4	11.11%
do	8	6.90%	scored	6	14.63%	would	4	11.11%
did	6	5.17%	are	4	9.76%	has	3	8.33%
was	6	5.17%	then	3	7.32%	are	3	8.33%
can	4	3.45%	will	3	7.32%	knows	3	8.33%
won	4	3.45%	was	2	4.88%	is	2	5.56%
wants	2	1.72%	knows	1	2.44%	will	2	5.56%
jumped	2	1.72%	helped	1	2.44%	does	1	2.78%
says	2	1.72%	can	1	2.44%	try	1	2.78%
will	2	1.72%	has	1	2.44%	was	1	2.78%
you	1	0.86%	would	1	2.44%	lives	1	2.78%
said	1	0.86%	taught	1	2.44%	makes	1	2.78%
where	1	0.86%	doesn't	1	2.44%	came	1	2.78%
we	1	0.86%	brought	1	2.44%	did	1	2.78%
knows	1	0.86%				do	1	2.78%
runs	1	0.86%				wants	1	2.78%
wrote	1	0.86%				then	1	2.78%
would	1	0.86%				among	1	2.78%
caught	1	0.86%						

Table 5.27 Comparison of the frequencies and percentage of different words occurring after "who" in interrogatives

According to Table 5.27, there seems to be a balanced proportion of grammatical and lexical items across the three sets of data. JTD has more grammatical words than those in STD and UTD. This may suggest that the basic sentence structures are provided at the beginner level. For example:

```
Who is your sister? (JTD)
Who is that boy over there? (STD)
Who are these individuals and what do… (UTD)
Who do you admire? (JTD)
Who has not wished to turn back the clock… (STD)
Who does Gates feel should make… (UTD)
Who can sing songs? (JTD)
Who can so properly be the inquisitors… (STD)
Who would pay the check? (UTD)
```

It is interesting to note that the be verb *is* has the highest frequency in JTD, while lexical items, particularly past tense verbs, have the highest frequency in both STD and UTD. For example:

```
Who is your sister? (JTD)
Who jumped highest? (JTD)
Who scored the two goals? (STD)
Who said that? (STD)
Who knows? (UTD)
Who pays for services or advice from a … (UTD)
```

Frequency of the words after "who" in subordinate clauses across the three sets of data

Table 5.28 shows the frequencies of the words occurring after "who" in subordinate clauses across the three sets of data.

JTD			STD			UTD		
word	**No.**	**%**	**word**	**No.**	**%**	**word**	**No.**	**%**
was	9	7.63%	are	92	12.64%	is	73	6.85%
had	8	6.78%	have	56	7.69%	are	50	4.69%
have	5	4.24%	had	26	3.57%	have	47	4.41%
are	5	4.24%	has	26	3.57%	had	45	4.22%
is	4	3.39%	is	23	3.16%	has	38	3.56%
she	3	2.54%	can	17	2.34%	was	22	2.06%
you	3	2.54%	were	15	2.06%	will	18	1.69%
live	3	2.54%	was	14	1.92%	studies	15	1.41%
saw	3	2.54%	would	14	1.92%	would	14	1.31%
play	2	1.69%	will	11	1.51%	were	14	1.31%
speak	2	1.69%	do	11	1.51%	works	12	1.13%
the	2	1.69%	gave	7	0.96%	can	12	1.13%
has	2	1.69%	want	7	0.96%	makes	10	0.94%
need	2	1.69%	came	6	0.82%	don't	9	0.84%
should	2	1.69%	said	6	0.82%	do	8	0.75%
saved	2	1.69%	was	6	0.82%	does	8	0.75%
listen	2	1.69%	helped	6	0.82%	could	7	0.66%
use	2	1.69%	made	5	0.69%	died	7	0.66%
participate	2	1.69%	say	5	0.69%	knows	7	0.66%
do	2	1.69%	we	4	0.55%	never	7	0.66%

Table 5.28 Comparison of the frequencies and percentage of different
words occurring after "who" in subordinate clauses

As Table 5.28 shown, be verbs are the most frequent words occurring after the word "who". All three sets of data share the two be verbs in the top five. Be verbs *are* predominant in STD at 12.64%, followed by *was* in JTD at 7.63%, and *is* at 6.85% for UTD. In this case, be verbs are more likely to be used as a form of evaluation of an event or a description of an activity. Examples are shown as follows:

```
Then, the little mermaid, who was very anxious to see whether…, (JTD)
…big white shark that attacks swimmmers who are spending their holidays
in a … (STD)
…also to clone the child, creating a twin who is an exact match for
bone-marrow… (UTD)
```

In the case of auxiliaries, JTD, STD, and UTD share two in the top five (have, had). This construction is used largely in past passive tense, indicating a type of language occurring predominantly in fiction. For example:

```
... and tomorrow of a wretched pilferer who had robbed a farmer's boy of...
(JTD)
...hanging a house breaker on Saturday who had been taken on Tuesday... (STD)
A man who has been very successful despite... (UTD)
...for the laundry and for the old woman who had grown close to us through
the... (UTD)
```

Similar to interrogatives, modals also can be found across the three sets of data, although in relatively small amounts. In most cases, marked meaning extensions for modal verbs need to be understood from their contexts. Examples of the modals are shown as follows:

```
We can't decide who should open it first. (JTD)
...there is nobody else in the village who can take it. (STD)
A mother who will never comfort the child who needs her. (UTD)
```

Frequency of the words after "whom" in interrogatives across the three sets of data

In the following sections, we look at the behavior of the word "whom" and how it appeared across the three sets of data. We also compare such behaviour with the previously analysed words.

Table 5.29 shows the frequencies of the words occurring after "whom" in interrogatives across the three sets of data.

JTD			STD			UTD		
word	No.	%	word	No.	%	word	No.	%
did	1	100.00%				are	1	100.00%

Table 5.29 Comparison of the frequencies and percentage of different words occurring after "whom" in interrogatives

According to Table 5.29, only grammatical words are found occurring after "whom" in interrogatives in JTD and UTD, and there are none in STD. Thus, the word "whom" has the lowest occurrence in the three sets of data. Compared to elicited data, this may also be the reason why learners hardly produce "whom" interrogatives. Examples are shown as follows:

```
Whom did he travel with? (JTD)
Whom are we trying to react with our... (UTD)
```

A Comparative Study of Wh-Words in Chinese EFL Textbooks, Elicited Native and Non-Native Speaker Data and Written Native and Non-Native Speaker Corpora

Frequency of the words after "whom" in subordinate clauses across the three sets of data

Table 5.30 shows the frequencies of the words occurring after "whom" in subordinate clauses across the three sets of data.

JTD			STD			UTD		
word	No.	%	word	No.	%	word	No.	%
I	4	36.36%	I	7	25.93%	he	8	17.39%
a	1	9.09%	he	5	18.52%	I	6	13.04%
he	1	9.09%	we	3	11.11%	one	5	10.87%
my	1	9.09%	were	2	7.41%	we	5	10.87%
they	1	9.09%	the	2	7.41%	you	4	8.70%
you	1	9.09%	a	1	3.70%	were	3	6.52%
the	1	9.09%	they	1	3.70%	they	2	4.35%
she	1	9.09%	to	1	3.70%	a	1	2.17%
			God	1	3.70%	pursuing	1	2.17%
			both	1	3.70%	to	1	2.17%
			is	1	3.70%	say	1	2.17%
			would	1	3.70%	have	1	2.17%
			shall	1	3.70%	every	1	2.17%
						if	1	2.17%
						became	1	2.17%
						everything	1	2.17%
						the	1	2.17%
						live	1	2.17%

Table 5.30 Comparison of the frequencies and percentage of different words occurring after "whom" in subordinate clauses

According to Table 5.30, the most frequent words occurring after "whom" in Extension 2 across the three sets of data are pronouns. There are largely found in JTD and STD, while the UTD has a wider variety of words including several lexical items. For such differences, one reason could be that sentence structures tend to be more complex and in turn offer a wider range and variety of word choices. Examples are shown as follows:

```
… you are like a young maiden, whom they had caught and strangled… (JTD)
…even go by the way that the man for whom I am named had his habit. (STD)
… and spoiled, except for the youngest, whom they called beauty. (UTD)
```

Frequency of the words after "whose" in interrogatives across the three sets of data

In the following sections, we look at the behavior of the word "whose" across the three sets of data. We also compare such behavior with the previously studied words.

Table 5.31 shows the frequencies of the words occurring after "whose" in interrogatives across the three sets of data.

JTD			STD			UTD		
word	**No.**	**%**	**word**	**No.**	**%**	**word**	**No.**	**%**
hat	3	20.00%	company	1	50.00%	opinion	1	25.00%
are	3	20.00%	is	1	50.00%	point	1	25.00%
is	3	20.00%				mother	1	25.00%
coat	1	6.67%				coat	1	25.00%
shirt	1	6.67%						
bike	1	6.67%						
shoes	1	6.67%						
sweater	1	6.67%						
schoolbags	1	6.67%						

Table 5.31 Comparison of the frequencies and percentage of different words occurring after "whose" in interrogatives

According to Table 5.31, grammatical words like *are* and *is* only occur in JTD and STD. This may suggest that such a question form is focused on primarily at the beginner levels. For example:

```
Whose are those shoes? (JTD)
Whose is this? (STD)
```

Lexical items are found across the three sets of data. In JTD, the word "whose" is largely followed by school-related word or personal belongs such as *schoolbag*, *coat*, and *shoes*. This is similar to that found in "which" interrogatives and again, possibly reflects the primary readship of the textbooks, for example:

```
Whose hat is this? (JTD)
Whose company operates Tokyo? (STD)
Whose opinion do you agree with more? (UTD)
```

Frequency of words occurring directly after "whose" in subordinate clauses across the three sets of data

Table 5.32 shows the frequencies of the words occurring after "whose" in subordinate clauses across the three sets of data.

JTD			STD			UTD		
word	No.	%	word	No.	%	word	No.	%
intimate	1	25%	families	3	8.33%	job	8	12.90%
world	1	25%	telephone	1	2.78%	husband	3	4.84%
hands	1	25%	beautiful	1	2.78%	life	2	3.23%
names	1	25%	mother	1	2.78%	parents	2	3.23%
			leg	1	2.78%	business	2	3.23%
			symbolic	1	2.78%	way	2	3.23%
			cultural	1	2.78%	children	2	3.23%
			honesty	1	2.78%	words	2	3.23%
			administration	1	2.78%	turn	1	1.61%
			political	1	2.78%	faith	1	1.61%
			choices	1	2.78%	child	1	1.61%
			little	1	2.78%	teachings	1	1.61%
			leaders	1	2.78%	skill	1	1.61%
			views	1	2.78%	encouragement	1	1.61%
			public	1	2.78%	family	1	1.61%
			fulfillment	1	2.78%	health	1	1.61%
			roots	1	2.78%	work	1	1.61%
			survival	1	2.78%	meanings	1	1.61%
			freedom	1	2.78%	fathers	1	1.61%

Table 5.32 Comparison of the frequencies and percentage of different
words occurring after "whose" in subordinate clauses

According to Table 5.32 shown, lexical items are the most frequent words occurring after "whose" across JTD, STD and UTD. Most lexical words are abstract nouns such as *freedom, faith, encouragement, public, administration,* and *honesty* which are more likely to relate to spirit and discipline. In addition, adjectives are also found in STD and UTD.

```
Then the others heard the secret, and very soon it became known to two
mermaids whose intimate friend happened to know who the prince was. (JTD)
I come before you tonight as a candidate for the Vice Presidency and as
a man whose honesty and integrity has been questioned. (STD)
```

In addition, there are concrete nouns are found in STD and UTD, such as *mother, leg, child,* and *skill.* For example:

```
Steven Spielberg, whose mother was a music teacher, was born in 1946 in
a small town in America.(STD)
...you have 22 millon Afro-Americans whose choices are being bound... (STD)
A person whose job is to examine and record the ... (UTD)
And parents whose child has a fatal disease like cancer might be able to
clone the child, creating a twin who is an exact match for bone-marrow
donation. (UTD)
```

Frequency of the words after "which" in interrogatives across the three sets of data

We now turn to the behavior of the word "which" in both interrogatives and subordinate clauses. The following sections investigate the similarities and differences across the three sets of data in terms of the words occurring after the word "which".

Table 5.33 shows the frequencies of the words occurring after "which" in interrogatives across the three sets of data.

JTD			STD			UTD		
word	**No.**	**%**	**word**	**No.**	**%**	**word**	**No.**	**%**
is	13	13.13%	subject	6	17.14%	of	19	50.00%
of	12	12.12%	one	4	11.43%	is	2	5.26%
would	7	7.07%	word	3	8.57%	method	2	5.26%
one	5	5.05%	grade	3	8.57%	areas	1	2.63%
sports	4	4.04%	is	2	5.71%	do	1	2.63%
kinds	4	4.04%	do	2	5.71%	side	1	2.63%
do	3	3.03%	of	2	5.71%	one	1	2.63%
language	3	3.03%	newspapers	2	5.71%	has	1	2.63%
picture	2	2.02%	part	2	5.71%	sport	1	2.63%
are	2	2.02%	room	1	2.86%	brand	1	2.63%
sweater	2	2.02%	school	1	2.86%	instrument	1	2.63%
colour	2	2.02%	places	1	2.86%	firm	1	2.63%
season	2	2.02%	games	1	2.86%	voices	1	2.63%
boy	2	2.02%	picture	1	2.86%	direction	1	2.63%
part	2	2.02%	ones	1	2.86%	career	1	2.63%

Table 5.33 Comparison of the frequencies and percentage of different words occurring after "which" in interrogatives

There are a large number of lexical items in terms of school-related words following "which": *sports, subject, grade, language, and method*. This may reflect the fact that the textbooks are aimed largely at teenager, for example:

```
Which sports are popular in your homework? (JTD)
Which language do you speak? (JTD)
Which grade are you in? (STD)
Which subject are you good at? (STD)
```

Only two types of grammatical words be verb (*is*) and auxiliary (*do*) are found across the three sets of data. For example:

```
Which is not true? (JTD)
Which is right? (UTD)
Which do you think is the most useful? (JTD)
Which do you find easiest/ most … (STD)
```

Only one type of modal is found in JTD, suggesting such collocation has low frequency occurrence in textbooks, for example:

```
Which would you prefer? (JTD)
```

Frequency of the words after "which" in subordinate clauses across the three sets of data

Table 5.34 shows the frequencies of the words occurring after "which" in subordinate clauses across the three sets of data.

JTD			STD			UTD		
word	**No.**	**%**	**word**	**No.**	**%**	**word**	**No.**	**%**
the	9	9.28%	we	28	6.09%	is	62	9.69%
was	6	6.19%	I	28	6.09%	the	30	4.69%
were	5	5.15%	is	27	5.87%	you	27	4.22%
they	5	5.15%	the	24	5.22%	he	20	3.13%
she	5	5.15%	will	24	5.22%	a	19	2.97%
is	5	5.15%	you	16	3.48%	one	18	2.81%
of	4	4.12%	are	13	2.83%	are	17	2.66%
we	4	4.12%	he	12	2.61%	we	17	2.66%
classmates	2	2.06%	was	11	2.39%	something	16	2.50%
he	2	2.06%	to	11	2.39%	people	13	2.03%
had	2	2.06%	have	10	2.17%	they	13	2.03%
would	2	2.06%	has	10	2.17%	I	13	2.03%
celebrate	2	2.06%	they	8	1.74%	it	10	1.56%
tasted	2	2.06%	our	7	1.52%	can	10	1.56%
you	2	2.06%	it	7	1.52%	was	9	1.41%
restaurant	2	2.06%	would	7	1.52%	means	8	1.25%
ones	2	2.06%	were	6	1.30%	has	7	1.09%
passed	1	1.03%	means	6	1.30%	there	7	1.09%
car	1	1.03%	has	5	1.09%	all	6	0.94%
pair	1	1.03%	must	5	1.09%	makes	6	0.94%

Table 5.34 Comparison of the frequencies and percentage of different words occurring after "which" in subordinate clauses

Table 5.34 shows that pronouns have a relatively high frequency in terms of grammatical words across the three sets of data. The pronouns "we" and "I" have the highest frequency in STD, for example:

```
...but people gave him a strange look which he didn't like... (JTD)
For the starter, which you eat with the smaller pair... (STD)
... about the lesson's main points, which he scans before the next class.
(UTD)
```

Similar to the word "where", pronouns are more likely to introduce the main clauses, completing the rest meaning of the sentence. In most cases, the construction is used as a kind of evaluation of an attitude or behaviour.

In the case of lexical items, JTD has the highest frequency with 7 in the top of 20, while there is only 1 lexical item in STD and 3 in UTD. This may suggest that subordinate clauses are provided with more lexical options at the beginner level, and vary in higher level textbooks. For example:

```
...400s that Mr. Perkin didn't know which car was his. (JTD)
...the afternoon we will visit the factory which makes minibuses and
trucks. (STD)
...is an early stage of development in which cells are busy dividing and
... (UTD)
```

The article "the" has a relatively high frequency across the three sets of data. This may again suggest that the word "which" is used to connect two main clauses, for example:

```
Over everything lay a peculiar blue radiance, as if it were surrounded
by the air from above, through which the blue sky shone, instead of the
dark depths of the sea. (JTD)
Presently they came in sight of land; she saw lofty blue mountains, on
which the white snow rested as if a flock of swans were lying upon them.
(STD)
And then the little mermaid went out from her garden, and took the road
to the foaming whirlpools, behind which the sorceress lived. (UTD)
```

It is interesting to note that only three modals (*can*, *must* and *would*) are found across the three sets of data. For example:

```
...for in each lies a glittering pearl, which would be fit for the diadem
of a... (JTD)
...tree went down, cut down by the water, which must have been three
metres... (STD)
There is no reason which can excuse the denial of that right. (UTD)
```

We have discussed the frequency lists of words occurring after "wh" words in three types of sentences across the three sets of data, encompassing how the frequency of co-occurring words appears across the three sets of data.

5.6 Discussion

5.6.1 Prototypes

The distribution of "wh" words as prototypes and extensions is shown in Table 5.35.

Wh-word	JTD (%)			STD (%)			UTD (%)			All books (%)		
	P	E1	E2	P	E1	E2	P	E1	E2	P	E1	E2
what	91	1	8	46	3	51	52	2	45	63	2	35
how	90	3	7	51	7	42	24	5	71	55	5	40
when	25	0	76	3	0	97	0	0	100	9	0	91
which	54	0	46	4	0	96	5	0	95	21	0	79
who	55	0	45	6	0	94	1	0	98	21	0	79
whom	8	0	93	11	0	89	0	0	100	6	0	94
why	82	0	18	71	0	29	53	0	47	69	0	31
whose	85	0	15	14	0	86	26	0	75	42	0	58
where	83	0	17	22	0	78	8	0	92	38	0	63
average	64	0	36	25	1	74	19	1	80	36	1	63

Table 5.35 Distribution of prototypes and extensions across three datasets

For convenience the original hypotheses are repeated here:

a) It is hypothesized that the textbook data will be largely prototypical as it relies on the intuition of textbook writers.
b) It is also hypothesized that textbook patterns will incline more towards non-prototypical structures according to proficiency level. For example, textbooks for university will be more non-prototypical than those for junior and senior schools.

The first hypostudy is not fully upheld. When all textbooks are viewed together, i.e., regardless of proficiency, prototypes occur frequently for only three of the nine "wh" words: *what, how,* and *why.* However, when the textbooks are viewed according to level a different picture emerges. For the lowest proficiency textbooks (JTD), prototypes dominate for seven of the nine "wh" words (*what, how, which, who, why, whose, where*). For the secondary school textbooks (STD), only two words (*how* and *why*) have more prototype structures. For the university textbooks (UTD), only two words (*what* and *why*) are found to contain more prototypical structures. Extension 2, i.e., subordinate clausal usage of "wh" words, predominates for seven of the nine "wh" words in both STD and UTD.

The above results suggest that the second hypostudy is upheld: at lower levels of proficiency (junior high school) textbook writers primarily provide prototype examples of "wh" words (on average 64%);

then, as proficiency increases, more extended examples are provided (senior high school and university provide 74% and 80% of E2 respectively).

5.6.2 Frequency of Words Occurring Immediately after "wh" Words in Terms of the Three Types of Sentences

Many of the words following "wh" words in interrogatives and subordinate clauses (declaratives are low-frequency and are followed by articles or lexical items) are grammatical in nature. These includes pronouns, auxiliaries, be verb, prepositions, and modals. For example:

Interrogatives:

```
How much have you learnt so far? (JTD)
How are you? (JTD)
What was the main cause of the … (UTD)
What do you know about his… (UTD)
When are you going off to Guangzhou? (STD)
When will you be satisfied? (STD)
Where could I have lost it? (UTD)
Where is the chimney? (STD)
Which would you prefer? (JTD)
Who are these individuals and what do… (UTD)
Who does Gates feel should make… (UTD)
Whom did he travel with? (JTD)
Whom are we trying to react with our… (UTD)
Whose are those shoes? (JTD)
Why are these statistics amazing? (UTD)
Why has the universe happened, and … (UTD)
```

Declaratives:

```
How embarrassing!
What a delicious supper! (STD)
```

subordinate clauses:

```
…between two amounts, which show how many times one contains the other…
(UTD)
That was how they saw things, at least. (UTD)
How did Yang lei say she could help? (JTD)
The other students guess what it is. (JTD)
They never asked what would happen to the world. (JTD)
When I begin to read, I had a sense of… (UTD)
…past long before a set of gears told us when to go to bed. (STD)
Say where the fire is. (STD)
Tell someone where you are going. (STD)
…but people gave him a strange look which he didn't like… (JTD)
```

```
There is a little pea which has taken root. (JTD)
...for in each lies a glittering pearl, which would be fit for the diadem
of a... (JTD)
Then, the little mermaid, who was very anxious to see whether..., (JTD)
...for the laundry and for the old woman who had grown close to us through
the... (UTD)
...there is nobody else in the village who can take it. (STD)
... you are like a young maiden, whom they had caught and strangled... (JTD)
Write and explain why you are the good person for this... (JTD)
```

The most frequent lexical items following "wh" words for all textbook types are shown in Table 5.36.

Wh-word	Interrogative	Declarative	Clausal
What	time, color, happened kind, makes, sort difference,	beautiful, fun, lovely horrible	time, happened, someone, kind
How	much, many, long	nice, creative, lucky, unlucky,	people, difficult, useful, hard, big
When	asked	_____	someone, people, suddenly
Where	_____	_____	people, religious, hear, milk
Which	sport(s), picture, part, subject	_____	means, makes, something, people
Who	said, knows wants, dies, pays	_____	do, studies, works makes, knows
Whom	_____	_____	pursing, became live, god
Whose	hat, coat, company	_____	job, families, husband
Why	school, build, get	_____	people, ambitious something,

Table 5.36 The most frequent lexical items associated with wh-words for all textbook types

what combines with a number of fixed expressions and collocations:

```
What happened to Zizzo and Zizza? (UTD)
What color is it? (JTD)
What time do you want to come? (STD)
```

How is strongly connected to qualifying words (e.g. *much, many, long*):

```
How much is it? (JTD)
How many students are there in your class? (STD)
```

```
How long have you been to Beijing? (UTD)
```

When occurs with *asked* (the only lexical word in top 20 lists):

```
When asked about the secret of ... (STD)
```
Which commonly occurs with school related words, such as subject, picture, room, places, game:
```
Which sport do you like most? (JTD)
Which places do you go to? (STD)
Which method do you think promotes... (UTD)
```

Who occurs with verbs (wanted, said, knows), especially in plural and past tense:

```
Who said these things about their day… (JTD)
Who helped to get things back to … (STD)
Who knows? (UTD)
```

Whose commonly occurs with nouns which mainly focus on personal items (school bag, sweaters, shoes, bags) and mental representation, such as *opinion*, *point*:

```
Whose hat is this? (JTD)
Whose company operates Todyo… (STD)
Whose opinion do you agree more… (UTD)
```

Why occurs with both verbs and nouns, such as *school*, *build*, and *get* and is primarily used for asking questions:

```
...with crops: pears, and date palms. "why school?" I asked my father.
(STD)
...research, it would seem not. So why build it? There are good political...
(UTD)
```

For *whom* and *where*, there are no adjacent lexical items across the data sets.

The lexical items occurring with *what* and *how* in declaratives are usually used in strongly positive or strongly negative evaluations:

```
What beautiful flowers!
What horrible weather!
How nice the classroom is!
```

How unbelievably boring life would be!

In subordinate clauses, *what* occurs with a similar group of lexical items to the interrogative form:

```
Write a story reporting what happened. (JTD)
...for a special dinner and explained what food she was planning to cook.
(STD)
```

How is mainly associated with only two kinds of adjectives: evaluative (*difficult, hard, useful, etc.*) and measuring adjectives *(wide, far, big, etc.)*:

```
...and she decided to test them to see how well she had been in her work.
(JTD)
He makes new friends and learns how important and difficult it is to be
a... (STD)
No matter how small, he never failed to... (UTD)
How good she has been in her work? (UTD)
```

When occurs with human nouns such as *people, someone, man*:

```
When someone else says that his... (JTD)
When smokers who are used to... (STD)
A time when people thought in terms of settling... (UTD)
```

Where occurs primarily with the noun *people*:

```
...a big building where people wait to get onto planes... (UTD)
...these are usually office jobs where people work with organizations...
(UTD)
```

Which seems strongly associated with verbs (*means, makes*) that indicate the more specific contents and concrete nouns (*classmates, people*):

```
...the afternoon we will visit the factory which makes minibuses and
trucks. (STD)
... study find words or phrases in the text which mean the same as the
following: (STD)
...when they remembered the scenes in which people were eaten by the
shark. (STD)
Decide which classmate is better for this job. (JTD)
```

Who are is connected with a wide variety of verbs (*do, study, works, makes*):

```
We fight about who plays with it first. (JTD)
He is a famous actor who plays the leading part in the new... (STD)
A kid who studies hard must stop teasing... (UTD)
```

Whom occurs with three verbs: *became, pursuing, live*. Interestingly, *whom* also occurs with *God*, indicating, perhaps, that this pronoun is associated with older forms of English to be found in the Bible:

```
...a small group of undergraduates for whom pursuing knowledge is the
most... (UTD)
...one of whom became the last Czarina of ... (UTD)
...folk fiddlers, to name only a few, all of whom live along the Mississippi...
(UTD)
```

The lexical words associated with *whose* mainly focus on objects belonging to the possessor, such as *jobs, family* and *husband*:

```
...like to approach the wife or mother whose husband or son has died
in... (STD)
A person whose job is to examine and record the ... (UTD)
An aunt whose family will fragment and fall.. (UTD)
```

Why occurs with a small range of nouns, such as *people, ambition, etc.*:

```
That's why ambitions need to be realistic. (JTD)
To explain why EQ is more important in life than... (UTD)
```

In this chapter, "wh" sentences in JTD, STD, and UTD textbooks were examined to see to what extent these sentences are central/basic wh-sentence type. The words that occur immediately after the "wh" word were then investigated. In the next chapter, elicited data from junior high, senior high, and university students in China as well as native speakers of English will be examined in a similar fashion and compared to the textbook findings that we have explored here. In the following chapters, we will look at the words occurring immediately after "wh" words in learners' elicited data, and written corpora data. We will also compare the behaviors of the words in these contexts.

Chapter Six

A Corpus-based Analysis of Data Elicited from Chinese-speaking Learners of English and Expert Users of English

6.1 Introduction

In this chapter, data is presented which has been drawn from Chinese-speaking learners of English and expert users of English. A total of 247 Chinese learners from Junior Middle School (JED), Senior High School (SED), University students (UED) and 50 native speakers (NS) were selected for the study. The main objectives of this part of the study are to investigate how much knowledge Chinese learners and English expert users have of English "wh" sentences, and to what extent they tend to produce prototypical, as opposed to more peripheral instances of them.

In the previous chapter, it was found that textbook writers primarily provide prototype examples of "wh" words (on average 64%) at lower levels of proficiency (junior middle school); then, as proficiency increases, more extended examples are provided (senior high and university textbooks contain 74% and 80% of E2 respectively).

One of the aims of this chapter is to explore the extent to which elicited data resembles textbook data. Two issues are investigated. Firstly, whether both Chinese-speaking learners of English and expert users of English predominantly produce prototypes and whether the production of prototypes is related to proficiency levels. In order to establish this, the number of prototypes produced by expert users of both Chinese and English at a similar age is compared. Secondly, the frequencies of the different words occurring immediately after the "wh" words are investigated. The methodology is described in the following sections.

6.2 Participants in the Study

The participants involved in the study were aged between 14 and 22 years old and were studying English as a foreign language (EFL) in China, or had English as their native language (NS). There were 67 EFL learners from the Far Eastern Junior Middle School (two student groups, aged 14-17),

126

60 from the Far Eastern Senior High School (two student groups, aged 17-20), and 120 from Xi'an Foreign Language University (five student groups, aged 20-21).

A total of 50 NS students, who are referred to as the expert users of English, participated in the study. There were 20 students from Edgbaston High School for Girls and 30 Undergraduates from Birmingham University. This was a convenience sample rather than a random sample.

The 120 university EFL learners had passed the College English Test (CET) either at level 4 or level 6. All Chinese college and university students must pass CET level 4 in order to graduate. Level 6 is considerably more difficult than Level 4. SED students are considered to be more proficient than JED students, but less proficient than UED students.

The native speaker (NS) users of English involved in this study have either prepared for or completed the General Certificate of Secondary Education (GCSE). This academic qualification is awarded in a specified subject and it is generally taken in a number of subjects by students aged 16 in secondary education in England, Wales, and Northern Ireland. Education to GCSE level is required before studying for A-levels, themselves a requirement for entry to university.

6.2.1 The Learning Contexts Of The Non-Native-Speaker Participants

As English is a compulsory subject from the 4th grade for Chinese elementary students (aged 7-8), all the participants had received a basic education in EFL.

Students at this level are taught English by a largely audio-lingual method, with a few explicit grammar instruction. Within a 45-minute class, most of the time is spent on reading and sentence construction. Occasionally, Chinese translation is used for explanations. After the class, students memorise the created sample sentences.

The ultimate goal of a senior high school student is to pass the university entrance exam. This exam includes grammar, vocabulary, listening, and essay writing in a foreign language, with a strong focus on grammar. Therefore, to some extent, the teaching approach in senior high school is determined by the content of university entrance exams. Learners at this level are taught via grammar-translation and audio-lingual methods, again focusing on grammar. Before these students reach university level, they should have learnt basic English grammar.

As English is taught at the university for only two years, the syllabus designers and materials writers try to develop learners' communicative skills, as well as their ability to use English lexis accurately and flexibly, rather than focusing on pattern memorization. Grammar instructions are given when complex sentences are encountered.

In contrast, NS users use English both in social communication and in an academic environment. Their use of English is sometimes considered as a perfect goal to which others who speak English as a foreign or second language might want to aspire.

6.3 Hypotheses

The hypotheses underlying this part of the study are as follows:

1) Both Chinese-speaking learners of English and expert users of English will primarily produce prototypes because this kind of elicited data is largely intuition driven.
2) Chinese-speaking learners of English will produce "wh" sentences that are even more central/basic than those produced by NS.
3) Chinese-speaking learners of English will produce more non-prototypical structures as proficiency increases (i.e., from JED to UED).
4). There will be similarities between textbook data and elicited data produced by non-native speakers, as both are driven by intuition and textbooks might be expected to influence NNS output.

6.4 Data Collection Procedures

The Chinese learners' data was collected after a normal class and NS speaker data was collected in the university library. All participants agreed to participate in the research. Participants were asked to handwrite five sentences containing each "wh" word (what, how, which, where, etc). These sentences were later digitalized to create a corpus of elicited data.

6.5 Data Processing

All the sentences written by participants were categorized into three groups ('prototype', 'extension 1' and 'extension 2') and the relative frequencies with which each group of students produced these three types of sentences were calculated. As we saw in Chapter 5, the interrogative was considered to be the prototype, the declarative was considered to be extension 1, and the subordinate clause was considered to be extension 2. These sentences were then saved in different excel files on the basis of their clause type.

Four sets of elicited data (corresponding to three levels of non-native speakers, as well as the native speakers) were analyzed in the same way. Not all students were able or willing to produce five sentences for each prompt. The numbers produced for each of the four sets are shown in Table 6.1. Table 6.1 also shows the number of occurrences of "wh" words across the four sets of elicited data.

Data set	No. of elicited sentences	No. of Participants	No. of average responses per participants
JED	2002	67	30
SED	1799	60	30
UED	4770	120	40
NS	1020	50	20
All learners	9591	297	32

Table 6.1 Number of wh-words across the four sets of elicited data

In the following sections I present the data for each of the sentence types that were produced.

6.5.1 Data Processing of the different sentence types

The data were processed using Wordsmith software. Each "wh" word is sorted in the centre and the sentences in which they occur are classified by clause type. Figure 6.1 shows the process of categorization.

Interrogative:		What	Is your name?
Declarative:		What	a beautiful flower it is.
Subordinate clause:	I don't believe	What	He says.

Figure 6.1 Categorization of "wh" sentences

The above category can be grammatically described as follows:

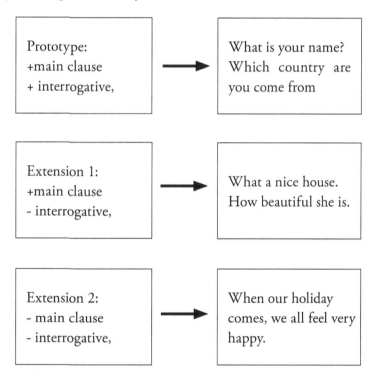

Figure 6.2 prototypes and extensions for "wh" sentences

For the prototype, subject-auxiliary inversion is obligatorily exhibited. An interrogative word involving "wh" words indicates a typical utterance. This utterance is used to turn the proposition into a question, as in *what is your name?* The proposition content can be expressed as *your name is what?* asked by a speaker who does not know the addressees' name, and wants to know what it is (Art and McMahon, 2006).

In extension 1, the "wh" word indicates an exclamative statement. It not only represents a typical utterance used to assert the proposition, but also contains a degree modifier (ibid). It is suggested that the utterance serves to express a speaker's affective stance or attitude towards some event or state of affairs (ibid). For example, *how smart she is*. Clearly it can be understood that this smartness is located at some point on a scale of smartness; the utterance also expresses the speakers' affective point of view, which, in this case, is positive.

In extension 2, "wh" words are usually introduced by a subordinate conjunction or a relative pronoun. The utterance is no longer describing a complete thought, so it does not stand alone, it must always be attached to a main clause to complete the meaning. For example: *When the holiday comes, we all feel very happy.* 'When' introduced by a subordinate conjunction which provide the condition of our happiness.

6.5.2 *Data Processing of Word Frequencies*

Having assembled the four sets of data categorized into three groups and saved in different excel files, the next task was to gather information about the first word on the right for each "wh" word among three different sentence types. This was done to allow a comparison between the sentences produced by the three levels of non-native speakers and the native speakers.

For each type of sentence, the words following "wh" words were manually scanned, and typed in a new column afterwards. The column was kept horizontal with the sample sentences. Example is shown below:

What	is your name?	is
What	can I do for you?	can
What	did you say on the phone?	did

Then, the typed columns were transferred to a new excel file to calculate the overall frequencies and their proportions. These were obtained by collecting the same words together and calculating the percentages in Excel. All four sets of data were processed in the same way.

In the third stage, the top 20 frequent words were drawn from the four original files in order to compare changes in frequency on the basis of the sentence types. The frequency totals of the words occurring after the "wh" words across the four sets of elicited data are shown later in the Results section.

6.6 *Prototypes and Extensions across the Four Elicited Datasets*

In this section, the results are presented and discussed. First, the prototypes and extensions of the different sentence types among the four sets of elicited data are presented. Second, the frequencies of the words occurring immediately after "wh" words are discussed.

As we saw in the introduction of this chapter, not all of the participants were able to produce five examples for each prompt. Since the four groups of participants varied in size, it was necessary to calculate the average number of sentences produced for each prompt by students at each level. Table 6.2 and Table 6.3 show the average number and the percentage of "wh" sentences produced for each prompt by students at each of four levels.

	Total size of data	what	how	where	when	why	who	whom	whose	which	Total
JED	3673	345(94)	344(94)	252(69)	261(71)	141(38)	245(67)	59(16)	128(35)	227(62)	2002(545)
SED	15780	281(18)	259(16)	166(11)	231(15)	218(14)	208(13)	43(3)	168(11)	225(14)	1799(114)
UED	7924	549(69)	510(64)	656(83)	501(63)	537(68)	526(66)	447(56)	523(66)	521(66)	4770(602)
NED	19595	191(10)	207(11)	127(6)	158(8)	168(8)	62(3)	29(1)	32(2)	46(2)	1020(52)
Total	46972	1366(29)	1320(28)	1201(26)	1151(25)	1064(23)	1041(22)	578(12)	851(18)	1019(22)	9591(204)

Table 6.2 Number of concordance lines of "wh" words across the three datasets (frequencies per 1000 words are shown in brackets)

Grade	JED			SED			UED			NS		
	Par	Tot	Ave	Par	Tot	Ave	Par	Tot	Ave	Par	Tot	Ave
what	67	345	5.1	60	281	4.7	120	549	4.7	50	191	3.8
how	67	344	5.1	60	259	4.3	120	510	4.3	50	207	4.1
where	67	252	3.8	60	166	2.8	120	656	2.8	50	127	2.5
when	67	261	3.9	60	231	3.9	120	501	3.9	50	158	3.2
why	67	141	2.1	60	218	3.6	120	537	3.6	50	168	3.4
who	67	245	3.7	60	208	3.5	120	526	3.5	50	62	1.2
whom	67	59	0.9	60	43	0.7	120	447	0.7	50	29	0.6
whose	67	128	1.9	60	168	2.8	120	523	2.8	50	32	0.6
which	67	227	3.4	60	225	3.8	120	521	3.8	50	46	0.9

Table 6.3 Average number of sentences produced for each prompt by students at each of the four levels

Note:

Par.: Participants

Tol.: Total number of responses

Ave.: Average number of responses per participant

Table 6.3 shows the total number of responses along with the average number of responses per participant across the four data sets. For ease of comparison, Table 6.4 summarises the average number of responses produced for each prompt by students at each level. It should be noted that elicited data from non-native speakers (junior, senior, and university) was collected in the classroom while native speakers were asked to complete the exercise in the university library, which is a slightly less restricted setting. Perhaps because of this non-restricted environment, some native speakers did not produce 5 responses for each prompt.

	what	how	where	when	why	who	whom	whose	which
JED	5.1	5.1	3.8	3.9	2.1	3.7	0.9	1.9	3.4
SED	4.7	4.3	2.8	3.9	3.6	3.5	0.7	2.8	3.8
UED	4.7	4.3	2.8	3.9	3.6	3.5	0.7	2.8	3.8
NS	3.8	4.1	2.5	3.2	3.4	1.2	0.6	0.6	0.9

Table 6.4 A comparison of the average number of sentences
produced for each prompt by students at each level

According to Table 6.4, the words *what* and *how*, produced the highest number of sentences for participants at all four levels. For the word *where*, the average number of sentences produced by university participants is slightly higher than those produced by junior high school participants, while senior participants and native speakers have an equal number of sentences produced. In the case of *when* and who, non-native speakers produced all equally while native speakers had the fewest number of sentences. For the word *why*, participants from university wrote more sentences than those in senior, native speakers, and junior. In the case of *whom, whose,* and *which*, university participants have the highest number of sentences, at around 4 sentences while native speakers have the fewest, at 1 sentence on average.

To sum up, participants from university have the highest number of sentences on average. Junior and senior participants have almost the same number of sentences. Native speakers have the fewest number of sentences produced on average for the words *whom, whose,* and *which*. An interesting feature of the results for participants is that *what* and *how* are easiest, closely followed by *when* and *where*. *Who, which,* and *why* are substantially more difficult and whom and whose seem to be the most difficult of all.

In the next stage of the study, the "wh" words were categorized into three types of sentence, namely, interrogative (Prototype), declarative (Extension 1) and subordinate clause (Extension 2) respectively, across the four sets of data.

Distribution of "what" sentences across the four sets of data

We now look at the distribution of "what" sentences across the four sets of data. The "What" sentence is markedly prototypical across the four sets of data. One possible reason for this might be that, apart from the textbooks' influence, "what" interrogative forms are one of the most commonly used constructions in our daily life. It is therefore more likely to be the most frequent constructions produced by the participants.

Table 6.5 and Figure 6.3 show the different types of "what" sentences in each data set.

	Prototype	%	Extension 1	%	Extension 2	%	total
JED	342	99%	3	1%	0	0	346
SED	184	65%	35	12%	62	22%	281
UED	479	87%	16	3%	54	10%	549
NS	141	74%	13	7%	37	19%	191
All ED	1146	84%	67	5%	153	11%	1366

Table 6.5 Different types of "what" sentences across four datasets

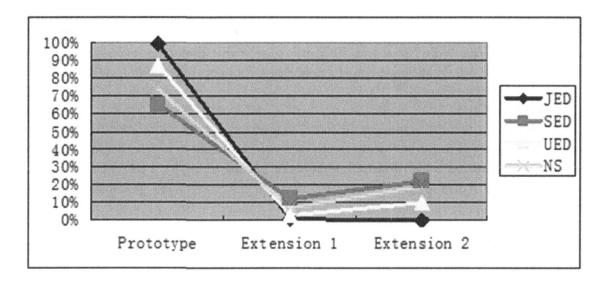

Figure 6.3 "what" sentence types across four sets of data

Table 6.5 and Figure 6.3 clearly show a predominance of prototypes for all four sets of elicited data, with 99% for JED, 87% for UED, 65% for SED, and 74% for NS respectively.

For Extension 1, SED has the highest percentage at 12%. US, UED and JED makes little use of Extension 1: US at 7%, 3% at UED, and JED at 1%.

Extension 2 occurs the most at SED, with approximately 22%, followed by NS, at 19%. Extension 2 is not found in JED. Examples of the different sentence types are shown below:

Prototypes:

```
What did you do last weekend? (JED)
What is the color of your bike? (SED)
What is the difference between them? (UED)
What can I do for you? (NS)
```

Extension 1:

```
What a pity. (JED)
What good weather. (SED
What a nice day!(UED)
What a stupid guy. (NS)
```

Extension 2:

```
What make my mother pound is that I am in good health. (SED)
What if you give me a red rose I will dance with you. (UED)
I know what I am doing. (NS)
```

Regardless of the fact that we found, in terms of textbook data that prototypes occurred more in JTD and UTD, while extension 2 largely occurred in STD, all four groups of participants predominately produced prototypical "what" sentences. This may suggest that prototypes generally reflect the conceptual understandings of certain constructions that seem to be stored in individuals' long-term memories.

It is interesting that non-native speakers are found to produce a steady volume of extension 1. One possible reason for this might be that textbooks contained abundant examples that influenced the way learners constructed "what" declaratives sentences. In contrast, native speakers hardly produce extension 1, which in turn suggests that examples provided in EFL textbooks are somehow artificial.

As for extension 2 in textbook data, this construction is largely found occurring in STD as it is more likely that complex sentence structure is introduced to help learners to build sentence construction skills. It is interesting to note that participants from senior high school produced more extension 2 sentences than other groups of participants, which corresponds to the textbook data as subordinate clauses are taught explicitly in class This may suggest that textbooks as a type of input play an important role in sentence construction.

Distribution of "how" sentences across the four sets of data

"How" sentences follow a similar pattern to "what" sentences, as prototypes are predominant across the four sets of data. Similar to the findings for "what" sentences, prototypes are largely produced by lower proficiency participants such as JED. As we move to a higher level, the proportion of prototypes declines steadily. Table 6.6 and Figure 6.4 show the different types of "how" sentences in each data set.

	Prototype	%	Extension 1	%	Extension 2	%	total
JED	331	96%	11	3%	2	1%	344
SED	186	72%	46	18%	27	10%	259
UED	383	75%	63	12%	64	13%	510
NS	139	67%	11	5%	57	28%	207
All ED	1039	79%	131	10%	150	11%	1320

Table 6.6 "how" sentences across the four datasets

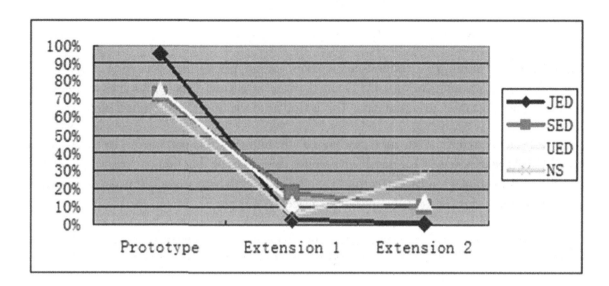

Figure 6.4 "how" sentence types across four sets of data

As Table 6.6 and Figure 6.4 show, prototypes (+interrogative, +main clause) predominate in JED, SED, UED and NS, at 96%, 72%, 75%, and 67% respectively. SED and UED have almost the same distribution for prototypes: with around 72% for SED and 75% UED.

Both JED and NS have few sentences of Extension 1, with around 3% (JED) and 5% (NS). The proportion of Extension 1 in SED, at 18% is 6% higher than in UED, at 12%.

Only two sentences of Extension 2 are found for JED, representing less than 1%. The proportion of Extension 2 was higher in both SED and UED, at 10% and 13% respectively. NS students produce the most for Extension 2, at 28%. Examples are shown below:

Prototypes:

```
How many people are there in your family? (JED)
How often do you swim? (SED)
How much money do you have? (UED)
How much money does the apartment cost to rent? (NS)
```

Extension 1:

```
How bad it is. (JED)
How fun it is. (SED)
How wonderful the picture is. (UED)
How exciting. (NS)
```

Extension 2:

```
No matter how tired I am, I will keep on. (JED)
I don't know how to deal with it. (SED)
```

```
This is the way how we solve the problem. (UED)
I do not know how to make this machine work. (NS)
```

In contrast to our findings for textbook data, "how" prototypes largely occur for JTD and STD, while extension 2 predominates for UTD. In the case of elicited data, prototypes are produced predominately across the four sets of data. This is similar to the findings for "what" sentences.

The proportion of extension 2 sentences produced by the four groups of participants increases steadily as proficiency levels increase. One possible reason for this might be that non-native speakers are able to produce more complex sentence structures as proficiency levels increase, whilst native speakers find it easier to produce this construction in the first place.

Similar to the findings for "what" sentences, more extension 1 sentences are produced by non-native speakers than native speakers. This may suggest that this construction is not a commonly used one in the native language context.

Distribution of "where" sentences across the four sets of data

"Where" sentences follow the same pattern as the previously analysed words "what" and "how", as prototypes largely occur across the four sets of data. It is interesting to note that participants from senior high school are likely to produce more extension 2 examples. This is similar to the findings for textbook data.

Table 6.7 and Figure 6.5 show the different types of "where" sentences across the four datasets.

	Prototype	%	Extension 1	%	Extension 2	%	total
JED	251	100%	0	0	1	0%	252
SED	120	72%	0	0	46	28%	166
UED	556	85%	0	0	100	15%	656
NS	109	86%	0	0	18	14%	127
All ED	1036	86%	0	0	165	14%	1201

Table 6.7 "where" sentences across each datasets

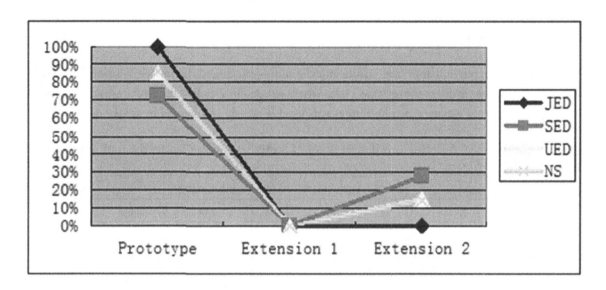

Figure 6.5 "where" sentence types across four sets of data

Table 6.7 and Figure 6.5 show that prototypes are predominant across the four sets of participants, with 100% for JED, 72% for SED, 85% for UED, and 86% for NS, for example:

```
Where can you find him? (JED)
Where did you go? (SED)
Where is the most proper place to go? (UED)
Where is your department? (NS)
```

Again, Extension 1 is absent from the four sets of data, suggesting that this form does not exist in the minds of participants.

Extension 2 subordinate clauses within SED (28%) account for almost double that found in UED (15%) and NS (14%):

```
It is a good place where I can have fun. (SED)
I do not know where the WC is. (UED)
The driver will tell you where to get off. (NS)
```

"Where" sentences for elicited data are different from that which was found in relation to textbook data. In the case of "where" prototypes, JTD and JED occur most frequently. This may suggest that textbooks mainly influence that learners' production. As for extension 2, this construction largely occurred in STD and UTD, which may partially explain why participants from senior high school have the highest proportion of extension 2 examples.

Distribution of "when" sentences across the four sets of data

We now look at the distribution of "when" sentences across the four sets of data in addition to comparing this to the previously studied words. "When" sentences are markedly different from the previously analysed words. Prototypes are largely produced by three SED, UED, and NS. This contrasts to the findings for previously studied words where prototypes are largely produced by all groups of participants.

It is interesting that participants from junior middle school produced the most extension 2 examples. This is similar to the findings for textbook data where extension 2 examples predominately occurred. This may suggest that learners' production at this level is largely influenced by textbooks.

Table 6.8 and Figure 6.6 show the different types of "when" sentences across the four datasets.

	Prototype	%	Extension 1	%	Extension 2	%	total
JED	123	47%	0	0	138	53%	261
SED	119	52%	0	0	112	48%	231
UED	331	66%	0	0	170	34%	501
NS	139	88%	0	0	19	12%	158
All ED	712	62%	0	0	439	38%	1151

Table 6.8 "when" sentences across each datasets

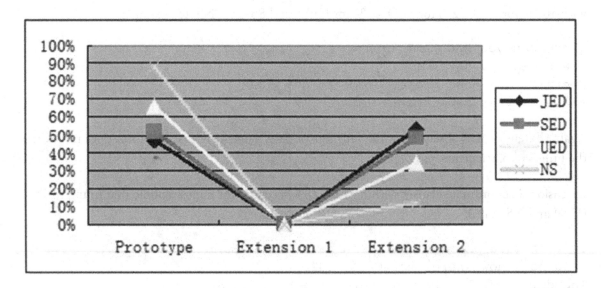

Figure 6.6 "when" sentence types across four sets of data

According to Table 6.8 and Figure 6.6, prototypes and Extension 2 are similar in proportion across JED and SED, while prototypes predominate in UED and NS.

Extension 1 is not found across the three datasets.

There is almost the same distribution for Extension 2 in JED and SED of around 53% (JED) and 48% (SED). NS and UED contain relatively fewer numbers of Extension 2, at 12% and 34%

Below are examples of prototype and Extension 2 across the three datasets:

Prototypes:

```
When are you going to Shanghai? (JED)
When do you want to go to school? (SED)
When did the air crash happen? (UED)
When will you leave for home? (NS)
```

Extension 2:

```
The boy was walking down the street when a UFO landed. (JED)
I remember the time when I met her. (SED)
Please think about the farmers when you want to waste food. (UED)
Then we will decide when to leave for Seattle. (NS)
```

"When" sentences are observed differently from the previously studied words. In contrast to the fact that prototypes predominate across the four sets of data for "what", "how", and "where", "when" prototypes largely occur at higher proficiency participants (SED, UED, and NS). Extension 2 is produced largely by lower proficiency participants (JED). This is corresponding to what we found in textbook data. This may suggest that learners stored the examples that provided in textbooks, and used them in their own sentence construction.

Distribution of "why" sentences across the four sets of data

We now move on to discuss the distribution of "why" sentences across the four sets of data. We will also compare the distribution with that from previously studied words.

Table 6.9 and Figure 6.7 show the different types of "why" sentences across the four datasets.

	Prototype	%	Extension 1	%	Extension 2	%	total
JED	139	99%	0	0	2	1%	141
SED	158	72%	0	0	60	28%	218
UED	426	79%	0	0	111	21%	537
NS	139	83%	0	0	29	17%	168
All ED	862	81%	0	0	202	19%	1064

Table 6.9 "why" sentences across each datasets

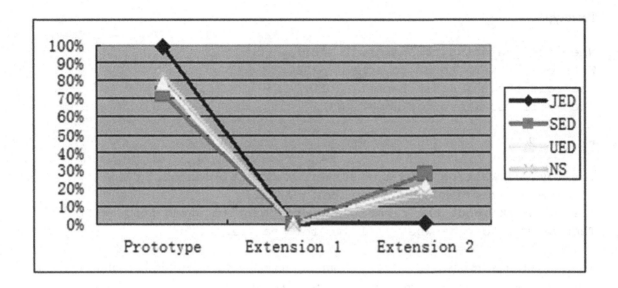

Figure 6.7 "why" sentence types across three sets data

As Table 6.9 and Figure 6.7 show, within the four data sets, prototypes predominate, with around 99% for JED, 83% for NS, 72% for SED, and 79% for UED. Extension 1 is not found across four datasets. Extension 2 has a relatively low frequency, with around 1% for JED, 17% for NS, 28% for SED and 21% for UED respectively. Examples of the sentence patterns are shown below:

Prototypes:

```
Why do you like banana? (JED)
Why not go shopping? (SED)
Why are you late again? (UED
Why would I lie to you? (NS)
```

Extension 2:

```
I want to know why it isn't right. (JED)
I don't know the reason why he has a beautiful hat. (SED)
It is a reason why she is the best. (UED)
That's why I wanted you to have a holiday. (NS)
```

"Why" sentences follow a similar pattern to the previously studied "what", "how", and "where" sentences, as prototypes are largely produced across the four groups of participants. In particular, prototypes are predominately produced by lower proficiency level participants from junior middle school.

Extension 2 is produced mainly by participants from senior high school and university. One possible reason for this might be that more complex sentences are taught at advanced level, which in turn influences the way learners construct their sentences.

This corresponds to the findings for textbook data that prototypes largely occur across three sets of data. This may suggest that the interrogative form is the most commonly used construction of which all the participants are aware.

Distribution of "who" sentences across the four sets of data

We now look at the distribution of "who" sentences. We will compare this word with the previously studied words, as well as "who" sentences in the textbook data.

Table 6.10 and Figure 6.8 show the different types of "who" sentences across the four datasets.

	Prototype	%	Extension 1	%	Extension 2	%	total
JED	240	98%	0	0	5	2%	245
SED	137	66%	0	0	71	34%	208
UED	407	77%	0	0	119	23%	526
NS	55	89%	0	0	7	11%	62
All ED	839	81%	0	0	202	19%	1041

Table 6.10 "who" sentence across each datasets

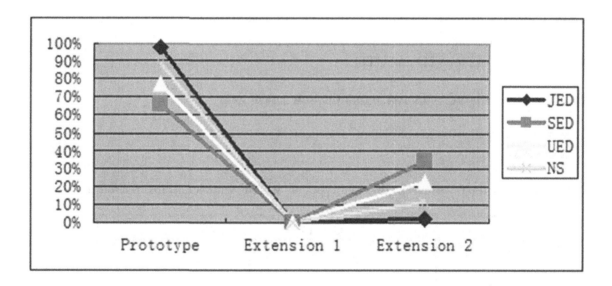

Figure 6.8 "who" sentence types across the four sets of data

Table 6.10 and Figure 6.8 clearly show that prototypes occur with a high frequency across all three datasets, with 98% for JED, 89% for NS, 66% for SED, and 77% for UED. Extension 1 is not found in three datasets. Extension 2 has relatively low frequency as expected: 2% (JED), 11% (NS), 34% (SED) and 23% (UED).

Examples are shown below:

Prototypes:

```
Who did you go to Hawaii with? (JED)
Who do you think the best? (SED)
Who is your favourite teacher? (UED)
Who's that guy over there? (NS)
```

Extension 2:

```
It must be him who often does bad things. (JED} It is his sister who
brought him up. (SED)
I don't know who you are. (UED)
Everybody who walks pass me sees it. (NS)
```

"Who" sentences follow a similar pattern to the previously analysed sentences such as "what", "how", "where", "why", and "who". Prototypical "who" sentences are favoured across the four groups of participants. This may suggest that this construction is well established in participants' linguistic knowledge.

As for extension 2, this construction is largely produced by participants from the senior high school. This matches the findings for the textbook data to the effect that this construction largely occurs in higher level textbooks for STD and UTD.

Distribution of "whom" sentences across the four sets of data

We now look at the distribution of "whom" sentences. We also compare this word with the previously studied words.

Table 6.11 and Figure 6.9 show the different types of "whom" sentences across the four datasets.

	Prototype	%	Extension 1	%	Extension 2	%	total
JED	54	92%	0	0	5	8%	59
SED	26	60%	0	0	17	40%	43
UED	218	49%	0	0	229	51%	447
NS	23	79%	0	0	6	21%	29
All ED	321	56%	0	0	257	44%	578

Table 6.11 "whom" sentences across datasets

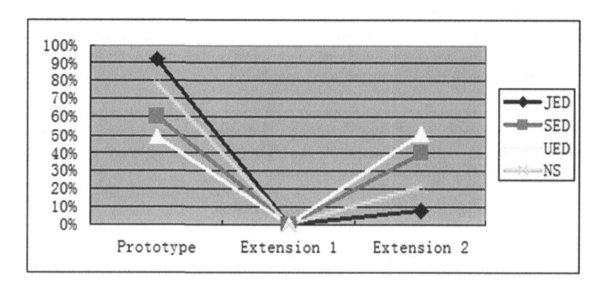

Figure 6.9 "whom" sentence types across the four sets of data

As Table 6.11 and Figure 6.9 show, the proportion of prototypes shows a gradual decline from 92% in JED, to 79% in NS, then 60% in SED and 49% in UED. In the absence of Extension 1, there is a corresponding increase in the proportion of Extension 2, from 8% in JED, to 21% in NS, then 40% in SED and 51% in UED

Examples are shown below:

Prototypes:

```
Whom do you go to school with? (JED)
Whom do you think is the best one to play with? (SED)
Whom will the teacher choose as our monitor? (UED)
To whom are you sending that? (NS)
```

Extension 2:

```
I don't know whom she loves. (SED)
He is a person whom I treated well. (UED)
That is the guy whom I met yesterday. (NS)
```

The "whom" word is different from the previously analysed words. As the data reveals, prototypes are largely produced by participants from junior middle school, senior high school, and native speakers. This contrasts with our findings from the textbook data to the effect that prototypes have the lowest level of occurrence across the three sets of data. One possible reason for this might be that participants are not familiar with this construction. The figures show that this construction has the fewest occurrences in textbook data. It appears that even native speakers are hesitant to construct such sentences. It is interesting that when participants construct this sentence type or they search for related examples from the long-term memory, they seem to construct the interrogative forms in a similar way to the other "wh" words. This may explain why prototypes predominate for the four groups of participants. Another possible explanation might be that some participants confuse the usage of "whom" with that of "who". It should be noted that they significantly produced "whom" sentences using a similar pattern to that of "who" sentences.

It is interesting to note that extension 2 sentences are mainly produced by participants from university. This may be attributed to the influence of textbooks. Textbooks at university adopt a style similar to newspaper articles or novels. It is predictable that "whom" extension 2 largely occurs in a written context and learners are well aware of this characteristic.

Distribution of "whose" sentences across the four sets of data

We now look at the distribution of "whose" sentences, as well as compare this word to the previously studied words. The "whose" sentences follow a similar pattern to the previously analysed words such as "what", "how", "where", "why", and "who".

Table 6.12 and Figure 6.10 show the different types of "whose" sentences across the four datasets.

	Prototype	%	Extension 1	%	Extension 2	%	total
JED	127	98%	0	0	2	2%	129
SED	129	77%	0	0	39	23%	168
UED	363	69%	0	0	160	31%	523
NS	32	100%	0	0	0	0	32
All ED	651	76%	0	0	201	24%	852

Table 6.12 "whose" sentences across each datasets

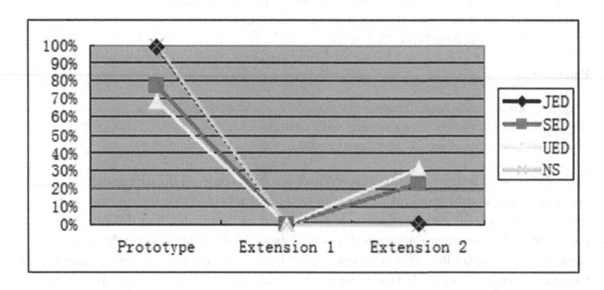

Figure 6.10 "whose" sentence types across the four sets of data

According to Table 6.12 and Figure 6.10, prototypes for three datasets have the highest frequency; however with a steady decrease for 100% for NS to 99% for JED, 77% for SED, and 69% for UED. Extension 1 cannot be found across all datasets. Extension 2 gradually increases across the three datasets, with 1% (JED), 23% (SED), and 31% (UED). Extension 2 in SED (23%) occurs less than that of prototype (77%), while Extension 2 in UTD (31%) reaches about half the number for prototype (69%). Extension 2 is not found in NS. Examples are shown below:

Prototypes:

```
Whose hat is on the window? (JED)
Whose homework is the best? (SED)
Whose pencils are these? (UED)
Whose drink is this? (NS)
```

Extension 2:

```
I want to know whose book has been forgotten. (JED)
He is just the one whose finger was cut. (SED)
I don't like the girl whose hair is too long. (SED)
```

"Whose" sentences follow a similar pattern to the previously studied words, with prototypes heavily produced across the four groups of the participants. This contrasts to the findings for textbook data which show that prototypes largely occur in lower level textbooks (JTD). A possible reason for this might be that participants over-generalize the "whose" interrogative form.

As for extension 2, this construction is produced mainly by participants from university. This may suggest that more complex sentence structures are taught in advanced level textbooks and thus learners have the knowledge to use this construction. This is similar to the findings for textbook data to the effect that this construction largely occurs in STD and UTD. It is interesting to note that this construction is not found in native speakers' data. This may suggest that the "whose" sentence is shown to be more central and basic and is known by the four groups of participants.

Distribution of "which" sentences across the four sets of data

We now look at the distribution of "which" sentences across the four sets of data. We also compare the usage of the word "which" to the previously studied words.

Table 6.13 and Figure 6.11 show the different types of "which" sentences across the four datasets.

	Prototype	%	Extension 1	%	Extension 2	%	total
JED	225	99%	0	0	2	1%	227
SED	120	53%	0	0	105	47%	225
UED	379	73%	0	0	142	27%	521
NS	39	85%	0	0	7	15%	46
All ED	763	75%	0	0	256	25%	1019

Table 6.13 "which" sentences across each datasets

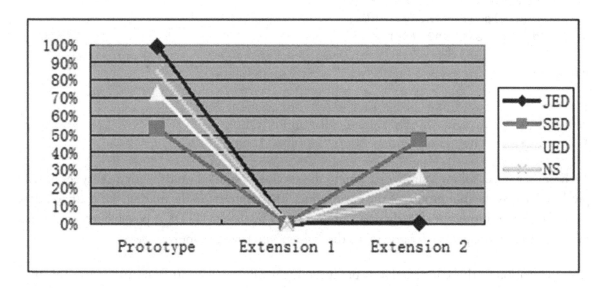

Figure 6.11 "which" sentence types across the four sets of data

As Table 6.13 and Figure 6.11 show, in terms of prototypes, JED and UED have high frequency, with 99% for JED, 85% for NS, and 73% for UED.

Again, Extension 1 is not found in any of the datasets.

Extension 2 has the highest frequency in SED, where it reaches 47%. Extension 2 in UED (27%) is half that of in SED (47%). There is almost the same distribution for prototypes and Extension 2 in SED, with 53% and 47%. NS has the fewest number of Extension 2, at 15%. Examples of the sentence patterns are shown below:

Prototypes:

```
Which book do you like? (JED)
Which do you like best? (SED)
Which colour do you like best? (UED)
Which version are you using? (NS)
```

Extension 2:

```
Should be Beijing, which is the capital of PRC, welcomes people from the
entire world (JED)
I don't know which question he can answer. (SED)
This is [a] big Bag which is very famous. (UED)
I can tell you more which are worse than this. (NS)
```

"Which" sentences have a similar usage pattern to the previously studied sentences such as "what", "how", "where", "why", "who", and "whose". The data shows that prototypes are largely produced across the four groups of participants. This contrasts with the findings for textbook data, with prototypes largely occurring in lower level textbooks (JTD). A possible reason for this might be that participants over-generalize the "whose" interrogative form because it is taught at the lower level and in turn stored in learners' long-term memory.

As for extension 2, this construction is mainly produced by participants from senior high school and university. This is similar to the findings for textbook data to the effect that this construction largely occurs in STD and UTD.

In conclusion there are three patterns that can be identified from the above discussion: 1) prototypes predominate across the four sets of data, for example, "what", "how", "where", "why", "who", "whose" and "which" sentences; 2) prototypes largely occur for participants at higher proficiency levels (SED, UED and NS), while extension 2 largely occurs at lower proficiency levels (JED), for example, "when" sentences; 3) prototypes largely occur in a mixed proficiency level (JED, SED, and NS), while extension 2 predominates for higher proficiency levels (UED), for example "whom" sentences.

In the last section, we have discussed the prototypes and extension structures of "wh" words. In the next section, we investigate the frequency of the different words that follow "wh" in interrogatives, declaratives, and subordinate clauses. This will give us a clear picture of which "wh" sentences are particularly likely to combine in terms of elicited sentences written by native speakers and language learners.

6.7 Frequency of the words Occurring Immediately after "wh" in interrogatives, declaratives, and subordinate clauses across the Four Elicited Datasets

As in the last chapter, we look at the words that occur immediately after the "wh" word in the three types of sentences. This is an investigation of colligation and collocation. We will look at the words immediately following the "wh" words as this often gives us a clear picture of the grammatical words that the "wh" words are particularly likely to combine with. We also look at the differences and similarities between NS and NNS in terms of the grammatical-lexical items that the "wh" words are particularly likely to combine with.

What

In this section, we look at the frequencies of words occurring immediately after "what" in interrogatives, declaratives and subordinate clauses. The discussion will focus on the differences and similarities in the way native speakers and non-native speakers use grammatical-lexical items to construct elicited sentences. The implications of the findings for L2 teaching and learning will also be discussed.

Frequency of the words occurring immediately after "what" in interrogatives across the four sets of data

Table 6.14 shows the frequencies of the words occurring immediately after "what" in interrogatives across the four sets of data. Due to the lack of space, only the top 20 words are shown.

JED			SED			UED			NED		
word	No.	%	word	No.	%	word	No.	%	word	No.	%
is	161	48.94%	is	105	51.47%	is	220	52.63%	is	39	27.86%
are	63	19.15%	are	35	17.16%	are	56	13.40%	do	23	16.43%
do	39	11.85%	do	16	7.84%	do	48	11.48%	are	12	8.57%
did	15	4.56%	can	10	4.90%	can	17	4.07%	can	8	5.71%
will	9	2.74%	did	7	3.43%	kind	9	2.15%	about	7	5.00%
should	8	2.43%	makes	6	2.94%	color	8	1.91%	did	6	4.29%
were	7	2.13%	kind	3	1.47%	did	7	1.67%	would	5	3.57%
about	6	1.82%	color	3	1.47%	makes	6	1.44%	happened	4	2.86%
does	4	1.22%	time	2	0.98%	about	5	1.20%	does	3	2.14%
was	4	1.22%	to	2	0.98%	would	5	1.20%	am	2	1.43%
color	2	0.61%	she	1	0.49%	does	4	0.96%	time	2	1.43%
time	2	0.61%	should	1	0.49%	class	4	0.96%	colour	2	1.43%
can	2	0.61%	else	1	0.49%	should	4	0.96%	for	2	1.43%
hobby	1	0.30%	would	1	0.49%	have	3	0.72%	shall	2	1.43%
the	1	0.30%	make	1	0.49%	day	3	0.72%	will	2	1.43%
kind	1	0.30%	about	1	0.49%	will	3	0.72%	size	2	1.43%
advise	1	0.30%	happen	1	0.49%	was	2	0.48%	seems	2	1.43%
sports	1	0.30%	happened	1	0.49%	to	2	0.48%	date	2	1.43%
happen	1	0.30%	will	1	0.49%	happened	2	0.48%	species	1	0.71%
it	1	0.30%	day	1	0.49%	could	1	0.24%	lesson	1	0.71%

Table 6.14 Comparison of the frequencies and percentage of different
words occurring after "what" in interrogatives

As Table 6.14 shows, the four sets of data have almost the same distribution, especially on be verbs and auxiliaries. *Is, are,* and *do* occur exclusively across the four sets of data. One possible reason for this might be that be verbs and auxiliaries are the basic "what" interrogative forms, and both native speakers and non-native speakers are aware of this. Examples are shown as follows:

```
What is the matter? (JED)
What is the date today? (SED)
What is your name? (UED)
What is the answer? (NED)
What are you doing? (JED)
What are you going to do? (SED)
What are they doing? (UED)
What are you doing? (NED)
What do you do? (JED)
What do you want? (SED)
What do you buy? (UED)
What did you say? (NED)
```

Learners from junior middle school produced fewer modal verbs than those from senior high school, university, and native speakers. One possible reason for this might be that textbooks for junior middle school have relatively fewer examples, and learners are not familiar with constructing interrogatives by using modals. In most cases, modal verbs contain an extension of meaning; it is possible that learners at a lower level are not sufficiently confident to produce these. Examples of modal verbs are shown as follows:

```
What should I do? (JED)
What will you do in the future? (SED)
What can I do for you? (UED)
What shall I wear? (NED)
```

Lexical items also have a similar distribution across the four sets of data. In most cases, all four groups of participants are likely to use fixed expressions and collocations, for example *what time...*, *what colour...* and *what else...* We have also found that there are many fixed expressions and collocations contained in the textbook; this may suggest that learners construct sentences containing such phrases because they have encountered them in their previous language exposure. In the case of native speakers, it is more likely that they have a wider range of vocabulary and they appear confident in using fixed expressions and collocations. Examples are shown as follows:

```
What advice do you have for Tom? (JED)
What color is it? (SED)
What impressed you most? (UED)
What kind of work is it? (NED)
What gift did you buy for mum?(NED)
```

Frequency of the words occurring immediately after "what" in declaratives across the four sets of data

Table 6.15 shows the frequencies of the words occurring after "what" declaratives across the three sets of data.

JED			SED			UED			NED		
word	No.	%	word	No.	%	word	No.	%	word	No.	%
a	3	100%	a	43	87.76%	a	13	100.00%	a	8	88.89%
			fun	3	6.12%				an	1	11.11%
			fine	2	4.08%						
			great	1	2.04%						

Table 6.15 Comparison of the frequencies and percentage of different words occurring immediately after "what" in declaratives

According to Table 6.15, the most frequent word is *a* across the four sets of data, indicating a high frequency of exclamatory expressions. For example:

```
What a foolish egg. (SED)
What fine weather. (SED)
What great idea. (SED)
What a fine day. (UED)
What a clever girl. (UED)
What a lovely dog. (UED)
What a sad day. (NED)
What a stingy man you are. (NED)
```

As the above examples show, learners' elicited sentences contain mistakes, such as 'what great idea', which should be written 'what a great idea'. It is interesting to note that learners at the beginner's level seem to produce the correct form. In contrast, those at a higher level are likely to make the most mistakes.

Because there is only one word occurring immediately after "what" interrogatives, it is necessary to look further to the right of the word in order to identify any differences across the four sets of data. It is interesting to note that most non-native speakers use declaratives in positive situations, which somehow can be considered to be a kind of compliment. In contrast, native speakers use declaratives in negative situations, which are used to express a negative opinion on an event. We have already seen these findings in the textbook data, suggesting that some examples provided in textbooks are somewhat artificial, and learners' production is influenced by this.

Frequency of the words occurring immediately after "what" in subordinate clauses across the four sets of data

Table 6.16 shows the frequencies of the words occurring after "what" in subordinate clauses across the four sets of data.

JED			SED			UED			NED		
Word	No.	%	word	No.	%	word	No.	%	word	No.	%
			I	17	23.61%	I	11	28.95%	I	8	28.57%
			you	15	20.83%	you	8	21.05%	you	4	14.29%
			to	8	11.11%	he	4	10.53%	happened	3	10.71%
			he	5	6.94%	to	3	7.89%	the	2	7.14%
			makes	5	6.94%	it	2	5.26%	we	2	7.14%
			is	3	4.17%	is	1	2.63%	to	2	7.14%
			she	3	4.17%	make	1	2.63%	people	2	7.14%
			surprised	2	2.78%	made	1	2.63%	that	1	3.57%
			surprise	2	2.78%	they	1	2.63%	is	1	3.57%
			make	2	2.78%	if	1	2.63%	age	1	3.57%
			difficulties	1	1.39%	has	1	2.63%	she	1	3.57%
			it	1	1.39%	goes	1	2.63%	a	1	3.57%
			kind	1	1.39%	knowledge	1	2.63%			
			should	1	1.39%	else	1	2.63%			
			fun	1	1.39%	we	1	2.63%			
			do	1	1.39%						
			bother	1	1.39%						
			bothered	1	1.39%						
			can	1	1.39%						
			the	1	1.39%						

Table 6.16 Comparison of the frequencies and percentage of different words occurring after "what" in subordinate clauses

As Table 6.16 shows, pronouns are the most frequent words occurring after "what" subordinate clauses across the three sets of data where subordinate clauses were produced (no subordinate clauses were produced by JED students). This is interesting as it is the opposite of what was found with interrogatives. Interrogative pronouns have the lowest occurrences across the four sets of data. One possible reason for this might be that pronouns are more likely to be a strong convention in "what" subordinate clauses than those in interrogatives. Examples are shown as follows:

```
I said what he wants to know. (SED)
What I want is to try my best. (UED)
I don't believe what he says. (UED)
I know what I am doing. (NED)
```

SED has a wider range of grammatical words and lexical items than UED. It is interesting to note that there are several forms of individual words. For example, make/makes, surprise/surprised, and bother/bothered. One possible explanation for this might be that after acquiring the basic sentence structures, it is more likely that learners are aware of using different forms of verbs in different contexts. Examples are shown as follows:

```
I will do it no matter what difficulties I will meet. (SED)
What surprises us is that a new English teacher comes. (SED)
What surprised me is that you are so silly. (SED)
What bothered is that you always go to school late. (SED)
There is an old saying that what goes around comes around. (UED)
```

NED has fewer lexical items than SED and UED. The lexical items native speakers produced are different from the other two groups of participants, for example *happened*, and *age*. It is interesting to note that these two lexical words do not appear in SED and UED. In contrast, lexical items occur frequently in "what" interrogatives. One possible reason for this might be that non-native speakers' elicited sentences largely rely on examples that are given in their textbooks, while native speakers are more aware of the conventions of the English language. Examples are shown as follows:

```
Guess what happened? (NED)
I have no idea of what happened last night. (NED)
```

How

In the following sections, we look at the frequencies of words occurring immediately following "how" in interrogatives, declaratives, and subordinate clauses. We also look at the differences and similarities between native speakers and non-native speakers in the ways they use different types of words.

Frequency of the words occurring immediately after "how" in interrogatives across the four sets of data

JED			SED			UED			NED		
word	No.	%	word	No.	%	word	No.	%	word	No.	%
is	68	20.42%	do	43	19.20%	Do	75	19.95%	is	36	19.67%
are	61	18.32%	are	34	15.18%	Are	56	14.89%	are	31	16.94%
old	40	12.01%	much	24	10.71%	is	37	9.84%	do	21	11.48%
often	30	9.01%	old	20	8.93%	can	36	9.57%	can	19	10.38%
do	30	9.01%	many	17	7.59%	much	27	7.18%	much	15	8.20%
many	27	8.11%	to	16	7.14%	old	26	6.91%	about	14	7.65%
long	22	6.61%	is	13	5.80%	to	21	5.59%	long	8	4.37%
much	20	6.01%	long	12	5.36%	many	20	5.32%	many	6	3.28%
about	11	3.30%	can	11	4.91%	about	18	4.79%	could	6	3.28%
far	6	1.80%	about	8	3.57%	long	18	4.79%	old	5	2.73%
can	5	1.50%	often	8	3.57%	could	7	1.86%	did	4	2.19%
was	5	1.50%	far	5	2.23%	does	6	1.60%	come	3	1.64%
to	4	1.20%	did	5	2.23%	come	6	1.60%	was	3	1.64%
it	2	0.60%	I	2	0.89%	did	3	0.80%	to	3	1.64%
will	1	0.30%	soon	2	0.89%	the	3	0.80%	tall	2	1.09%
did	1	0.30%	tall	1	0.45%	often	3	0.80%	should	2	1.09%
			you	1	0.45%	deep	2	0.53%	far	1	0.55%
			does	1	0.45%	would	2	0.53%	soon	1	0.55%
			could	1	0.45%	will	2	0.53%	would	1	0.55%
						far	2	0.53%	does	1	0.55%
						soon	2	0.53%	bad	1	0.55%

Table 6.17 Comparison of the frequencies and percentage of different words occurring after "how" in interrogatives

According to Table 6.17, Be verbs in JED have the most frequent word across the four sets of data. For example:

```
How are you? (JED)
How are you feeling today? (SED)
How are you? (UED)
How was the concert? (NED)
```

As expected, there are frequent occurrences of quantifying words like *often*, *much*, *many*, *long*, and *far*. SED and UED share 5 words in the top 7: *do*, *are*, *much*, *old*, and *to*. Such quantifying words can be considered somewhat formulaic and can be easily stored in learners' minds. It is interesting that the quantifying words can also be found in the textbook data. This may suggest that textbooks as one type of input play an important role in learners' language acquisition processes. It is also interesting to note that non-native speakers tend to use countable nouns such as *pen*, and *students* to follow quantifying words, while native speakers are more likely to use uncountable nouns such as *time* to follow quantifying words. One possible reason for this might be that non-native speakers are not very confident of using quantifying words with countable and uncountable nouns. Examples are shown as follows:

```
How much are these jeans? (JED)
How much does it cost? (SED)
How much is it? (UED)
How much are these, please?(NED)
How many pens do you have? (JED)
How many hours do you work? (SED)
How many students in the class? (UED)
How many times shall I tell you?(NED)
How long have you been collecting shells? (JED)
How long have you finish homework? (SED)
How long will it take? (UED)
How long is it going to last?(NED)
How far is it? (JED)
How far it is? (SED)
How far is it from your home to your school? (UED)
```

The phrase "how to" occurs across the four sets of data. It seems that this phrase is used formulaically and is more likely to be used in the on-line production. It is interesting to note that this phrase occurs more frequently than in NED. One possible reason for this might be L1 transfer. The phrase "how to" is used frequently in the Chinese language as it is the most commonly used collocation in the Chinese language. Examples are shown as follows:

```
How to make apple pie? (JED)
How to enrich your knowledge? (SED)
How to make a good friend and keep our relationship? (UED)
how to use computer?(NED)
how to solve laptop problems?(NED)
```

In the case of modal verbs, native speakers tend to use modals to indicate a kind of blaming or questioning, for example:

```
How could you do that? (NED)
How can you do that? (NED)
```

In contrast, non-native speakers tend to write sentences that can be easily traced back to the examples that are shown in their textbooks. In many cases, the sentences that they produced are similar to those for the textbook data. This may suggest that learners' working memories have a strong relationship with long-term memory, particularly in on-line production. Examples are shown as follows:

```
How can you understand me? (SED)
How can we predict the future? (NED)
```

Frequency of the words occurring immediately after "how" in declaratives across the four sets of data

Table 6.18 shows the frequencies of the words occurring after "how" in declaratives across the four sets of data.

JED			SED			UED			NED		
word	**No.**	**%**	**Word**	**No.**	**%**	**word**	**No.**	**%**	**word**	**No.**	**%**
beautiful	5	41.67%	Beautiful	20	42.55%	beautiful	24	41.38%	clumsy	1	25.00%
strange	2	16.67%	Fun	5	10.64%	fine	4	6.90%	exciting	1	25.00%
smart	2	16.67%	Clever	5	10.64%	deep	3	5.17%	fresh	1	25.00%
far	1	8.33%	Great	1	2.13%	nice	3	5.17%	beautiful	1	25.00%
boring	1	8.33%	Cheerful	1	2.13%	lovely	2	3.45%			
			Pretty	2	4.26%	delicious	2	3.45%			
			Lovely	2	4.26%	great	2	3.45%			
			Crazy	1	2.13%	big	2	3.45%			
			Happy	1	2.13%	difficult	1	1.72%			
			Interesting	1	2.13%	serious	1	1.72%			
			Cool	1	2.13%	friendly	1	1.72%			
			Big	1	2.13%	small	1	1.72%			
			Perfect	2	4.26%	terrible	1	1.72%			
			Shy	1	2.13%	elegant	1	1.72%			
			Fine	1	2.13%	well	1	1.72%			
			Funny	1	2.13%	ridiculous	1	1.72%			
			Wonderful	1	2.13%	funny	1	1.72%			
						fresh	1	1.72%			
						interesting	1	1.72%			
						wonderful	1	1.72%			
						foolish	1	1.72%			
						luck	1	1.72%			
						clever	1	1.72%			

Table 6.18 Comparison of the frequencies and percentage of different words occurring after "how" in declaratives

According to Table 6.18, non-native speakers produce more declarative sentences than native speakers in general. One possible reason for this might be that there are many examples listed in textbooks, and learners are influenced by them. In addition, a much greater number of lexical words are found across the three datasets. The most frequent word is *beautiful* for JED, SED, and UED. This is consistent with what we have found for textbook data. UED contains a wider range of lexical words. One possible reason for this might be that learners at a higher level have a larger vocabulary, particularly in adjectives. Examples are shown as follows:

```
How beautiful it is. (JED)
How beautiful the scene is. (SED)
```

```
How boring it is. (JED)
How smart. (JED)
How clever he is. (SED)
How smart you are. (SED)
How stunning she is. (UED)
How funny it is. (UED)
How beautiful the flower is. (UED)
How exciting? (NED)
How beautiful the flower is. (NED)
```

We have found that for "what" declaratives, non-native speakers tend to use declaratives to express positive thoughts or ideas, while native speakers are more likely to use them to express negative thoughts or ideas. In contrast, despite the fact that there are a small number of examples produced by native speakers, most of the adjectives have positive meanings. This is consistent with the idea that non-native speakers use declaratives to express positive thoughts or ideas, however, we might need to study more native speakers' sentences to prove the idea that they tend to use declaratives to express negative ideas.

Frequency of the words after "how" in subordinate clauses across the four sets of data

Table 6.19 shows the frequencies of the words occurring after "how" in subordinate clauses across the four sets of data.

JED			SED			UED			NED		
word	**No.**	**%**	**word**	**No.**	**%**	**word**	**No.**	**%**	**word**	**No.**	**%**
To	18	72.00%	beautiful	5	41.67%	to	21	63.64%	to	10	76.92%
difficult	3	12.00%	strange	2	16.67%	we	2	6.06%	he	1	7.69%
Much	1	4.00%	smart	2	16.67%	it	2	6.06%	clumsy	1	7.69%
Hard	1	4.00%	far	1	8.33%	and	1	3.03%	you	1	7.69%
He	1	4.00%	boring	1	8.33%	they	1	3.03%			
Warm	1	4.00%	bad	1	8.33%	I	1	3.03%			
						things	1	3.03%			
						he	1	3.03%			
						hard	1	3.03%			
						did	1	3.03%			
						could	1	3.03%			

Table 6.19 Comparison of the frequencies and percentage of different words occurring after "how" in subordinate clauses

According to Table 6.19, the phrase *how to* is the most frequent collocation in JED, UED and NED, suggesting that both native speakers and non-native speakers use this phrase to link the main clauses. It is interesting to note that the phrase *how to* occurs more frequently in non-native speakers' sentences in terms of "how" interrogatives. Examples are shown as follows:

```
I don't know the problem how to solve. (SED)
I don't know how to finish the work. (UED)
You should learn how to entertain yourself and enjoy your life. (NED)
Mother and I decided that you should learn how to keep your own rooms
neat and not make a mess wherever you go. (NED)
```

It is interesting to note that quite a few lexical items are found to follow "how" subordinate clauses, such as *beautiful, strange, difficult, hard* and *clumsy*. One possible explanation we can offer is that both native speakers and non-native speakers store "how" declaratives as fixed expressions while they construct subordinate clauses. This may suggest that people not only store individual words but also semi-phrases or sentences as a type of formulaic language. It is considered to be important for L2 language teaching and learning as learners can choose these stored words, phrases or sentences to construct sentences in accordance with their contexts. Examples are shown as follows:

```
No matter how tired I am, I will keep on. (JED)
No matter how interesting I really don't like it. (SED)
No matter how hard, I will clime the mountain. (UED)
I know, but you can't imagine how clumsy he is. (NED)
```

Where

We now turn to look at the frequencies of words occurring immediately after "where" in interrogatives, and subordinate clauses. We also look at the differences and similarities between native speakers and non-native speakers in the way they use different types of words.

Frequency of the words occurring immediately after "where" in interrogatives across the four sets of data

Table 6.20 shows the frequencies of the words occurring after "where" in interrogatives across the four sets of data.

JED			SED			UED			NED		
word	**No.**	**%**	**word**	**No.**	**%**	**Word**	**No.**	**%**	**word**	**No.**	**%**
is	68	24.64%	is	47	30.13%	is	115	31.42%	is	24	32.00%
are	49	17.75%	are	34	21.79%	are	68	18.58%	are	16	21.33%
do	32	11.59%	do	26	16.67%	do	47	12.84%	did	8	10.67%
are	17	6.16%	did	14	8.97%	did	31	8.47%	does	7	9.33%
did	10	3.62%	will	8	5.13%	will	20	5.46%	do	5	6.67%
were	8	2.90%	can	5	3.21%	can	19	5.19%	shall	4	5.33%
does	6	2.17%	were	5	3.21%	have	14	3.83%	have	2	2.67%
has	5	1.81%	does	3	1.92%	shall	13	3.55%	will	2	2.67%
you	4	1.45%	I	3	1.92%	does	10	2.73%	can	2	2.67%
was	4	1.45%	you	2	1.28%	the	7	1.91%	to	1	1.33%
will	1	0.36%	should	2	1.28%	should	4	1.09%	am	1	1.33%
can	1	0.36%	the	2	1.28%	I	3	0.82%	in	1	1.33%
am	1	0.36%	have	2	1.28%	were	2	0.55%	on	1	1.33%
it	1	0.36%	would	1	0.64%	we	2	0.55%	the	1	1.33%
there	1	0.36%	my	1	0.64%	could	2	0.55%			

Table 6.20 Comparison of the frequencies and percentage of different words occurring after "where" in interrogatives

Similar to "when" interrogatives, words immediately following the word *where* are only grammatical words. It is interesting to note that four datasets share four words in the top five (*is, did, are, do*). 'Where' interrogatives collocate with a wider range variety of grammatical words than 'when' interrogatives. These include 'be' verbs, auxiliaries, and modals. Both native speakers and non-native speakers tended to produce a large proportion of sentences which containing these basic grammatical words. Examples are shown as follows:

```
Where is his dog? (JED)
Where is your mother? (SED)
Where is the hospital? (UED)
Where is the train station? (NED)
Where are you going? (JED)
Where are you from? (SED)
Where are you come from? (UED)
Where are my keys? (NED)
Where do you live? (JED)
```

```
Where do you live? (SED)
Where did you buy these delicious cakes? (UED)
Where do you want to go? (UED)
Where did you find it? (UED)
Where do you keep thumbtacks and paper clips? (NED)
```

Frequency of the words after "where" in subordinate clauses across the four sets of data

Table 6.21 shows the frequencies of the words occurring after "where" in subordinate clauses across the four sets of data.

JED			SED			UED			NED		
word	No.	%	word	No.	%	word	No.	%	word	No.	%
your	1	100.00%	I	19	32.20%	you	10	16.39%	you	8	61.54%
			the	8	13.56%	I	10	16.39%	I	2	15.38%
			is	7	11.86%	he	7	11.48%	to	1	7.69%
			you	5	8.47%	the	6	9.84%	we	1	7.69%
			there	3	5.08%	to	6	9.84%	the	1	7.69%
			it	3	5.08%	there	4	6.56%			
			near	3	5.08%	it	3	4.92%			
			to	2	3.39%	we	3	4.92%			
			my	2	3.39%	his	2	3.28%			
			has	1	1.69%	her	1	1.64%			
			he	1	1.69%	they	1	1.64%			
			she	1	1.69%	give	1	1.64%			
			no	1	1.69%	did	1	1.64%			
			people	1	1.69%	has	1	1.64%			
			we	1	1.69%	used	1	1.64%			
			in	1	1.69%	she	1	1.64%			
						in	1	1.64%			
						have	1	1.64%			
						near	1	1.64%			

Table 6.21 Comparison of the frequencies and percentage of different words occurring after "where" in subordinate clauses

According to Table 6.21, pronouns have the high frequency for SED, UED and NED., for example:

```
The place where I live is very beautiful. (SED)
Where you lived is the most beautiful place in our city. (UED)
I know where you live. (NED)
You reach a point in any project where you just want to get the thing
finished. (NED)
```

It is interesting to note that the word *there* occurred frequently in the idiom: *where there is a will, there is a way,* which emphasise the formulaic nature of the lexicon and also the influence of EFL in China. In addition, both native speakers and non-native speakers were aware of the fact that the word "where" indicates more detailed information about a location, it is therefore in most cases, the main clauses are followed by a location noun such as *place, park,* and *home.* On the other hand, native speakers seem more flexible when constructing "where" subordinate clauses. In most cases, the word "where" is used to link two clauses. In contrast, learners seem not very confident about this usage. Examples are shown as follows:

```
I want to go to the place where there are a lot of mountains. (SED)
It was my home where gave me the most wonderful memory. (UED)
You reach a point in any project where you just want to get the thing
finished. (NED)
```

When

In the following sections, we look at the frequencies of words occurring immediately after "when" in interrogatives, and subordinate clauses. We also look at the differences and similarities between native speakers and non-native speakers in the way they use different types of words.

Frequency of the words occurring immediately after "when" in interrogatives across the four sets of data

Table 6.22 shows the frequencies of the words occurring after "when" in interrogatives across the four sets of data.

JED			SED			UED			NED		
word	No.	%	word	No.	%	word	No.	%	word	No.	%
are	35	26.12%	did	53	35.33%	will	77	22.99%	is	42	30.00%
do	32	23.88%	will	29	19.33%	did	65	19.40%	can	35	25.00%
did	19	14.18%	do	18	12.00%	do	39	11.64%	will	16	11.43%
is	12	8.96%	were	11	7.33%	is	24	7.16%	did	14	10.00%
the	9	6.72%	is	10	6.67%	you	24	7.16%	are	13	9.29%
were	6	4.48%	are	6	4.00%	shall	20	5.97%	do	11	7.86%
will	6	4.48%	does	5	3.33%	does	20	5.97%	shall	4	2.86%
does	6	4.48%	shall	4	2.67%	can	17	5.07%	she	3	2.14%
was	6	4.48%	can	4	2.67%	are	13	3.88%	does	2	1.43%
should	1	0.75%	you	3	2.00%	the	8	2.39%			
it	1	0.75%	the	2	1.33%	I	6	1.79%			
this	1	0.75%	it	2	1.33%	to	4	1.19%			
			should	2	1.33%	were	3	0.90%			
			I	1	0.67%	my	3	0.90%			
						have	2	0.60%			
						should	2	0.60%			
						it	2	0.60%			
						could	2	0.60%			
						must	1	0.30%			
						would	1	0.30%			
						we	1	0.30%			
						was	1	0.30%			

Table 6.22 Comparison of the frequencies and percentage of different words occurring after "when" in interrogatives

According to Table 6.22, the only words which come after "when" interrogatives are grammatical words, including *be* verbs, auxiliaries, modals, and pronouns. JED provides basic grammatical words, and gradually increases as proficiency level improves. One possible reason for this might be that textbooks tend to provide the basic interrogative form at lower levels, and some complex sentence structures appear as proficiency level increases. In most cases, this reflects communicative daily dialogues. Such sentences are short and easily to memorize, and learners can store them in their long-term memory. Examples are shown as follows:

```
When are you going? (JED)
When is your birthday? (SED)
When are you getting up everyday? (UED)
```

```
When did it start? (JED)
When do you eat dinner? (SED)
When do you go home? (UED)
When should I go to work? (JED)
When will you come to my house? (SED)
When can you come? (UED)
When he arrived home? (JED)
When it start? (SED)
When you will come back? (UED)
```

Frequency of the words after "when" in subordinate clauses across the four sets of data

Table 6.23 shows the frequencies of the words occurring after "when" in subordinate clauses across the four sets of data.

JED			SED			UED			NED		
word	No.	%	word	No.	%	word	No.	%	word	No.	%
the	45	30.20%	I	82	56.94%	I	47	34.31%	I	5	26.32%
I	45	30.20%	we	11	7.64%	the	34	24.82%	the	3	15.79%
he	15	10.07%	he	10	6.94%	you	12	8.76%	you	3	15.79%
she	12	8.05%	the	9	6.25%	we	8	5.84%	other	2	10.53%
you	12	8.05%	you	7	4.86%	he	6	4.38%	she	2	10.53%
a	10	6.71%	my	5	3.47%	it	6	4.38%	to	1	5.26%
my	6	4.03%	it	4	2.78%	my	5	3.65%	they	1	5.26%
your	1	0.67%	she	3	2.08%	to	3	2.19%	be	1	5.26%
we	1	0.67%	her	1	0.69%	his	2	1.46%	he	1	5.26%
her	1	0.67%	a	1	0.69%	a	2	1.46%			
alien	1	0.67%	and	1	0.69%	everything	2	1.46%			
			all	1	0.69%	she	2	1.46%			
			mother	1	0.69%	is	1	0.73%			
			watching	1	0.69%	they	1	0.73%			
			crossing	1	0.69%	a	1	0.73%			
			shall	1	0.69%	our	1	0.73%			
			should	1	0.69%	their	1	0.73%			
			listening	1	0.69%	holiday	1	0.73%			
			playing	1	0.69%	there	1	0.73%			
			someone	1	0.69%	someone	1	0.73%			
			most	1	0.69%						

Table 6.23 Comparison of the frequencies and percentage of different words occurring after "when" in subordinate clauses

According to Table 6.23, all four datasets have relatively higher frequencies of pronouns. It is more likely that pronouns are used to introduce the main subject. This might be one of the restricted collocations of "when" subordinate clauses. Examples are shown as follows:

```
I fall sleep when I watch TV. (JED
I remember the time when I met her. (SED)
When I was a young child, I like to play tolls. (UED)
It is 9:00 when you should get up. (SED)
You can come to my home when you are free. (UED)
```

Lexical items such as *alien*, *watching*, and *holiday* are found across three datasets, for example:

```
When alien was in the museum, I call the TV station. (JED)
When watching TV, my mum came back. (SED)
When holiday comes, we all fell very happy (UED)
```

Why

We now turn to look at the frequencies of words occurring immediately after "why" in interrogatives, and subordinate clauses. We also look at the differences and similarities between native speakers and non-native speakers in terms of the ways in which they use different types of words.

Frequency of the words occurring immediately after "why" in interrogatives across the four sets of data

Table 6.24 shows the frequencies of the words occurring after "why" in interrogatives across the four sets of data.

JED			SED			UED			NED		
Word	No.	%	word	No.	%	word	No.	%	word	No.	%
do	124	46.27%	do	50	26.18%	do	80	23.12%	don't	48	28.74%
are	30	11.19%	are	31	16.23%	are	55	15.90%	are	36	21.56%
not	26	9.70%	did	29	15.18%	did	30	8.67%	not	30	17.96%
don't	22	8.21%	not	16	8.38%	not	29	8.38%	do	18	10.78%
is	19	7.09%	don't	14	7.33%	don't	24	6.94%	is	18	10.78%
does	17	6.34%	you	9	4.71%	you	22	6.36%	did	5	2.99%
did	12	4.48%	I	8	4.19%	is	18	5.20%	can't	4	2.40%
you	4	1.49%	does	6	3.14%	should	12	3.47%	didn't	4	2.40%
open	2	0.75%	didn't	5	2.62%	didn't	12	3.47%	am	2	1.20%
his	1	0.37%	isn't	5	2.62%	does	12	3.47%	this	1	0.60%
join	1	0.37%	the	3	1.57%	can't	8	2.31%	would	1	0.60%
played	1	0.37%	haven't	2	1.05%	the	8	2.31%			
he	1	0.37%	there	2	1.05%	am	5	1.45%			
isn't	1	0.37%	were	2	1.05%	I	4	1.16%			
Your	1	0.37%	isn't	1	0.52%	she	3	0.87%			
Were	1	0.37%	am	1	0.52%	it	3	0.87%			
didn't	1	0.37%	it	1	0.52%	we	3	0.87%			
Was	1	0.37%	people	1	0.52%	can	2	0.58%			
Should	1	0.37%	can	1	0.52%	me	2	0.58%			
can't	1	0.37%	was	1	0.52%	haven't	2	0.58%			
doesn't	1	0.37%	sky	1	0.52%	doesn't	1	0.29%			

Table 6.24 Comparison of the frequencies and percentage of different words occurring after "why" in interrogatives

According to Table 6.24, native speakers and non-native speakers are different in terms of their most frequently used words. The most frequently word that non-native speakers use is *do*. In contrast, the most frequent word that native speakers use is negative form *don't*. One possible reason for this might be that "why" interrogatives are usually used to formulate suggestions, a fact which the non-native speakers were unaware of. As we see from chapter 5, although textbooks provide many examples of negative forms, when learners were given examples of the "wh" words, it seems has less production as we expect. In addition, "why" interrogatives with negative forms are also commonly used in Chinese Language. One possible reason for this might be that learners focused on the quantity of sentences they have to produce; instead, they probably need more time to consider the sentence structures. Examples are shown as follows

```
Why do you do that? (JED)
Why do you think so? (SED)
Why do you like swimming? (UED)
Why don't you go to school? (JED)
Why don't you like playing basketball? (SED)
why can't you speak? (UED)
Why don't you take the initiative? (NED)
```

It is interesting to note that lexical items only occur for JED and SED. This construction contains mistakes as learners at lower levels still need more time and effort to acquire the structures. In addition, this construction tends to express a kind of blaming or request intonation. This may because the meaning of the word "why" directly asks reasons. Examples are shown as follows:

```
Why open the door? (JED)
Why join music club? (JED)
Why sky is blue? (SED)
Why make yourself so upset? (UED)
```

Frequency of the words after "why" in subordinate clauses across the four sets of data

Table 6.25 shows the frequencies of the words occurring after "why" in subordinate clauses across the four sets of data.

JED			SED			UED			NED		
word	No.	%	word	No.	%	word	No.	%	word	No.	%
I	1	100.00%	he	20	33.90%	I	33	42.86%	you	12	42.86%
			I	19	32.20%	he	16	20.78%	I	13	46.43%
			you	12	20.34%	you	14	18.18%	they	2	7.14%
			she	4	6.78%	she	5	6.49%	we	1	3.57%
			there	1	1.69%	we	3	3.90%			
			the	1	1.69%	her	1	1.30%			
			we	1	1.69%	there	1	1.30%			
			do	1	1.69%	money	1	1.30%			
						winter	1	1.30%			
						got	1	1.30%			
						the	1	1.30%			

Table 6.25 Comparison of the frequencies and percentage of different
words occurring after "why" in subordinate clauses

According to Table 6.25, pronouns mainly follow "why" subordinate clauses across the four datasets. These findings are similar to what we found in the textbook data. One possible reason for this might be that learners' elicited sentences are largely influenced by the examples that are shown in textbooks. Examples are shown as follows:

```
It is very important for you to know why she is sad. (SED)
```

```
I don't know why he is so angry. (UED)
That's why I wanted you to have a holiday and brought you on this trip. (NED)
```

SED and UED have a relatively wider range of word choices, including lexical items.

```
Who can tell me that why study so hard now. (SED)
This is why winter is not so cold in Kun Ming. (UED)
```

Who

In the following sections, we look at the frequencies of words occurring immediately after "who" in interrogatives, and subordinate clauses. We also look at the differences and similarities between native speakers and non-native speakers in the way they use different types of words.

Frequency of the words occurring immediately after "who" in interrogatives across the four sets of data

Table 6.26 shows the frequencies of the words occurring after "who" in interrogatives across the four sets of data.

JED			SED			UED			NED		
word	**No.**	**%**	**word**	**No.**	**%**	**word**	**No.**	**%**	**word**	**No.**	**%**
is	153	68.00%	is	78	44.57%	is	175	49.30%	is	24	42.11%
are	33	14.67%	are	25	14.29%	do	45	12.68%	are	5	8.77%
do	6	2.67%	do	23	13.14%	are	45	12.68%	do	5	8.77%
it	4	1.78%	will	10	5.71%	can	23	6.48%	was	3	5.26%
played	3	1.33%	can	8	4.57%	will	8	2.25%	sent	3	5.26%
am	3	1.33%	did	7	4.00%	am	5	1.41%	did	2	3.51%
can	3	1.33%	am	3	1.71%	knows	4	1.13%	else	2	3.51%
fight	2	0.89%	wants	2	1.14%	comes	4	1.13%	am	1	1.75%
wears	2	0.89%	finished	2	1.14%	did	4	1.13%	likes	1	1.75%
went	1	0.44%	it	2	1.14%	it	3	0.85%	plays	1	1.75%
dance	1	0.44%	he	2	1.14%	would	3	0.85%	smells	1	1.75%
has	1	0.44%	was	1	0.57%	wants	3	0.85%	send	1	1.75%
sing	1	0.44%	has	1	0.57%	have	2	0.56%	will	1	1.75%
cleaned	1	0.44%	broke	1	0.57%	should	2	0.56%	knows	1	1.75%
want	1	0.44%	damage	1	0.57%	makes	2	0.56%	cares	1	1.75%
else	1	0.44%	stands	1	0.57%	gives	1	0.28%	should	1	1.75%
gave	1	0.44%	won	1	0.57%	he	1	0.28%	would	1	1.75%
murdered	1	0.44%	bother	1	0.57%	she	1	0.28%	had	1	1.75%
were	1	0.44%	make	1	0.57%	you	1	0.28%	has	1	1.75%
open	1	0.44%	you	1	0.57%	had	1	0.28%	can	1	1.75%

Table 6.26 Comparison of the frequencies and percentage of different
words occurring after "who" in interrogatives

According to Table 6.26, the most frequent words following the word "who" across the four datasets are be verbs (*is*, *are*) and auxiliaries (*do*). It seems that there are no major differences in using grammatical words across the four sets of data. One possible reason for this might be that "who" interrogatives follow the basic rules of question forms, as well as L1 transfer. Most grammatical words that follow the word "who" can be found in their equivalent translation in the Chinese language. Examples are shown as follows:

```
Who is your mother? (JED)
Who is your friend? (SED)
Who is that girl over there? (NED)
Who was it on the phone? (NED)
Who are you watching for? (JED)
Who are you talking about? (SED)
Who are you? (NED)
Who do you want to have a dinner with? (JED)
Who do you prefer? (SED)
Who did this? (NED)
```

It is interesting to note that lexical items, in particular verbs, are found in a large proportion with this construction across the four sets of data. Verbs are also found less in the present and past tense. It seems that such sentence constructions occur largely in spoken discourse, especially in daily conversation. We have seen that textbooks at a lower level tend to provide conversations that contain such construction; it is more likely that learners stored the sentence structure in their long-term memory. Examples are as follows:

```
Who save the cat? (JED)
Who got the report card? (JED)
Who wants to go with me? (SED)
Who break the vase? (SED)
Who come from Beijing? (UED)
Who make you so sad? (UED)
Who plays doctor? (NED)
Who smells in there? (NED)
Who send it? (NED)
```

Feifei Zhang

Frequency of the words occurring immediately after "who" in subordinate clauses across the four sets of data

Table 6.27 shows the frequencies of the words occurring after "who" in subordinate clauses across the four sets of data.

JED			SED			UED			UED		
word	**No.**	**%**	**word**	**No.**	**%**	**word**	**No.**	**%**	**word**	**No.**	**%**
is	2	40.00%	is	22	27.16%	is	26	27.37%	is	3	27.27%
in	1	20.00%	always	5	6.17%	I	14	14.74%	he	1	9.09%
open	1	20.00%	I	5	6.17%	the	6	6.32%	that	1	9.09%
play	1	20.00%	he	4	4.94%	stand	3	3.16%	will	1	9.09%
			you	3	3.70%	had	2	2.11%	has	1	9.09%
			go	2	2.47%	are	2	2.11%	prefer	1	9.09%
			wears	2	2.47%	helped	2	2.11%	walks	1	9.09%
			win	2	2.47%	wear	2	2.11%	travel	1	9.09%
			did	2	2.47%	has	2	2.11%	had	1	9.09%
			wants	1	1.23%	you	2	2.11%			
			gave	1	1.23%	it	2	2.11%			
			tell	1	1.23%	wears	1	1.05%			
			didn't	1	1.23%	called	1	1.05%			
			comes	1	1.23%	tell	1	1.05%			
			won	1	1.23%	dress	1	1.05%			
			set	1	1.23%	dressed	1	1.05%			
			treats	1	1.23%	contribute	1	1.05%			
			treat	1	1.23%	was	1	1.05%			
			do	1	1.23%	invent	1	1.05%			
			cares	1	1.23%	stands	1	1.05%			

Table 6.27 Comparison of the frequencies and percentage of different words occurring after "who" in subordinate clauses

According to Table 6.27, grammatical words such as be verbs, auxiliaries and pronouns occurring immediately after "who" subordinate clauses have almost the same proportion across the four sets of data. It is interesting to note that *is* is the most frequent word occurring after "who" subordinate clauses across the four sets of data. In addition, this is similar to what we found for "who" interrogatives. One possible explanation for this might be that the be verb *is* is restricted construction that can be used in both interrogatives and subordinate clauses. Examples are shown as follows:

```
I don't know who is your father. (JED)
Who is the best should be discussed. (SED)
I wonder who is that.(NED)
```

168

In addition, there are many lexical items that are used by both native speakers and non-native speakers. This is similar to what we have found for "who" subordinate clauses. This may suggest that these two sentence types have a similar restricted collocation and construction. Most of the lexical items are verbs, in particular the present and past tense. Examples are shown as follows:

```
My brother is a person who likes playing very much.. (UED)
He is the man who has a pretty daughter. (UED)
She asked who want to stay here. (SED)
Those who wear yellow cloths are Mr.Lee (UED)
She is a beautiful who comes from England. (UED)
Everybody who walks past me sees it. (NED)
I have quite a few friends who travel in and out of here. (NED)
```

Whom

In the following sections, we look at the frequencies of words occurring immediately after "whom" in interrogatives, and subordinate clauses. We also look at the differences and similarities between native speakers and non-native speakers in the way they use different types of words.

Frequency of the words occurring immediately after "whom" in interrogatives across the four sets of data

Table 6.28 shows the frequencies of the words occurring after "whom" in interrogatives across the four sets of data.

JED			SED			UED			NED		
word	No.	%	word	No.	%	word	No.	%	word	No.	%
is	27	54.00%	do	32	68.09%	do	72	35.82%	did	8	36.36%
were	7	14.00%	is	4	8.51%	did	25	12.44%	does	3	13.64%
are	4	8.00%	are	3	6.38%	is	19	9.45%	are	3	13.64%
can	3	6.00%	did	2	4.26%	are	18	8.96%	were	3	13.64%
come	2	4.00%	does	1	2.13%	will	13	6.47%	do	2	9.09%
will	2	4.00%	have	1	2.13%	you	9	4.48%	to	1	4.55%
playing	1	2.00%	will	1	2.13%	should	9	4.48%	should	1	4.55%
use	1	2.00%	here	1	2.13%	can	8	3.98%	is	1	4.55%
could	1	2.00%	you	1	2.13%	I	7	3.48%			
your	1	2.00%	has	1	2.13%	does	6	2.99%			
has	1	2.00%				she	3	1.49%			
						were	3	1.49%			
						have	3	1.49%			
						would	2	1.00%			
						am	1	0.50%			
						was	1	0.50%			
						the	1	0.50%			
						had	1	0.50%			

Table 6.28 Comparison of the frequencies and percentage of different words occurring after "whom" in interrogatives

Compared to the textbook data, the words following "whom" have a wider variety of grammatical words across the four sets of data. It is interesting to note that lexical items only occur for JED. Similar to what we have found for textbook data, "whom" sentences have the least occurrences among the "wh" sentences for textbook data and elicited data. Learners are not sure what to write about, and even native speakers lack the confidence to produce "whom" sentences. In addition, most of the sentences they produce seem to follow a similar pattern of other "wh" interrogatives, particularly the "who" interrogatives. One possible reason for this might be that in most cases, "whom" sentences occur in relatively formal contexts as well as in written discourse. Although textbooks at a higher level contain several examples, the sentence structures are not the ones people use in their daily life, and it seems learners need more examples and practice to grasp this construction. Examples are shown as follows:

```
Whom is your mother? (JED)
Whom is Tom's mother? (SED)
whom is the little boy? (UED)
whom were you talking about? (NED)
```

```
Whom can swim alone? (JED)
Whom can it belong to? (SED)
whom will you like with? (UED)
Whom has the rule? (JED)
Whom do you want to go with? (SED)
whom do you turn to for help? (UED)
Whom did you recommend for the job? (NED)
Whom playing on the tree? (JED)
```

Frequency of the words after "whom" in subordinate clauses across the four sets of data

Table 6.29 shows the frequencies of the words occurring after "whom" in subordinate clauses across the four sets of data.

JED			SED			UED			NED		
word	No.	%	word	No.	%	word	No.	%	word	No.	%
is	3	75.00%	I	9	37.50%	I	50	31.65%	the	2	50.00%
to	1	25.00%	is	4	16.67%	you	27	17.09%	very	1	25.00%
			are	2	8.33%	is	17	10.76%	you	1	25.00%
			he	2	8.33%	he	10	6.33%			
			chess	1	4.17%	we	6	3.80%			
			dress	1	4.17%	the	5	3.16%			
			like	1	4.17%	she	4	2.53%			
			the	1	4.17%	will	3	1.90%			
			she	1	4.17%	are	3	1.90%			
			you	1	4.17%	should	3	1.90%			
			can	1	4.17%	this	2	1.27%			
						her	2	1.27%			
						was	2	1.27%			
						they	2	1.27%			
						dress	2	1.27%			
						always	2	1.27%			

Table 6.29 Comparison of the frequencies and percentage of different words occurring after "whom" in subordinate clauses

According to Table 6.29, the most frequent words occurring after "whom" are pronouns. Modals (can for SED and will for UED), and lexical items (dress for SED and dress for UED) are for SED and UED. Examples are as follows:

```
I don't know whom's meaning. (JED)
It is Tom whom is made to cry by you. (SED)
It is Kack whom you supposed to believe in. (SED)
She is a girl through whom I learnt a lot. (UED)
She is washing whom dress a skirt. (SED)
Let's invite someone whom used to be a writer. (SED)
```

```
This is my sister whom dresses a red skirt. (UED)
I don't know whom will be the winner. (UED)
```

As we can see from the above examples, "whom" sentences that learners produce are likely to follow a similar pattern to "who" sentences. One possible reason for this might be that learners have not grasped the 'whom' form as "whom" sentences have the lowest occurrences in textbooks., so they rely on their knowledge of the 'who' form which they perceive to be similar. Again, this is strong evidence that textbooks are an important input that influences learners' production. Elicited sentences were collected in an environment that participants need to produce sentences with a given task. In most cases, learners tend to produce sentences that are stored in their long-term memories. Because there are fewer examples provided in textbooks, and there are fewer restricted collocations introduced in textbooks, learners seem to have less knowledge of how to construct 'whom' sentences from their explicit knowledge.

Whose

In the following sections, we look at the behaviour of the word "whose" and how it appeared in native speakers and non-native speakers' elicited sentences.

Frequency of the words occurring immediately after "whose" in interrogatives across the four sets of data

Table 6.30 shows the frequencies of the words occurring immediately after "whose" in interrogatives across the four sets of data.

JED			SED			UED			NED		
word	No.	%	word	No.	%	word	No.	%	word	No.	%
is	38	29.46%	book	25	15.15%	book	37	11.78%	bag	3	9.09%
pen	12	9.30%	pen	18	10.91%	pen	29	9.24%	turn	2	6.06%
book	8	6.20%	name	8	4.85%	bag	16	5.10%	coat	2	6.06%
pencil	6	4.65%	shirt	7	4.24%	mother	9	2.87%	house	2	6.06%
are	5	3.88%	clothes	5	3.03%	name	9	2.87%	shoes	2	6.06%
the	4	3.10%	pencil	5	3.03%	shoes	9	2.87%	clothes	2	6.06%
your	4	3.10%	father	4	2.42%	clothes	8	2.55%	do	1	3.03%
bike	3	2.33%	money	4	2.42%	coat	7	2.23%	trousers	1	3.03%
bag	3	2.33%	homework	4	2.42%	house	5	1.59%	keys	1	3.03%
cat	3	2.33%	coat	4	2.42%	hair	5	1.59%	job	1	3.03%
basketball	3	2.33%	bag	4	2.42%	cat	5	1.59%	are	1	3.03%
with	2	1.55%	dictionary	3	1.82%	dictionary	4	1.27%	book	1	3.03%
cup	2	1.55%	gift	3	1.82%	bike	4	1.27%	letter	1	3.03%
it	2	1.55%	the	2	1.21%	purse	4	1.27%	watch	1	3.03%
does	2	1.55%	idea	2	1.21%	songs	4	1.27%	shirt	1	3.03%
hat	2	1.55%	class	2	1.21%	pencil	4	1.27%	telling	1	3.03%
father	2	1.55%	songs	2	1.21%	dress	4	1.27%	won	1	3.03%
			box	2	1.21%	duty	4	1.27%	made	1	3.03%
						money	3	0.96%	got	1	3.03%
						eyes	3	0.96%	wearing	1	3.03%

Table 6.30 Comparison of the frequencies and percentage of different words occurring after "whose" in interrogatives

According to Table 6.30, grammatical words such as *is*, *are*, and *does* only occurred in JED. This may suggest that learners over-generalize the question forms as they may follow a similar pattern to "who" interrogative forms. Examples are shown as follows:

```
Whose is this notebook? (JED)
Whose are your teachers? (JED)
whose are these shoes? (NED)
Whose did they do? (JED)
whose do these things belong to? (NED)
```

It is interesting to note that almost all the words following "whose" are lexical items: *T-shirt, pencil, friend, sister, pen,* and *name*. It has also been found that there are many concrete nouns occurring in lower textbook data. Such school-related words are introduced at beginner level. Another reason for this might be that learners have paid attention to the environment where they were when the elicited data were collected. Non-native speakers' data were collected in classrooms, learners are more likely to produce sentences by using the examples around them. Examples are shown as follows:

```
Whose T-shirt is red? (JED)
Whose friend are they? (SED)
Whose pen is put in the desk? (UED)
Whose shirt is so dirty? (NED)
```

Frequency of the words after "whose" in subordinate clauses across the four sets of data

Table 6.31 shows the frequencies of the words occurring after "whose" in subordinate clauses across the four sets of data.

JED			SED			UED			NED		
word	**No.**	**%**	**word**	**No.**	**%**	**word**	**No.**	**%**	**word**	**No.**	**%**
book	1	50%	door	1	2.56%	work	1	1.25%			
hat	1	50%	hair-cut	1	2.56%	action	1	1.25%			
			color	1	2.56%	sister	1	1.25%			
			father	1	2.56%	door	1	1.25%			
			are	1	2.56%	bag	1	1.25%			
			clothes	1	2.56%	handbag	1	1.25%			
			car	1	2.56%	ability	1	1.25%			
			mother	1	2.56%	performance	1	1.25%			
			words	1	2.56%	knowledge	1	1.25%			
			backpack	1	2.56%	feeling	1	1.25%			
			knowledge	1	2.56%	turn	1	1.25%			
			blood	1	2.56%	mother	1	1.25%			
			son	1	2.56%	owner	1	1.25%			
			heart	1	2.56%	point	1	1.25%			
			care	1	2.56%	head	1	1.25%			
			can	1	2.56%	background	1	1.25%			
			turn	1	2.56%	handwriting	1	1.25%			
			characters	1	2.56%	son	1	1.25%			
			party	1	2.56%	responsibility	1	1.25%			
			cup	1	2.56%	fur	1	1.25%			

Table 6.31 Comparison of the frequencies and percentage of different words occurring after "whose" in subordinate clauses

According to Table 6.31, lexical items are the most frequent words occurring after "whose". Most lexical words are abstract nouns such as *knowledge, characters, responsibility, performance, ability* and *money,* while there are many concrete nouns related to personal life found in non-native speakers' sentences. This is similar to what we found for textbooks. Only the modal word *can* is found in SED. Examples are shown as follows:

```
That's the man whose house was burnt down. (SED)
It's a horse whose window faces east. (UED)
I want to know whose knowledge is the richest in the class. (SED)
I like to make friends whose character like me. (SED)
It's a stuff that we really can't find out whose money it is. (UED)
Do you think the girl whose performance is the best? (UED)
I appreciate this professor whose knowledge is very broad. (UED)
He is a man whose idea is very particular. (UED)
```

This is a situation of concrete nouns versus abstract nouns. The sentences that learners produced are stored in their long-term memories, and most of the structures they produce are similar to what appeared in the textbook data.

Which

In the following sections, we look at the frequencies of words occurring immediately after "which" in interrogatives, and subordinate clauses. We also look at the differences and similarities between native speakers and non-native speakers in the way they use different types of words.

Frequency of the words occurring immediately after "which" in interrogatives across the four sets of data

Table 6.32 shows the frequencies of the words occurring after "which" in interrogatives across the four sets of data.

JED			SED			UED			NED		
word	No.	%	word	No.	%	word	No.	%	word	No.	%
isn't	73	36.50%	one	32	20.13%	one	66	18.70%	way	7	20.59%
is	23	14.50%	is	28	17.61%	is	43	12.18%	one	3	8.82%
one	12	11.50%	do	17	10.69%	do	35	9.92%	game	2	5.88%
color	8	6.00%	book	9	5.66%	color	21	5.95%	book	2	5.88%
do	7	4.00%	kind	6	3.77%	country	15	4.25%	window	2	5.88%
pen	6	3.50%	way	5	3.14%	book	13	3.68%	number	1	2.94%
T-shirt	3	3.00%	pen	5	3.14%	class	11	3.12%	version	1	2.94%
book	3	1.50%	color	5	3.14%	kind	8	2.27%	piece	1	2.94%
flower	2	1.50%	subject	3	1.89%	pen	7	1.98%	coat	1	2.94%
are	2	1.00%	fruit	3	1.89%	city	7	1.98%	place	1	2.94%
country	2	1.00%	picture	2	1.26%	subject	5	1.42%	bus	1	2.94%
another	2	1.00%	country	2	1.26%	teacher	4	1.13%	of	1	2.94%
floor	2	1.00%	teacher	2	1.26%	room	4	1.13%	cake	1	2.94%
movie	2	1.00%	room	2	1.26%	place	4	1.13%	dress	1	2.94%
food	1	1.00%	dog	2	1.26%	house	4	1.13%	kind	1	2.94%
girls	1	0.50%	are	2	1.26%	school	4	1.13%	hotel	1	2.94%
you	1	0.50%	clothes	2	1.26%	person	4	1.13%	colour	1	2.94%
the	1	0.50%	team	2	1.26%	food	4	1.13%	type	1	2.94%
statement	1	0.50%	sports	1	0.63%	style	3	0.85%	movie	1	2.94%
box	1	0.50%	kite	1	0.63%	season	3	0.85%	fruit	1	2.94%
answer	1	0.50%	I	1	0.63%	job	3	0.85%	car	1	2.94%
man	1	0.50%	food	1	0.63%	bag	3	0.85%	bank	1	2.94%
		0.50%	caught	1	0.63%	car	3	0.85%	sport	1	2.94%

Table 6.32 Comparison of the frequencies and percentage of different words occurring after "which" interrogatives

According to Table 6.32, the negative form *doesn't* only occur for JED, and it is the most frequent word occurring after "which" interrogatives. One possible reason for this might be that this form is introduced in textbooks or is provided in examples given by teachers. In most cases, learners memorise examples that are provided in textbooks or examples that are given by teachers. Because these examples are focused on in the classroom, learners are more likely to store them in their long-term memory. This may also explain why there are so many similar sentences produced by learners. For example:

```
Which isn't true? (JED)
```

It is interesting to note that the word *is* has a high frequency in SED and UED, in contrast, there are none for NED. This may suggest that learners might be over-generalising the "which" interrogative forms. According to the above discussion, it is noted that the words occurring after each "wh" word vary in accordance with their own structures. Learners may remember the rule when they first got to know the sentences, while as more sentence types and rules are introduced, it is somewhat confusing for learners as learners seem to memorise the examples to understand the sentence structure better. Examples are shown as follows:

```
Which is cheaper? (SED)
Which is the right one I should choose, the red or the blue? (UED)
```

Similar to "whose" sentences, a large number of lexical items are found following the word "which", in particular concrete nouns: *color, country, floor, girls, sports, pen, teacher,* and *kite.* Compared to "whose" sentences, "which" sentences are even more related to people's daily life. One possible reason for this might be that "which" interrogatives have restricted collocation and are used to ask more specific questions related to the interlocutors' daily life. Examples are shown as follows:

```
Which color do you like? (JED)
Which county will win the next world cup? (JED)
Which teacher comes first? (SED)
Which pen do you like most? (SED)
Which sports do you like best? (UED)
Which role do you want to play in this TV? (UED)
```

Also, the word *one* ranks among the most frequent words for SED and UED. This is considered to be used as a fixed expression in which the meanings of the word *one* vary in accordance with the main subjects. Native speakers are more likely to use fixed expressions such as *which version…, which way….*

```
Which one do you like? (JED)
Which one is the right one? (SED)
Which one do you want to get? (UED)
which way shall we go? (NED)
Which version are you using? (NED)
```

Frequency of the words after "which" in subordinate clauses across the four sets of data

Table 6.33 shows the frequencies of the words occurring after "which" in subordinate clauses across the four sets of data.

JED			SED			UED			NED		
word	No.	%	word	No.	%	word	No.	%	word	No.	%
the	1	50.00%	is	37	37.37%	I	12	14.29%	she	2	40.00%
is	1	50.00%	you	10	10.10%	is	22	26.19%	are	1	20.00%
			I	9	9.09%	one	6	7.14%	dress	1	20.00%
			are	4	4.04%	are	4	4.76%	includes	1	20.00%
			has	4	4.04%	you	3	3.57%			
			was	4	4.04%	my	3	3.57%			
			makes	4	4.04%	we	2	2.38%			
			he	4	4.04%	always	2	2.38%			
			my	3	3.03%	opens	1	1.19%			
			make	2	2.02%	were	1	1.19%			
			always	1	1.01%	gave	1	1.19%			
			it	1	1.01%	given	1	1.19%			
			under	1	1.01%	animal	1	1.19%			
			question	1	1.01%	may	1	1.19%			
			one	1	1.01%	appears	1	1.19%			
			does	1	1.01%	too	1	1.19%			
			doctor	1	1.01%	could	1	1.19%			
			let	1	1.01%	located	1	1.19%			
			answer	1	1.01%	lives	1	1.19%			
			surrounded	1	1.01%	suit	1	1.19%			

Table 6.33 Comparison of the frequencies and percentage of different words occurring after "which" in subordinate clauses

According to Table 6.33, pronouns have a relatively high frequency among the grammatical words. Pronouns are more likely to be used to introduce main clauses that complete the meaning of sentences. SED and UED have almost the same distribution in terms of grammatical words and lexical items. For JED, learners produce fewer "which" subordinate clauses. One possible reason for this might be that learners have been introduced to the sentence structures only recently and they need more time to digest and produce examples. This may also suggest that the L2 learning process is dynamic, and learners may need to incorporate new information together with existing information. Examples are shown as follows:

```
I don't like this cup which he likes. (SED)
You can choose the way which you like. (SED)
He likes drawing, which he doesn't regard as his profession. (UED)
```

There are two types of lexical items i.e. nouns and verbs occurring after "which" subordinate clauses. It is more likely that the meaning is completed when using a noun to introduce the main clause, for example

```
I don't know which question he can answer. (SED)
I want to know which animals can stay longest in a bottle. (UED)
```

In contrast, it is more likely to describe a current situation when using verbs to introduce the main clause. For example:

```
Xi'an is a beautiful city which has a lot of interests. (SED)
In the basket there are quite many apples, some of which have gone bad.
(UED)
I like the red one which looks like a princess. (SED)
```

6.8 Discussion

6.8.1 Prototypes

Table 6.34 shows the distribution of "wh" words as prototypes and extensions.

Wh-word	JED (%) P	E1	E2	SED (%) P	E1	E2	UED (%) P	E1	E2	NED (%) P	E1	E2
what	99	1	0	65	12	22	87	3	10	74	7	19
how	96	3	1	72	18	10	75	12	13	67	5	28
when	47	0	53	52	0	48	66	0	34	88	0	12
which	99	0	1	53	0	47	73	0	27	85	0	15
who	98	0	2	66	0	34	77	0	23	89	0	11
whom	92	0	8	60	0	40	49	0	51	79	0	21
why	99	0	1	72	0	28	79	0	21	83	0	17
whose	98	0	2	77	0	23	69	0	31	100	0	0
where	100	0	1	72	0	28	85	0	15	86	0	14

Table 6.34 Distribution of prototypes and extensions across three datasets

For convenience the original hypotheses are repeated here:

1). It is hypothesized that when learners use "wh" words, they will primarily produce prototypes as this kind of elicited data is largely intuition driven.
2). It is also hypothesized that when learners use "wh" words, they will produce more non-prototypical structures as proficiency increases (i.e., from JED to UED).
3). Finally, it is suggested that there will be similarities between textbook data and elicited data as both are driven by intuition.

The first hypostudy is fully upheld. Regardless of the level of proficiency, seven of the nine "wh" words (*what, how, where, who, whose, why,* and *which*) predominate for prototypes. However, when proficiency is considered, for junior school students, prototypes predominate for eight "wh" words, except the word *when*. When moved to a higher level, for example senior school students, prototypes predominate for six "wh" words: *what, how, who, why, whose,* and *where*. For the university students, prototypes predominate for six "wh" words: *what, how, which, who, why,* and *where*. In the case of Extension 2, three words are outstanding for more occurrences than prototypes: *when* for JED, *when,* and *which* for SED, and *whom* for UED. For the native speakers, prototypical structures predominate for all the "wh" words.

The table shows that the second hypostudy is not fully upheld: The prototype is very strong in the elicited datasets at an average of 92% for JED, 65% for SED, and 73% for UED. While proficiency increases, students occasionally produce the clausal structures (senior high students and university students provide 31% and 25% of E2 respectively).

The above results show that the third hypostudy is not upheld: at the lower level of proficiency, textbooks and elicited data are both prototypically predominant (on average 64 % for JTD and 92% for JED), then, as the proficiency increases, more extended examples are provided in textbooks with senior high and university providing 74% and 80% of E2 respectively). However, senior high and university students still primarily produce prototypes (on average 65% for SED and 73% for UED).

6.8.2 *Frequency of Words Occurring Immediately after "wh" Words in Terms of the Three Types of Sentences*

The situation for grammatical words in elicited data is similar to those in textbooks. These grammatical words following "wh" words in interrogatives and subordinate clauses (declaratives are low frequency and are followed by article or lexical items) are commonly used words. Below are examples for pronouns, auxiliaries, be verb, prepositions, and modals:

Interrogatives:

```
How do you? (JED)
How are you feeling today? (SED)
How could you do that? (UED)
What is your name? (JED)
What are you doing? (SED)
What do they buy? (UED)
When is your birthday? (JED)
When do you eat dinner? (SED)
When do you like to go to bed? (UED)
Where is your coat? (JED)
Where did you buy these delicious cakes? (SED)
Where are you coming from? (UED)
Which should I like? (JED)
Which does come first? (SED)
```

Which <u>can</u> you play? (UED)
Who is the man over there? (JED)
Who <u>are</u> you talking about? (SED)
Who <u>did</u> that? (UED)
Whom <u>is</u> your mother? (JED)
Whom <u>can</u> it belong to? (SED)
Whom <u>do you</u> turn to for help? (UED)
Whose <u>is</u> this notebook? (JED)
Whose <u>are</u> your teachers? (JED)
Why <u>did</u> you do that? (JED)
Why <u>don't</u> you go to school? (SED)
Why <u>can't</u> you speak? (UED)

Declaratives:

How boring it is. (JED)
How smart he is. (SED)
How funny it is. (UED)
What fine weather. (SED)
What a clever girl. (UED)
Subordinate Clauses:
I don't know how <u>much</u> it is. (SED)
I really don't know how <u>could</u> you get it that way. (UEDI said what <u>he</u> wants to know. (SED)
What <u>I</u> want is to try my best. (UED)
When <u>I</u> watched TV, what were you doing? (JED)
I remember the time when <u>I</u> met her. (SED)
When <u>I</u> was a young child, I liked to play tolls. (UED)
It is in the park where <u>I</u> lost my key. (SED)
Where <u>you</u> lived is the most beautiful place in our city. (UED)
I want to buy the pants which <u>are</u> in red. (JED)
I think the computer which <u>is</u> on the desk is beautiful. (SED)
It's an object which <u>is</u> soft and sweet. (UED)
I don't know who <u>is</u> your father? (JED)
Who <u>is</u> the best should be discussed. (SED)
My brother is a person who <u>likes</u> playing very much.. (UED)
It is Kack whom <u>you</u> are supposed to believe in. (SED)
She is a girl through whom <u>I</u> learnt a lot. (UED)
It is very important for you to know why <u>she</u> is sad. (SED)
I don't know why <u>he</u> is so angry. (UED)

The most frequent lexical items following "wh" words for elicited data types are shown in Table 6.35:

"Wh" word	Interrogative	Declarative	Subordinate clausal
What	time, colour, kind, happen	fun, fine, great	make, surprise, bother, difficulty
How	much, many, long, old, about	beautiful, fine, clever, smart	much, bad, loud strange, boring, smart
When	_____	_____	alien, mother, holiday, watching, crossing, listening, playing
Where	_____	_____	people, give, used
Which	colour, pen, book, food, country, teacher	_____	make, give, appears, let, answer
Who	play(ed/s), want(ed), make(s), give (gave)	_____	wear, help, wants, gave, called, dress(ed), treat(s)
Whom	come, play(ing), use	_____	chess, dress, like
Whose	pen, book, pencil, bag, clothes, money	_____	door, father, mother, son knowledge, background, characters, responsibility,
Why	open, people, play	_____	name, colour, ability, clothes performance, father, daughter, mother

Table 6.35 The most frequent lexical items associated with "wh" words for elicited data types

As Table 6.35 shows, in terms of interrogative, *what* associates with a number of fixed expressions and collocations: *what* combines with a number of fixed expressions and collocations:

```
What time do you go to school? (JTD)
What happened to his brother? (STD)What colour do you like best? (UTD)
```

How is strongly connected to qualifying words (e.g. *much, many, long*) and fixed expression:

```
How much is that bag? (JTD)
How many people are there in your family? (STD)
How long will the meeting last? (UTD)
How about having a picnic this weekend? (UED)
```

For *when* and *where*, there are no adjacent lexical items across the data sets.

Many nouns commonly occurring with *which* relate to objects inside the classroom such as *pen*, book, and teacher, or to a number of general domains such as *food, colour, country,* and *season*:

```
Which colour do you like best? (JED)
Which food do you like best? (JED)
Which season do you prefer? (SED)
Which country would you like to travel to? (UED)
```

Who occurs with verbs (want, play, give, and help), especially in plural forms and the past tense:

```
Who played basketball? (JED)
Who wants to try? (JED)
Who gives you my book? (UED)
Who helped you at that time? (SED)
```

Whom occurred with verbs (i.e. come, playing, and use):

```
Whom is playing the tree? (JED)
Whom come to the play today? (SED)
Whom used the bathroom? (UED)
```

Many nouns commonly occurring with whose relate to personal items (pen, book, pencil, bag, and clothes):

```
Whose book is it? (JED)
Whose pen? (JED)
Whose colour is more beautiful? (SED)
Whose clothes do you like? (SED)
Whose pencil is this? (UED)
Whose bag is on the desk? (UED)
```

Why occurs with both verbs and nouns, such as *open*, *play*, and *people*, and is primarily used for asking questions:

```
Why open the window in the evening? (JED)
Why play in the ground? (JED)
Why people don't like winter? (SED)
```

The lexical items occurring with *what* and *how* in declaratives are usually used in strongly positive or strongly negative evaluations:

```
What fine weather. (JED)
How horrible your handwriting is. (JED)
How beautiful the flowers are. (SED)
```

In clauses, *what* occurs with a similar group of lexical items as in the interrogative form:

```
What makes me angry is that she wasn't careful to do it. (SED)
```

I will do it mo matter what <u>difficulties</u> I will meet. (SED)
What <u>makes</u> us suffer makes us strong. (UED)
How is commonly associated with only two kinds of adjectives: evaluative (*bad, strong, boring, loud, and smart, etc.*) and measuring adjectives (*much*):

I know how <u>much</u> it means to me. (SED)
You can not imagine how <u>loud</u> a noise the dog can make. (UED)
You never know how <u>strong</u> the winder is. (SED)
I know how <u>boring</u> you are. (UED)
you can not imagine how <u>smart</u> his brother is. (UED)

When occurs with both nouns (*mother, alien,* and *holiday*) and verbs especially in (*watching, crossing, listening,* and *playing*):

The girl was shopping when the <u>alien</u> got out. (JED)
When <u>mother</u> came in, I was watching TV. (SED)
I will take good rest when the <u>holiday</u> comes. (UED)
When <u>watching</u> TV, my mum came back. (SED)
When <u>playing</u> basketball, I feel really excited. (SED)
When <u>listening</u> to the music, I feel so comfortable. (SED)
When <u>crossing</u> the road, please watch the light signal. (SED)
Where occurs with both verb (*give* and *used*) and noun *people:*
I like to go to a park where <u>people</u> are few. (SED)
I lie in a place where <u>used</u> to be a farmland. (UED) It was my home where <u>gave</u> me the most wonderful memory. (UED)

Which seems strongly associated with verbs (*let, make, and appears,*) that indicate the more specific contents:

He has been gone which <u>makes</u> me happy. (SED)
I like that which <u>lets</u> me feel comfortable. (SED)
She likes the gift which <u>appears</u> very expensive. (UED)

Who is connected with a wide variety of verbs (*wear, helped, wants, gave, called, dressed, and treats*):

Martin Luther King who gave a speech 'I have a dream' to black…. (SED)
Li Feng is a person who treats others always as friend. (SED)
He wanted to know the girl who dressed in a yellow skirt. (UED)
Yesterday the one who helped an old man is me. (UED)

Whom occurs with a noun: *dress* and a verb *like:*

The girl whom <u>dresses</u> skirt is my younger sister. (SED) I like making friends with whom <u>like</u> travelling. (SED

The lexical words associated with *whose* mainly focus on objects belonging to the possessor, such as *father, mother,* and *son*. Interestingly, *whose* also connected with abstract nouns such as *knowledge, background, characters,* and *responsibility*:

```
I want to know whose father is a skier. (SED)
This is the form whose background should write down. (SEDI want to know
whose knowledge is the richest in the class. (SED)
I am a teacher whose responsibility is to teach students. (UED)
```

Why occurs with two nouns (*money* and *winter*) and a verb (*got*):

```
People confuse why winter in my hometown is so hot. (UED) This is the
reason why money is so important. (UED)
I don't know why got angry suddenly. (UED)
```

In the next chapter, "wh" sentences from the both native and non-native speakers written corpora will be examined in a similar format. The analysis of the authentic language corpora attempts to see to what extent the prototypes and extension structures are reflected in natural occurring language.

Chapter Seven

A Comparison of "Wh" Sentences in Two Corpora of Written English: One Produced by Chinese-Speaking Learners of English and One Produced by Expert Users of English

7.1 *Introduction*

We have discussed the idea that cognitive processes such as categorization can influence the ways in which learners construct "wh" sentences. In this chapter, we investigate to what extent the prototype is represented in written discourse. The chapter sets out to compare and contrast a corpus of written language produced by Chinese-speaking learners of English with a corpus of written language produced by expert users of English. The focus is on the prototype and extension structure of "wh" sentences within these two corpora.

As we saw in Chapter 2, learning to write in a foreign language presents a considerable challenge to many learners. Unlike the elicited sentences discussed in Chapter 6, learners may spend more time and effort on writing a paper. It is therefore likely that the grammatical and lexical patterns which appear in these texts will be more grammatically 'accurate' and therefore different from the elicited data. It is therefore interesting to investigate the extent to which prototypes are represented in written language and what rules learners adhere to when they create written texts. In this chapter, we focus again on the functions of three different types of "wh" sentences: interrogative, declarative and subordinate clauses (which we refer to respectively as 'prototype', 'extension 1' and 'extension 2'). The focus is also on the contextual functions performed by these different types of "wh" sentences within the paragraphs.

The chapter focuses in particular on how the different types of "wh" sentences appear in texts which are produced by expert users of English and EFL learners. The chapter sets out to offer a comparison between expert users and EFL learners in the way prototypes are represented in written texts, together with the grammatical and lexical patterns they choose. It is hoped that this will describe their similarities and differences which may eventually reflect the complexity and flexibility of the target language. The findings may be used by teachers to help EFL learners to understand more choices that native speakers make in specific situations.

In this chapter, three issues are investigated. Firstly, we investigate the extent to which the three types of "wh" sentences are represented in the written corpora of both Chinese-speaking learners of English and expert users of English. More specifically, the analysis will be focused on the polysemous nature of each "wh" word on the basis of its usage (prototype interrogatives, extended declaratives, and extended subordinate clauses). In addition, we also look at the contextual functions of the three types of sentences in the contexts in which they occur. Finally, we investigate the frequencies of the different words occurring immediately after the "wh" words in terms of three types of sentences.

7.2 The Corpora Used for this Chapter

For the written corpus of expert users of English, the corpus is LOCNESS (LOUVAIN CORPUS OF NATIVE ENGLISH ESSAYS). LOCNESS is a corpus of native speakers' essays made up of British Pupils' A level essays, British University Students' essays, and American University Students' essays, with a total of 324,304 words.

For the written corpus of Chinese-speakers of English, the WECCL (Written English of Chinese Learners) was chosen from the SWECCL (Spoken and Written English of Chinese Learners corpus of non-native speakers). The SWECCL corpus comprises 200 million words of written and spoken English collected from Chinese learners of English. The sub-corpora WECCL (Written English of Chinese Learners) has approximately 100 million words collected from nine different varieties of students majoring in English.

7.3 Research Procedure

As we have seen above, the purpose of this chapter is to investigate the written corpus of writing by Chinese-speaking learners of English and expert users of English with the reference to the prototype and extension structure of "wh" sentences. In order to obtain this information, the following research procedure was developed.

7.3.1 Data Sample

The study analysed the polysemous nature of each "wh" word in the two corpora; the WECCL corpus and the LOCNESS corpus respectively. A search for each "wh" word produced a total of 44,611 concordance lines, with 40,019 concordance lines for the WECCL, and 4,592 for the LOCNESS. As these two corpora are of different sizes, and have considerable differences, the data selected will be presented as normalised figures which, on the basis of the smaller quantity, were calculated as approximately 10% of the occurrences of concordance lines of each "wh" word from WECCL. This method has three advantages. Firstly, the data for WECCL is a random sample so the analysis of the results can be considered reasonable; secondly, because the study focuses on a particular linguistic structure, investigating the ways in which similar structures in written texts are produced by two groups of writers, it is easier to compare these two corpora at a relatively similar number; thirdly, it is reasonable and would not be a time-consuming task to analyse such an amount of language. Table 5.1 shows the numbers of the concordance lines after the selection of the two corpora for each "wh" word.

Wh-words	WECCL	LOCNESS
what	790	698
how	458	435
when	965	843
why	227	238
which	637	1137
whose	13	24
where	63	286
who	370	910
whom	9	21
Total	3532	4592

Table 7.1 The number of the concordance lines after the selection of the two corpora for each "wh" word

7.3.2 *The prototypical Senses and Extended Senses of "wh" words*

The corpus data were accessed using version 4.0 of *WordSmith* Tools (Scott 2000), and the concordance lines with each "wh" word were categorized into three groups, namely prototype, extension 1 and extension 2, in order to find out the relative frequencies which each corpus has of these three types of sentences. The interrogative was considered to be the prototype, the declarative was extension 1 and the subordinate was extension 2.

These sentences were then saved in different excel files on the basis of their clause type.

Interrogative:		What	Is your name?
Declarative:		What	a beautiful flower it is.
Subordinate clause:	I don't believe	What	He says.

Having assembled the two sets of data categorized into three groups and saved in different excel files, the next task was to gather information about the frequencies of words occurring after each "wh" word on the basis of three different sentence types. This was done to allow a comparison between the two corpora, with the reference to the words frequently occurring after each "wh" word among different sentence types.

7.3.3 Words Occurring Immediately after Each "wh" Word in Terms of the Three Different Sentence Types

For each type of sentence, the words following immediately "wh" words were manually scanned, and later typed in a new column. The column was kept horizontal with the sample sentences. An example is shown below:

What	is your name?	is
What	can I do for you?	can
What	did you say on the phone?	did

7.4 Results

In this section, the results are presented and discussed. Firstly, the prototypes and extensions of the different sentence types among the two corpora are presented. Secondly, the frequencies of the words occurring after "wh" words are discussed. Thirdly, the contextual functions of the three types of "wh" sentences in the texts are discussed.

7.4.1 Prototypes and Extension structures across the two corpora

As we saw in the introduction, a search for each "wh" word produced a total of 44,611 concordance lines, with 40,019 concordance lines for the WECCL, and 4,592 for the LOCNESS. Because the two corpora varied so significantly in size only 10% of the WECCL concordance lines were used. The numbers of concordance lines found for each "wh" word across the two corpora are illustrated in Table 7.2:

	Total size of data	what	how	where	when	why	who	whom	whose	which	Total
LOCHNESS	324401	698(2)	435(1)	286(1)	843(3)	238(1)	910(3)	21(0)	24(0)	1137(4)	4592(14)
WECCL	245350	797(3)	495(2)	63(0.)	965(4)	227(19)	370(2)	9(0)	13(0)	637(3)	3532(15)
Total	569751	1495(3)	930(2)	349(1)	1808(3)	465(1)	1280(2)	30(0)	37(0)	1774(3)	8124(14)

Table 7.2 Number of concordance lines of "wh" words across the two corpora (frequencies per 1000 words are shown in brackets)

Since the two corpora vary in size, a reasonable comparison could be made by simply calculating the average number and percentage of "wh" concordance lines occurring in each corpus. Table 7.3 and Table 7.4 show the average number and percentage of each "wh" concordance line occurring in each corpus.

Corpus	LOCNESS			WECCL		
	No.Occ	Tot	**Per**	No.Occ	Tot	**Per**
what	698	4,592	**0.15**	794	4002	**0.20**
how	435	4,592	**0.95**	495	4002	**0.12**
where	286	4,592	**0.06**	63	4002	**0.02**
when	843	4,592	**0.18**	965	4002	**0.53**
why	238	4,592	**0.05**	227	4002	**0.24**
who	910	4,592	**0.20**	370	4002	**0.09**
whom	21	4,592	**0.01**	9	4002	**0.00**
whose	24	4,592	**0.01**	13	4002	**0.00**
which	1137	4,592	**0.25**	637	4002	**0.16**

Table 7.3 Average number of concordance lines occurring for each corpus

Note:

No.Occ.: Number of occurrence

Tol.:Total number of occurrence

Per.:Percentage of occurrence

Table 7.3 shows the total number of concordance lines of each "wh" word along with the average number of occurrences across the corpora. For ease of comparison, Table 7.4 summarises the average number of each "wh" concordance line occurring for each corpus.

	what	how	where	when	why	who	whom	whose	which
LOCNESS	0.15	0.95	0.06	0.18	0.05	0.20	0.01	0.01	0.25
WECCL	0.20	0.12	0.02	0.53	0.24	0.09	0.00	0.00	0.16

Table 7.4 A comparison of the average number of each "wh" concordance line occurring for each corpus

According to Table 7.4, "wh" words in the WECCL have relatively higher occurrences than those occurring in the LOCNESS, in particular the words *how, who, which, whom, whose,* and *when*. For the words *what, when,* and *why,* the LOCNESS has the higher number of occurrences. In the case of *whom,* and *whose,* the average numbers of concordance lines in the WECCL have the fewest occurrences, representing almost a nought.

In the next stage of the study, the "wh" words were categorized into three types of sentence, namely, interrogative (Prototype), declarative (Extension 1) and subordinate clause (Extension 2) respectively, across the two corpora.

Distribution of "what" sentences across the two corpora

We will now look at the distribution of "what" sentences across the two corpora. We will also compare the distribution of "what" sentences in written corpora to EFL textbook and elicited data. Table 7.5 and Figure 7.1 show the different types of "what" sentences in each corpus.

	Prototype	%	Extension 1	%	Extension 2	%	total
LOCNESS	96	14%	1	0.1%	601	86%	698
WECCL	125	16%	14	2%	651	82%	790
All	221	15%	15	1.%	1252	84%	1488

Table 7.5 Different types of "what" sentences across the two corpora

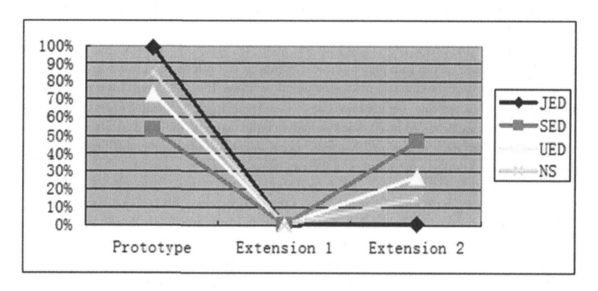

Figure 7.1 "what" sentence types across the two corpora

Table 7.5 and Figure 7.1 clearly show a predominance of extension 2 subordinate clauses for the two corpora, with 86% for LOCNESS and 82% for the WECCL respectively. For prototypes, the WECCL has a slightly higher percentage at 16% than those in the LOCNESS at 14%. Extension 1 occurs most often in the WECCL, with approximately 2%, followed by the LOCNESS, only at 0.1%.

Examples of the different sentence types are shown below:

Prototypes:

```
What will you do after that? (WECCL)
What should we say? (LOCNESS)
```

Extension 1:

```
What a great invention the mobile phone is! (WECCL)
What a terrible thing. (LOCNESS)
```

Extension 2:

```
Just try to make out what will happen after an American married a
Chinese. (WECCL)
What is needed is a large increase in road tax and tax on fuels to make
car travel more expensive. (LOCNESS)
```

As we have seen from the above discussion, extension 2 subordinate clauses predominate across the two corpora. One possible reason for this might be that the distribution of "what" sentences in written corpora has a strong relationship to the purpose of the written language it appears in. It has been shown that written English tends to contain more complex sentences that include subordinate clauses (Carter and McCarthy 1997). They argue that this is because writers have more time to reflect on what they want to say and can thus present more complex ideas. Both native speakers and non-native speakers' corpora reflect the characteristics of academic writing. This is different from that found in textbook data and elicited data. For textbook data, extension 2 largely occurs in STD, as the complex sentence structures are provided by textbook writers to build learners' ability to construct sentences. In the case of elicited data, extension 2 has fewer occurrences and it is predictable that extension 2 subordinate clauses are rarely produced in daily language.

In contrast, prototypes have a low frequency across the two corpora. This is also different from the findings for textbook data and elicited data. For textbook data, prototypes largely occur for JTD and UTD. In the case of elicited data, prototypes predominate across groups of participants. One possible reason for this might be that prototypical interrogatives rarely occur in written corpora compared with other sentences as they reflect sporadic online production where language is produced in quick short bursts, and also prototypical interrogatives represent direct questions that indicate a typical features of spoken interaction.

Extension 1 has the fewest occurrences across the two corpora. This is consistent with the findings for textbook data and elicited data. This may suggest that extension 1 declaratives constitute an unusual construction which is rarely used in different varieties of language contexts. In English, 'which' tends to be used in subordinate clauses, rather than 'what'.

Distribution of "how" sentences across the two corpora

We will now look at the distribution of "how" sentences across the two corpora. The pattern of the distribution of "how" sentences is similar to that of the previously studied "what" sentences.

Table 7.6 and Figure 7.2 show the different types of "how" sentences in each corpus

How

	Prototype	%	Extension 1	%	Extension 2	%	total
LOCNESS	81	19%	5	1%	349	80%	435
WECCL	132	29%	37	8%	289	63%	458
All	213	24%	42	5%	638	71%	893

Table 7.6 Different types of "how" sentences across the two corpora

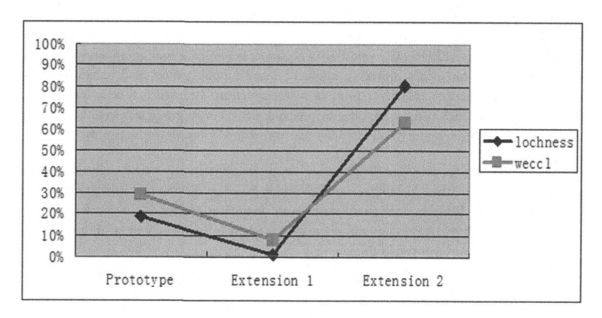

Figure 7.2 "how" sentence types across the two corpora

As Table 7.6 and Figure 7.2 show, extension 2 (-interrogative, -main clause) has the highest distribution in the LOCNESS, at 80% and 63% for the WECCL. Extension 2 has almost 4 times the distribution than prototypes in the LOCNESS, but in the case of the WECCL, Prototypes occur with half the frequency of the extension 2. Both corpora contain few prototypes, however the proportion of prototypes in WECCL, at 29%, is higher than in LOCNESS, at 19%. Only a few sentences of Extension 1 are found in the LOCNESS, representing less than 1%. The proportion of Extension 1 was lower in both corpora, at 1% for the LOCNESS and 8% for the WECCL respectively. Examples are shown below:

Prototypes:

```
And how are they communicating? (LOCNESS)
"How about your examination today? (WECCL)
```

Extension 1:

```
How passive are they. (LOCNESS)
How wonderful it would be! (WECCL)
```

Extension 2:

```
It is simply a matter of how far he can push the people before they
react...(LOCNESS)
...make students aware of how important the issue is. (WECCL)
```

Similar to the findings for "what" sentences, extension 2 "how" subordinate clauses predominate across the two corpora. This shows that non-native speakers have an awareness of extension 2 uses which resembles that of native speakers. This contrasts with the findings for textbook data and elicited data. For textbook data, extension 2 largely occurs in higher level textbooks UTD. In the case of elicited data, extension 2 has a small proportion of occurrences across the four groups of participants. One possible reason for such a difference might be that textbook writers tend to provide more complex sentence structures as learners' proficiency levels increase. Learners may store well-selected prototypical schemas such as those provided by textbook writers or language teachers in their long-term memory, suggesting prototypical examples have a strong relationship with memory.

Elicited data is likely to be linked to the processes that produced it. In other words, researchers have a clear purpose in mind when selecting research questions. Based on the bias inherent in the purpose, elicited data is more likely to arise from participants' long-term memories. In contrast, written production from both native speakers and non-native speakers is more likely to be affiliated to the style and aim of the writing it comes from.

It is interesting to note that extension 1 declarative clauses appear significantly in the WECCL. This is consistent with findings for textbook data and elicited data, as there are abundant examples of extension 1. Thus the non-native speakers appear to have been influenced by the textbook language.

In the case of prototypes, it is more likely that the interrogative forms are commonly used in our daily life in spoken language. For this reason, both native speakers and non-native speakers significantly produce prototypes for elicited data, which appears to resemble spoken rather than written language.

Distribution of "where" sentences across the two corpora

We will now look at the distribution of "where" sentences across the two corpora. We will also compare "where" sentences to the previously studied sentences, as well as the distribution within textbook data and elicited data.

Table 7.3 and Figure 7.3 show the different types of "where" sentences in each data set.

where

	Prototype	%	Extension 1	%	Extension 2	%	total
LOCNESS	13	5%	0	0%	273	95%	286
WECCL	7	11%	0	0%	56	89%	63
All	20	6%	0	0%	329	94%	349

Table 7.7 Different types of "where" sentences across the two corpora

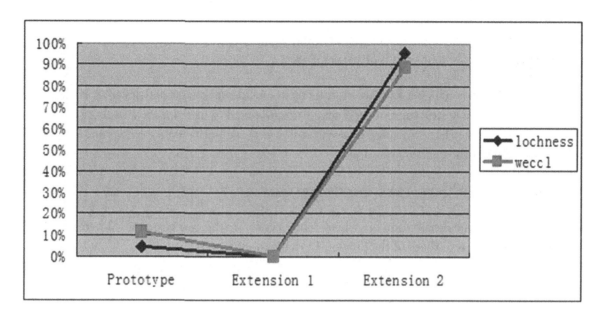

Figure 7.3 "where" sentence types across the two corpora

As Table 7.7 and Figure 7.3 show, within the two corpora, Extension 2 predominates, with around 95% for the LOCNESS, and 89% for the WECCL. Extension 1 is not found across two datasets. Prototype has a relatively low frequency, with around 5% for the LOCNESS, and 11% for the WECCL respectively. Examples of the sentence patterns are shown below:

Prototype:

```
Where would it stop? (LOCNESS)
Where are my friends? (WECCL)
```

Extension 2:

```
This is where 'drag hunting' becomes involved. (LOCNESS)
Find out where it comes from... (WECCL)
```

"Where" sentences follow a similar pattern to "what" and "how" sentences, as extension 2 subordinate clauses predominate across the two corpora. One possible reason for this might be that "where" subordinate clauses are used more frequently in written language on the grounds that they carry extra information to enrich the text's contents. Written discourse tends to serve a more transactional function than spoken discourse (where relationship-building is arguably more important). This is perhaps one reason why we have more subordinate clauses in the corpora as they tend to carry information.

The distribution of "where" sentences is different in textbook data and elicited data. For textbook data, prototypes largely occur in lower level textbooks, such as JTD, while extension 2 predominates for higher level textbooks, such as STD and UTD. One possible reason for this difference might be that textbooks at lower levels tend to focus on basic daily conversation; therefore the prototypical examples

195

are more likely to be recognised by learners. In addition, the prototypical "where" sentences are used frequently in native speakers' daily contexts. This may explain the reason that this construction occurs predominately across the four groups of participants.

In contrast, textbooks at a higher level are more likely to include newspaper articles or an extract from a novel, and the sentence structures of these texts are considered to be complex. It is more likely that extension 2 subordinate clauses are used in a written context, and both native speakers and non-native speakers are aware of the contexts of using it.

Distribution of "when" sentences across the two corpora

We will now look at the distribution of "when" sentences across the two corpora. "When" sentences follow a similar pattern to those of the previously analysed sentences.

Table 7.8 and Figure 7.4 show the different types of "when" sentences across the two corpora.

when

	Prototype	%	Extension 1	%	Extension 2	%	total
LOCNESS	8	1%	0	0%	835	99%	843
WECCL	1	0%	0	0%	964	100%	965
All	9	1%	0	0%	1799	99%	1808

Table 7.8 Different types of "when" sentences across the two corpora

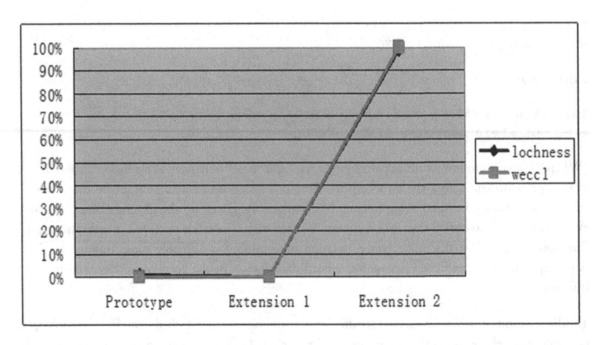

Figure 7.4 "when" sentence types across the two corpora

Table 7.8 and Figure 7.4 show that Extension 2 is predominant across the two corpora, with approximately 99% for the LOCNESS, and 100% for the WECCL, for example:

```
When the dogs finally find a scent the hunt begins. (LOCNESS)
He would smile back when I caressed him. (WECCL)
Extension 1 is absent from the two sets of data, suggesting that this
form does not exist in the written language that students produced. Few
prototypes occur across the two corpora, representing approximately 1%
in the LOCNESS and less than 1% in the WECCL, for example:

When does drug overpricing stop? (LOCNESS)
Then how can they live alone when they grow up?(WECCL)
```

"When" sentences follow a similar pattern to "what", "how", and "where" sentences. In this case, "when" extension 2 subordinate clauses are presented significantly across the two corpora. One possible reason for this might be the fact that both corpora were complied of academic essays, which have been found to contain more subordinate clauses.

The distribution of "when" sentences across the two corpora is similar to that found for textbook data, as extension 2 predominates across the three sets of textbooks. One possible reason for this might be that "when" subordinate clauses could be considered to be an important grammatical element during language acquisition and textbook writers therefore tend to provide more examples for this construction. In fact the first subordinate clause that is introduced in lower level textbooks is 'when'. This might be because it is easy to teach.

The distribution of "when" sentences across the two corpora is different from the findings for elicited data in terms of the distribution of prototypes. In the case of elicited data, extension 2 subordinate clauses are largely produced by participants at lower levels (JED). It is interesting to note that this construction is introduced in lower level textbooks (JTD). One possible reason for this might be that textbooks are one of the most important types of input in the L2 language acquisition process in terms of influencing the way learners construct sentences. In addition, the "when" sentence is also found to be the most frequently occurring sentence type across the textbook data.

Distribution of "why" sentences across the two corpora

We will now look at the distribution of "why" sentences across the two corpora. The distribution of "why" sentences differs from the patterns established by the previously studied "wh" sentences.

Table 7.9 and Figure 7.5 show the different types of "why" sentences across the two corpora.

why

	Prototype	%	Extension 1	%	Extension 2	%	total
LOCNESS	71	30%	0	0 %	167	70%	238
WECCL	135	59%	0	0 %	92	41%	227
All	206	44%	0	0%	259	56%	465

Table 7.9 Different types of "why" sentences across the two corpora

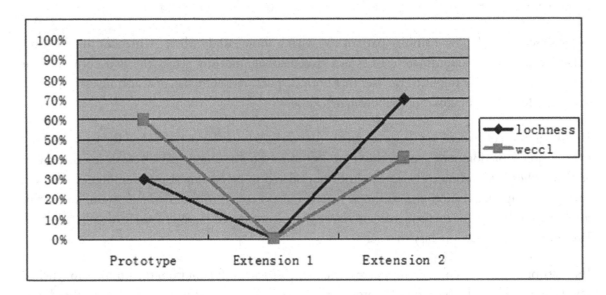

Figure 7.5 "why" sentence types across the two corpora

According to Table 7.9 and Figure 7.5, for the word *why*, the case is slightly different. Similar to the words *what*, *how*, and *when*, Extension 2 again predominates in the LOCNESS, with around 70%, while for the WECCL, the prototype (60%) has a slightly higher distribution than Extension 2 (41%). This may suggest that the use of *why* in non-native speakers' written language is largely based on a spoken format. In most cases, prototypes are used to indicate new topics which have the function of attracting the reader as well as helping the writers themselves to interact.

Extension 1 is not found across the three datasets.

Examples are shown as follows:

Prototypes:

```
Why is British rail so unreliable? (LOCNESS)
Why did you copy others? (WECCL)
```

Extension 2:

```
...that is why they are paid so highly. (LOCNESS)
What we must do is that we should know why we learn English and how to
learn English. (WECCL)
```

"Why" sentences are markedly different from the previously studied sentences because extension 2 subordinate clauses largely occur in the LOCNESS. In contrast, prototype interrogative occur primarily in the WECCL. One possible reason for this might be that, as we have seen earlier from textbook data, prototypical structures predominate across three sets of textbooks. In the case of elicited data, prototypical structures are also predominately produced by all groups of participants. It is predictable that non-native speakers' written production may be influenced by textbook data. In addition, we can say the prototypical structures of "why" sentences are somewhat relied on excessively by non-native speakers.

Distribution of "who" sentences across the two corpora

We now move on to discuss the distribution of "who" sentences across the two corpora. "Who" sentences follow a similar pattern to "what", "how", "where", and "when" sentences as extension 2 subordinate clauses predominate across the two corpora.

Table 7.10 and Figure 7.6 show the different types of "who" sentences in each data set.

who

	Prototype	%	Extension 1	%	Extension 2	%	total
LOCNESS	7	1%	0	0%	903	99%	910
WECCL	11	3%	0	0%	359	97%	370
All	18	1%	0	0%	1262	99%	1280

Table 7.10 Different types of "who" sentences across the two corpora

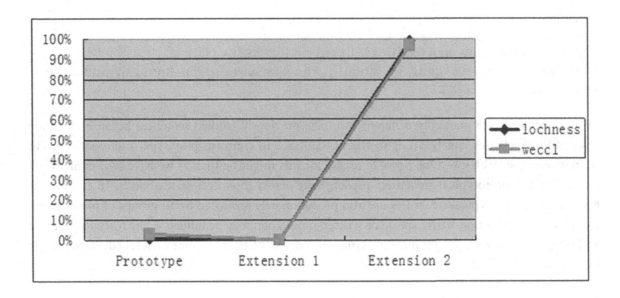

Figure 7.6 "who" sentence types across the two corpora

Table 7.10 and Figure 7.6 clearly show that Extension 2 occurs with a high frequency across the two datasets, with 99% for the LOCNESS, and 97% for the WECCL. Extension 1 is not found in the two datasets. Prototype has relatively low frequency as expected: 1% (LOCNESS), and 3% (WECCL). Examples are shown below:

Prototype:

```
Who won? (LOCNESS)
If I and your mother fall into the water together, who will you save
first? (WECCL)
```

Extension 2

```
For commuters who regularly travel long distances rail transport should
be made more appealing, more comfortable and cheaper. (LOCNESS)
It seems that the upper class people who run these hunts think they own
everything, the land, the fox. (WECCL)
```

"Who" sentences follow a similar pattern to the previously analysed "what", "how", "where", and "when" sentences. Extension 2 subordinate clauses are favoured by both native speakers and non-native speakers in terms of written language.

The distribution of "who" sentences is different from that found for textbook data and elicited data. For textbook data, extension 2 subordinate clauses largely occur in higher level textbooks (STD and UTD) as more complex structures are introduced to help learners to build their skills in sentence construction. In contrast, prototypes only predominate in the lower level textbooks (JTD), suggesting that this construction is more important for learners at beginner level.

In the case of elicited data, extension 2 subordinate clauses are hardly produced by four groups of participants. One possible reason for this might be that subordinate clauses are more difficult to produce than interrogatives. In addition, elicited data for both non-native speakers and native speakers was collected after class or randomly in a library. It is therefore likely that the participants choose to write the quickest and easiest sentences.

Distribution of "whom" sentences across the two corpora

We now move on to discuss the distribution of "whom" sentences across the two corpora. "Whom" sentences follow a similar pattern to "what", "how", "where", "when" and "who" sentences as extension 2 subordinate clauses predominate across the two corpora.

Table 7.11 and Figure 7.7 show the different types of "whom" sentences in each data set.

whom

	Prototype	%	Extension 1	%	Extension 2	%	total
LOCNESS	2	10%	0	0%	19	90%	21
WECCL	0	0%	0	0%	9	100 %	9
All	2	7%	0	0%	28	93%	30

Table 7.11 Different types of "whom" sentences across the two corpora

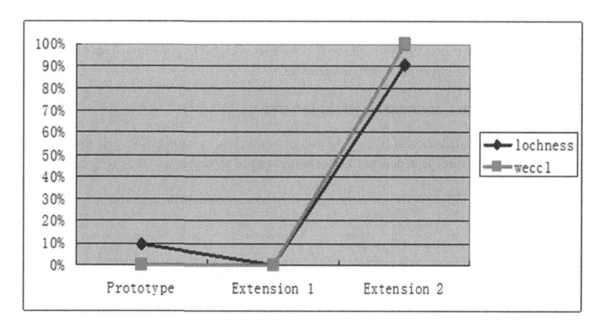

Figure 7.7 "whom" sentence types across the two corpora

As Table 7.11 and Figure 7.7 show, Extension 2 for the two datasets has the highest frequency, at 90% for the LOCNESS and almost 100% for the WECCL. Extension 1 cannot be found across all

Feifei Zhang

datasets. There are only two prototype sentences identified from the LOCNESS, at only 10% while there are none in the WECCL. Examples are shown as follows:

Extension 2:

```
According to Sartre, for whom actions defined life, Hugo was therefore a
failure...(LOCNESS)
It's certainly not a problem of whom to blame. (WECCL)
```

Prototype:

```
whom is he or she appealing to? (LOCNESS)
For whom is there a payoff? (LOCNESS)
```

Although "whom" sentences have the lowest number of occurrences across the two corpora, the distribution of "whom" sentences follow a similar pattern to the previously studied sentences, as extension 2 subordinate clauses predominate across the two corpora. We have noticed that the occurrence of "whom" sentences has the lowest number of occurrences for textbook data, elicited data and written corpora. It is possible that "whom" sentences are one of the unusual types of sentences that people hardly used in both daily life and academic contexts.

The distribution of "whom" sentences is similar to that found for textbook data, as extension 2 subordinate clauses predominately occur. This may suggest that "whom" subordinate clauses are commonly used in an academic written context. In the case of elicited data, extension 2 subordinate clauses are largely produced by participants at higher levels (UED). In contrast, prototypical structures are largely produced by participants at junior middle school, senior high school, and also by native speakers. One possible reason for this might be that learners at higher level are more likely to produce complex sentence structures as presented in textbooks.

Distribution of "whose" sentences across the two corpora

We now look at the distribution of "whose" sentences across the two corpora. We will also compare the distribution of "whose" sentences to the previously studied sentences.

Table 7.12 and Figure 7.8 show the different types of "whose" sentences in each data set.

whose

	Prototype	%	Extension 1	%	Extension 2	%	total
LOCNESS	0	0%	0	0%	24	100 %	24
WECCL	1	8%	0	0%	12	92%	13
All	1	3%	0	0%	36	97%	37

Table 7.12 Different types of "whose" sentences across the two corpora

202

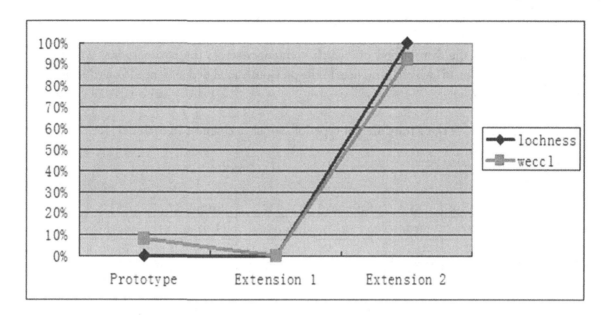

Figure 7.8 "whose" sentence types across the two corpora

Table 7.12 and Figure 7.8 show that extension 2 is predominant among the two corpora, with 100% for the LOCNESS, and 92% for the WECCL, for example:

Passengers whose life seems to revolve around annoying others... (LOCNESS)

So we can't easily tell whose duty it is. (WECCL)

Again, Extension 1 is absent from the two corpora, suggesting that this form does not exist in the written language corpora. The prototype cannot be found from the LOCNESS, while there is only one prototype sentence identified from the WECCL, representing a distribution at 8%:

Whose fault it is? (WECCL)

The distribution of "whose" sentences is similar to the previously studied "what", "how", "where", "when", "who" and "whom" sentences, as extension 2 subordinate clauses predominate across the two corpora. This may suggest that "whose" subordinate clauses are commonly used in an academic written context and both native speakers and non-native speakers are aware of them.

The distribution of "whose" sentences across the two corpora is different from that found for textbook data and elicited data. For textbook data, extension 2 subordinate clauses largely occur for higher level textbooks (STD and UTD), suggesting that more complex sentence structures are introduced to help learners to recognize the variability of the target language's linguistic structures. In the case of elicited data, extension 2 subordinate clauses are hardly produced by the four groups of participants. In contrast, prototypical structures are significantly produced.

Distribution of "which" sentences across the two corpora

We will now discuss the distribution of "which" sentences across the two corpora. We will also compare the distribution of "which" sentences to the previously analysed sentences, as well as textbook data and elicited data.

Table 7.13 and Figure 7.9 show the different types of "which" sentences in each data set.

which

	Prototype	%	Extension 1	%	Extension 2	%	total
LOCNESS	0	0%	0	0 %	1136	100%	1137
WECCL	26	4%	0	0 %	611	96%	637
All	27	2%	0	0 %	1747	98%	1774

Table 7.13 Different types of "which" sentences across the two corpora

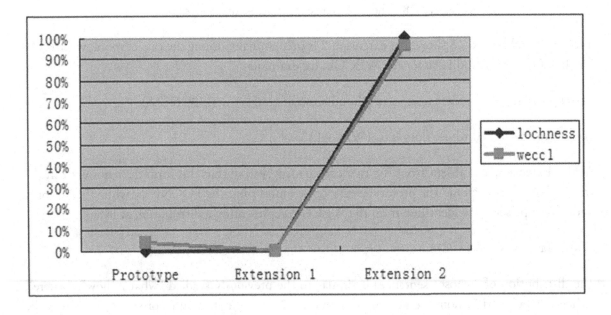

Figure 7.9 "which" sentence types across the two corpora

As Table 7.13 and Figure 7.9 show, in terms of Extension 2, two corpora have a high frequency, with 100% for the LOCNESS, and 96% for the WECCL. Again, Extension 1 is not found in any of the corpora. The two corpora have the fewest number of prototypes, while the WECCL has a slightly higher frequency than those in the LOCNESS, with only 4% at the WECCL, and less than 1% at the LOCNESS. Examples are shown as follows:

Prototypes:

```
Which one do you prefer? (WECCL)
```

Extension 2:

```
The severe shortage of revenue which is spent in doing up the image of
the railway...(LOCNESS)
It is an impressive lesson Mom gives me which I will always remember.
(WECCL)
```

The distribution of "which" sentences is similar to the previously studied "what", "how", "where", "when", "who", "whom", and "whose" sentences, as extension 2 subordinate clauses predominate across the two corpora. This may suggest that "which" subordinate clauses are commonly used in an academic written context and both native speakers and non-native speakers are aware of them.

The distribution of "whose" sentences across the two corpora is different from that found for textbook data and elicited data. For textbook data, extension 2 subordinate clauses largely occur for higher level textbooks (STD and UTD), suggesting that more complex sentence structures are introduced in higher level textbooks. For elicited data, prototypical structures predominate across the four groups of participants, suggesting that prototypes have a strong influence in people's minds.

In conclusion, there are two patterns that can be identified from the above discussion: 1) extension 2 subordinate clauses predominate across the two corpora, for example, "what", "how", "where", "when", "who", "whom" "whose" and "which" sentences; 2) extension 2 subordinate clauses largely occur in the LOCNESS, while prototypical interrogatives largely occur in the WECCL, for example, "why" sentences. As the discussion suggests, although prototypes have a strong influence on people's minds, the sentence types of "wh" words still vary in accordance with the intention and level of the written text. Genre can override more general prototypicality effects.

We begin this section by discussing the extent to which the analysis of three types of sentences appears in written texts that are produced by expert users of English and EFL learners. Given our data, most "wh" words have a high frequency in extension 2 subordinate clauses in written discourse, in terms of both native speakers and non-native speakers. As the analysis shows, for the words *when, which, whose, where, who* and *whom*, both the native speakers and non-native speakers exhibit a similar trend in terms of the three types of sentences in the two corpora. The written discourse in the two corpora shows a high level of preference for subordinate clauses. Therefore, extension 2 (subordinate clauses) can be considered to be the predominant sentence type that occurrs in written discourse. In terms of the words *what* and *how*, three types of sentences occur in a relatively high proportion in non-native speakers. For example, the word *what* occurs 16% in prototypes, 2% in extension 1, and 82% in extension 2 while the word *how* appears 29% in prototypes, 8% in extension 1, and 63% in extension 2. It is interesting to note that in the case of the word *why*, written corpora from non-native speakers have a relatively high proportion of prototypes compared with extension 2, with 59% (prototypes) and 41% (extension 2).

Different between NS and NNS data can also be explained in terms of contextual function. In the following sections, I discuss the contextual functions of the three types of "wh" sentences in which they occur.

7.4.2 *Contextual Functions of the Three Types of "Wh" Sentences Across the Two Corpora*

Native and non-native speaker language use can be expected to vary in terms of function as well as form. It is useful to be aware of both types of variation if the aim of the instructor is to help learners produce written texts that resemble those produced by native speakers. In this study, the native speakers were found to make use of a wider variety of functions than the non-native speakers. In order to illustrate this, let us begin by looking at the functions of the prototypes and extensions in the two corpora.

7.4.2.1 Examples of native and non-native writers in terms of the contextual functions expressed by "wh" sentences

In order to examine the functions of the words in each corpus, the corpus data were accessed using version 4.0 of *WordSmith* Tools (Scott 2000) to provide a search for each "wh" word. In order to identify the contextual functions of the three types of "wh" sentences, I used a tool called "file view" to trace back the original written transcription, establishing the investigation of different types of "wh" sentences use in context. Table 7.14 gives the general functions of the three types of "wh" sentences that were identified from the two corpora.

Sentence types	Functions
Prototypes	·Provide the topics; ·Express the writer's emotions or beliefs; ·Attract the reader to the following content; ·Enhance the argumentation (in most cases, they are used to support the writer's argument).
Extension 1	·Provide further illustration or description, allowing the context to become more interesting and vivid; ·In most cases, it is used in negative situations by native speakers, and used in positive situations by non-native speakers.
Extension 2	·A response to the topic; ·Provides the solutions for potential questions; ·highlights the topic, sets the argument by providing the writer's own opinion, and also provides the context and the use of phrasal verbs.

Table 7.14 The general functions of the three types of "wh" sentences identified from the two corpora

Examples of "wh" sentences from the native and non-native speaker corpora are given below, along with their functions. These are simply examples.

<u>what</u>

Examples 1a and 1b show the use of "what" words in prototypes in the LOCNESS and WECCL:

1a. Traffic jams are becoming larger and more frequent. Trains are never on time. Everybody always has a complaint about some part of the transport system in the United Kingdom. <u>What is wrong, and what can we do about it?</u> (LOCNESS)

1b. In potted landscape making, you should bend the branches when the plants are young. Because when the plants become older, it's hard to bend or can't be bent at all. The some principles<sp-priciple>, we should not wait the pollution become so serious that we have to find some way to overcome it. Under that occasion, we should put into more time, financial resources, labour power, material resources to develop new technology to solve the pollution. And may be we can't find out the effective measures in a short time, <u>then what should we do?</u> (WECCL)

In both of these examples, the "what" sentences are used to express the writers' beliefs and emotions. The use of the question form not only emphasizes the topics such as *the traffic jam* in example a and *pollution* in example b, but also provides the outlines of the contents for the following paragraphs, so that the readers can assume that the solutions are provided in the next paragraphs.

Example 1c and 1d shows the use of "what" words in extension 1:

1c<u>. what a stupid unethical theory it is.</u> The fact that Pangloss remains adamant in his belief of philosophical optimism could also demonstrate Voltaire's low opinion on those who believe in it. (LOCNESS)

1d. Though I don't know who is the father of mobile telephone, I still admire and appreciate him from the bottom of my heart. <u>What a great invention mobile phone is!</u> Everybody dreams to have one because it is so convenient in communicating. Own a mobile phone, the times wait a long queue after a IC card telephone has gone, you can make a call at any time and any place, if you want. And your family and friends can easily find you, especially there are some emergencies. And you may not believe, it can save people's lives. (WECCL)

In example c, extension 1 is used to express the writer's opinion in a negative way. It provides a strong argument which the writer holds. In example d, the writer uses extension 1 to express the positive attributes of the mobile phone, as well as elaborating on the reasons to have a mobile phone.

Example 1e and 1f show the use of "what" words in extension 2:

> 1e. Solutions for these problems in Britain have been fairly unimaginative and unsuccessful. Park and ride schemes are common to discourage people from taking their cars into city centres as are pedestrian streets and one way systems but they have done little to relieve the problem. The average speed of traffic in Central London is no faster than that of 200 years ago when horse drawn carriages were being used. <u>What is needed is a large increase in road tax and tax on fuels to make car travel more expensive.</u> Encourage the use of bikes with schemes like the "Green Bike Scheme" proposed in Exeter where bikes can be picked up and used and dropped off at various points around the city for free. (LOCNESS)
>
> 1f. and <u>what matters most should be parents-children mutual attitude during communication.</u> That is trying to befriend each other. (WECCL)

In example 1e, the use of the *what* subordinate clause recalls the topic as well as providing the potential solutions to this problem, such as increasing the road tax, and encouraging people to try to use other forms of transportation. The idea that these things are 'needed' is foregrounded in this particular construction. In example 1f, the thing that 'matter's most' is foregrounded.

How

Examples 2a and 2b show the use of "how" words in prototypes in the LOCNESS and WECCL:

> 2a. Many people agreed with this but did not wish to see any 'White Elephants' constructed. Sports teams, clubs, social groups and communities applied for cash for new facilities and then John Major announced some profits would be used for the construction of a British Academy of Sport. However, people were worried that the money would not be evenly spread, would the North-South divide be a factor? <u>How would the Naitonal Heritage * decide what a good cause would be?</u> Could any money fall into the wrong hands, or be wasted? These were all major talking points and arguments raged about distribution of money from the Lottery.(Locness)
>
> 2b. Our real purpose to learn English is to communicate. Reading also can communicate, but you just communicate with the author in some senses. Reading is much easier than communicating, for example, when you don't understand a sentence, you can read it many times until you get it and you can look up the new words in a dictionary. However, when you are communicating with someone, you must understand what he says very quickly, if you even can't listen to him clearly, how <u>can the communication go on?</u> (WECCL)

In example 2a, the use of the prototype question form attracts the attention of the reader, causing him or her to focus on the main topic. The writer gives a general description of the situation in which many sports teams, clubs, social groups and communities applied for the money and a problem arose as to how the money should be given to each group. The use of a question here emphasises this topic and makes the reader think for themselves about the issue. Consistently, the reader is encouraged to make inferences and accesses his or her understanding in light of the situation and aims or purposes of the text. In example 2b, the use of prototype question expresses the writer's emotion and opinions. After a description of the definition of communication, the writer attempts to build an argument that oral communication is more difficult than written communication. As we can see, the theme in example 2a is clear, and can be easily traced. In example 2b the writer does not give a clear description of the situation, the theme is ambiguous in that the reader might be confused about whether the main topic is learning English or a different means of communication. Native speakers' writing is considered to be more structured and understandable.

Example 2c and 2d shows the use of "how" words in extension 1:

2c. When Candide is forced to join the Bulgar army and is whipped for his attempt at desertion, he sees for himself the futility of warfare and <u>how fruitless and destructive it all is.</u> (Locness)

2d. You don't have to walk for several streets to find a telephone to make a call. You can take your cell-phone out of your pocket and use it anytime at anywhere. <u>How convenient!</u> (WECCL)

In example 2c, the use of the declarative (extension 1) *how fruitless and destructive it all is.* provides further emphasis that Candide hates the warfare. Based on the description, the writer attempts to set a description-discussion pattern. In this short paragraph, such patterns can be found in two aspects: a description of Candide's negative view of being a soldier (*When Candide is forced to join the Bulgar army*) and Candide's attempts to escape such a life several times lead to a discussion or judgement that Candide hates warfare. Accordingly, the writer discusses the matter further by using the declarative to evaluate the situation, based on the previous manifested texts. In addition, the use of the declarative allows the context to become more interesting, as well as strengthening the statement that the writer may want to reveal the fact that warfare should be abandoned and reinforcing the sympathy aspect of being a soldier. In example 2d, the use of the declarative expresses the writer's emotion as he or she thinks the mobile phone is a convenience for daily life. The declarative used in native speakers' writing appears to be mainly a means of illustration or description. It relates the context tightly and naturally. On the other hand, the declarative used in non-native speakers' writing appears to be more of a complement which advocates the writer's opinion.

Example 2e and 2f show the use of "how" words in extension 2:

2e. Firstly you could see that the introduction of computers has made us think more because of all the programmes used on them. <u>It can take quite sometime learning how to use them.</u> Besides, as soon as one programme or computer is brought out it becomes out of date because people are <?immiediately?> thinking about how to improve it. After all it was man that invented the computer. Computers can't replace the human brain (not yet anyway!).(LOCNESS)

2f. It is different from our native language. <u>Because the people around you speak the same language, you can learn how to speak it easily.</u> But if you speak English among Chinese people, you will find it hard to make progress in your speaking. So in this case, it is wise to learn to read in English at first.

In example 2e, the use of the subordinate clause (extension 2) provides the context and potential question relating to the main topic. The writer first introduces the computer, then the programmes, then follows with a description of how to use the computer and how to improve it. The use of the subordinate allows the writer to provide more detail to support his or her argument. In example 2f, the use of the subordinate clause illustrates the situation. The writer attempts to build a scene that learning a language with native speakers is easier than learning a language with non-native speakers. *How to speak it easily* is complementary to the subject phrase *you can learn*.

<u>when</u>

Examples 3a and 3b show the use of "when" words in prototypes in the LOCNESS and WECCL:

3a. As a nursing student, the indications of this are ominous, patients I treat will not receive proper care because they are afraid of it costing too much for them to take their medicine. I don't want to be the one to tell them that they can't have a certain medicine because they cant afford it. Because of this, these Federal price regulatory board are necessary to keep fairness on the mind of the pharmaceutical industry. If companies like Merck and Upjohn don't look at who they are serving, the Mothers, Fathers and children of America, they will lose business. Yes, it is morally ethical for drug companies to make a profit, but where is the limit? <u>When does drug overpricing stop?</u> It is up to the American people to decide. (Locness)

3b. <u>When "lifelong education" can be spreaded from western countries to China?</u> It is obvious that young people accepte it easily, but to the old, they couldn't understand, why should they accept such a strange idea? (WECCL)

In example 3a, the use of the prototype question highlights the topic that the price of medicine is incredibly high, and that people cannot afford it. In addition, the use of the question here expresses the writer's emotion in which he or she strongly disagrees with such phenomena. In example 3b, the question considers the topic of lifelong education in China. The use of the question at the beginning of a paragraph has its benefits. Readers can clearly understand the theme of the paragraph.

Examples 3c and 3d show the use of "when" words in extension 2 in the LOCNESS and WECCL:

3c. There have been many demonstrations by activists when fox hunting is taking place and although I do not agree with some of the animal activists methods I am in this case of the strong opinion that fox hunting should be banned in the United Kingdom. My reasons for this are as follows.(LOCNESS)

3d. In old China, the education which was received by a common people was from the school, and it only lasted for a few years. When one man finished his study in school, he would never come back to school as a student again. They thought that they had learned all knowledge they needed.(WECCL)

In example 3c, the "when" subordinate clause is interpreted in relation to an explanation and illustration of the events, namely, many demonstrations. *When* provides detailed information about the demonstrations. It also highlights the topic and provides the background of the paragraph. In example 3d, the subordinate clause provides an example, allowing the topic sentence to be exclusively discussed. In addition, the clause indicated by "when" provides the situation and condition for the main clause *he would never come back to school as a student again.*

why

Examples 4a and 4b show the use of "why" words in prototypes in the LOCNESS and WECCL:

4a. British rail is notoriously slow, late and expensive and the hype of rail travel and steam trains is long since gone with many old tracks being dismantled. If we are to alleviate the roads in Britain them we must encourage rail travel in Britain and we should be opening new lines not closing old ones. Perhaps the privatisation of British Rail will produce a more competitive service but I fear that it will result in the closure of smaller less profitable lines and only a better service on the main routes. <u>Why is British rail so unreliable?</u> Most of the world besides Britain seems to run a reliable service even developing countries. Few efforts have been made to make the fares cheaper and a more desirable form of family travel, with the Family railcard really being a non-starter.(LOCNESS)

4b.Traditions<sp-Tranditions> and Modernization are seemed to be in conflict. Traditions<sp-Tranditions> are back-looking while modernization is forward-looking. They are seemed that will never include each other and can not be a mixture under any conditions. Furthermore, the preservation of tradition<sp-trandition> will even slow down the pace of modernization. <u>But, why not change our points of view little?</u> look at some examples that have already existed in the reality, we can get a different conclusion. (WECCL)

In example 4a, the use of the prototype question highlights the fact that British rail has problems. After explicitly discussing the problems, the writer uses a question to express his or her disappointment. In example 4b, the writer provides a general description of the two social phenomena: traditions and modernization. The use of the question here attracts the reader to focus on the writer's opinion.

Examples 4c and 4d show the use of "why" words in extension 2 in the LOCNESS and WECCL:

4c. Despite computers saving time, they do everything for you at the touch of a button, solve the most difficult sums, check for spelling errors on essays, letters and other documents and much more. <u>This is why it could be said we don't use our brains as much.</u> (LOCNESS)

4d. This expression is more humorous than just say I want you to stand treat. Because always when students gather to have a meeting, the initiator will invite others to eat. Therefore, this expression was formed. <u>Now, no mather why you want to stand treat, or be treated, you could use "bao gao."</u> (WECCL)

Both "why" sentences make most sense in concluding and highlighting the topic. However, in example 4c, the two segments seem to have a logical problem. The first sentence may make sense if we delete the word *despite*. In example 4d, the writer gives a detailed description of the definition, the "why" sentence is used to clarify the topic, allowing the readers to understand better.

which

Examples 5a show the use of "which" words in prototypes in the WECCL:

5a. <u>Which skill of English is more important for Chinese learner?</u> Some people say is reading, and some say is speaking. Yes, both of them are important. But if I may say in this way, I think is thinking. (WECCL)

The "which" prototype cannot be found in the LOCNESS corpus. In example 5a, the question used as the beginning of the paragraph, provides the topic sentence. The use of the phrase *which skill* classifies and narrows down the main subject *English*.

Examples 5b and 5c show the use of "which" words in extension 2 in the LOCNESS and WECCL:

5b. The Fifth Republic inherited the limitations and dissatisfaction of the Fourth. The education system needed immediate modernisation and democratization. <u>The first reform which aimed at achieve these was the Berthoin reform which was issued by decree under de Gaulle's emergency powers with no opportunity for parliamentary debate.</u>(LOCNESS)

5c. Nowadays, most people agree that there is a generation gap between children and parents. <u>It's like a wall standing between the two generations, which makes it difficult for them to communicate with each other.</u> (WECCL)

The "which" subordinate clauses in both examples make a lot sense in explaining and describing the event although they are different in detail. In example 5b, the first *which* and second *which* are both used as defining and demonstrating the first reform and the Berthoin reform. In example 5c, the first segment in the "which" subordinate clause provides the reason for the second segment *which makes it difficult for them to communicate with each other*. The second segment is more likely to be the cause or consequence of the first segment. This is different from example 5b, which is more likely to present the truth rather than the judgement.

where

Examples 6a and 6b show the use of "where" words in prototypes in the LOCNESS and WECCL:

6a. This form of genetic engineering allows the parents to choose their own child. Therefore, couples who only want boys could do so. However, if a couple could only love one gender of child should they have one? Although in principle the idea of choosing children is not a bad one, <u>where would it stop?</u> If this is acceptable then choosing blonde hair and blue eyes may also become acceptable. This could lead to a total change in the population. Also, if for any reason the treatment should go wrong and the wrong gender is conceived, the parents may find it hard to love the child. However, in China, for example, the one child law has meant that many baby girls have been killed for want of a boy. Therefore, if the parents could ensure that they have a boy, it would save many deaths, so in that case choosing the gender of a child before conception would be preferable. (LOCNESS)

6b. But sometimes we just complain too often. Even very trivial matters will lead into a quarrel. Sometimes parents and children seriously negotiate over the matter of dressing while or in pink. When I look back into my remote rebellious past, I can't help laughing at myself. I was so eager to show that I grew up and could decide everything. <u>But where do I get my daily necessities?</u> Who feeds me? Still my parents.(weccl)

In example 6a, the "where" question is used as a way of expressing the writer's idea. The writer uses the question to highlight his or her opinion and also can be seen as a process. Following the "where" question, the writer gives several negative examples to support his or her idea. Notice that it is not easy to see which is the topic. Instead, the writer uses a pattern of *arising the question-giving examples-discusses the consequences*. In example 6b, after a detailed discussion of the generation gap, the "where" question indicates the writer's opinion that children should respect their parents. Again, the topic and the writer's opinion emerge as the question is used.

Examples 6c and 6d show the use of "where" words in extension 2 in the LOCNESS and WECCL:

6c. It cannot help but be noticed that Britain's roads are becoming increasingly unsavoury places. <u>Congestion is a severe problem, particularly in urban areas, where it is very difficult - almost impossible in fact -to create new road systems to cope with the taffic.</u> A journey into Lancaster, for example, may only take ten minutes when the roads are quiet, but can take three-quarters of an hour during the 'rush-hour'. Congestion is certainly not a problem that will go away; the number of cars on Britain's roads is increasing constantly. The M25 has already been dubbed 'the biggest car-park in Europe', and if current trends continue, the number of cars using it will double by 2030.(LOCNESS)

6d. American parents tend to give enough freedom to their children. So American children can just do what he or she wants, which suit their instinct of curiosity and playing. They are given opportunities to develop their talent in all dissections, though sometime they would be ignorantly blind. As a result, most American children have happy childhood. And as they grow older, they will come to concerntrate on one or more things for the rest of their life. <u>No matter where they will finally reach, the most important thing is that they are always confident with their own decisions.</u>(WECCL)

In example 6c, the use of the "where" subordinate clause makes sense of defining and illustrating the traffic problems in urban areas. The writer uses the subordinate clause to provide more useful information. In example 6d, the "where" subordinate clause is used as a logical reasoning device as well as signaling the hypostudy that American parents give their children more freedom.

whose

Examples 7a show the use of "whose" words in prototypes in the WECCL:

7a. <u>Whose fault it is?</u> The lights go out. The music goes up. The audience shut their mouths and immerse themselves into the great love story. The beautiful fairy-like heroine turns around and gives a sweet smile on the screen. Suddenly, a vulgar rings breaks the whole atmosphere. Mobile phone! (WECCL)

In example 7a, the "whose" prototype sets the scene which makes the reader more inclined to follow the text. The writer attempts to activate the topic that the mobile phone destroys daily life to some extent by describing a scene which is familiar to most people. The question used here is more likely to build a cognitive link between the writer and the reader.

Examples 7b and 7c show the use of "whose" words in extension 2 in the LOCNESS and WECCL:

> 7b. <u>I believe that the whole concept of a National Lottery is flared, and, despite the sums donated to charity and the few big winners whose lives are genuinely improved, on the whole it has caused more misery than happiness.</u> Abolition may be too much to hope for, but I think that the system should be closely looked at before the license is renewed. (LOCNESS)
>
> 7c. <u>I have a relative whose son is a college student in a big city in China.</u> She says she bought her son a expensive mobile phone, but she could not get in touch with hi by phone most of the time. But one day she received a letter said that her son had been the "King of Short Message<sp-Massage>" because he sent 2000 or more short messages<sp-massages> during one month!(WECCL)

In example 7b, the "whose" subordinate clause provides a description and judgement of the subject *few big winners*. The writer gives his or her opinion about the National Lottery by using such a description as a support. In addition, there is a contrast between the detailed illustration of the few winners as opposed to the main theme that most people who play the National Lottery are unhappy. In example 7c, the "whose" subordinate clause is used as an attributive clause, providing a kind of description of the writer's relative.

who

Examples 8a and 8b show the use of "who" words in prototypes in the LOCNESS and WECCL:

> 8a. Another problem is that of understaffing, both on trains and at stations. This leads to an increase in fare dodging, which is now quite possible unintentionally - with ticket offices closed at both ends of the journey, and no guard, <u>who are you supposed to pay</u>? (locness)
>
> 8b. But sometimes we just complain too often. Even very trivial matters will lead into a quarrel. Sometimes parents and children seriously negotiate over the matter of dressing while or in pink. When I look back into my remote rebellious past, I can't help laughing at myself. I was so eager to show that I grew up and could decide everything. But where do I get my daily necessities? <u>Who feeds me?</u> Still my parents.(WECCL)

In example 8a, the use of the question *Who are you supposed to pay?* creates a connection between the problem and the potential consequence. The weakness of the train service may cause inadequate income from train fares. The writer uses the question to express his or her opinion that the train service has its problems. In example 8b, the use of the question *Who feeds me?* brings in the writer's opinion, based on his or her experience. The readers may naturally interact with such experience in light of the situation that the generation gap between parents and children is obvious.

Examples 8c and 8d show the use of "who" words in extension 2 in the LOCNESS and WECCL:

> 8c.Boxing, nowadays has a certain aura about it and the atmosphere is almost electric when there is a title fight. <u>The number of people who enjoy the sport far outweigh those who dislike it.</u>(LOCNESS)
>
> 8d. May be the world's competition is fierce, we must believe that a degree certificate just can reflect only one's academic achievements but not all abilities essential for successful career. <u>There are many successful people in the history who have little education.</u> What we need is the ability not the degree certification. And it is wrong to think that one's promotion is primarily decided by whoever one has obtained a graduate degree or not. (WECCL)

In example 8c, the writer attempted to use a subordinate to set a comparison between those people who like watching boxing and those who dislike it. The writer first described the situation of boxing as a great entertainment for a number of people, enhancing his or her argument by using a subordinate clause. In addition, it is clear that the topic and the writer's favourable opinion of boxing are drawn out. In example 8d, the writer tends to use a subordinate clause to express his or her opinion that a degree certificate is not as important as one's ability. The subordinate clause used here can be considered as giving the example that there are many successful people in history who did not have a degree or certification. In addition, the writer uses the subordinate clause to build a connection between the texts and the reader. The reader has to articulate such knowledge on the basis of his or her own experience. This text can be seen as a successful piece of writing. The topic and arguments are clear and logical.

<u>Whom</u>

Examples 9a show the use of "whom" as a prototype in the LOCNESS corpus:

> 9a. <u>When the person attempting suicide is crying out, whom is he or she appealing to?</u> Most of the time, he or she is appealing to his or her family or friends. What part does the family play in the matter of the person's suicide? The family is often forgotten when discussing suicide except when a writer makes the family the basis for his or her argument. (LOCNESS)

The writer attempts to build a question-answer pattern to illustrate his or her idea. The first segment *when the person attempting suicide is crying out* provides the situation or background for the second segment *whom is he or she appealing to*. The "whom" question corresponds to the event which is described in the first segment.

Examples 9b and 9c show the use of "whom" words in extension 2 in the LOCNESS and WECCL:

9b. Another problem with having a test tube baby could arise from the egg donation. <u>if an egg is donated by a friend, the donater could want rights over a child whom they may see as their own.</u> A child who was a test tube baby may grow up with identicty problems due to this. A particularly bad example of this relates to eggs taken from aborted foetus. A child growing up with the knowledge of having come from an aborted foetus - something which has never technically been alive could be left with psychological problems.(LOCNESS)

9c. Nowadays the use of mobile phone has become very popular. When you are walking in the street, varieties of mobile phones will jump into your eyes. Different people have different styles of mobile phones. Girls like some tiny and charming ones while businessmen prefer to what have may functions. Mobile phone has been used in every area of social life by different social stratums. <u>From college teachers to factory workers, from the bosses of multinational corporations to the sellsmen<sp-salesmen> on the street, all of whom may have mobile phones.</u>(WECCL)

In example 9b, the writer uses the "whom" subordinate clause to create a possibility of an event that the donors might want to keep and educate their own children. The word "whom" refers to the object *a child*. In example 9c, the word "whom" refers to the subject noun phrase a group of people, namely college teachers, factory workers, bosses, and salesmen. In this case, the subordinate clause is used to create the context, allowing the text to be more interesting.

We have discussed the examples of "wh" sentences used in their functions with reference to native and non-native speaker written corpora. In the next section, I discuss the frequency of words occurring immediately after "wh" sentences across the two corpora.

7.4.3   *Frequency of the Words after "Wh" in Interrogatives, Declaratives, and Clauses across the Two Corpora*

We have discussed the fact that frequency of exposure plays an important role in the process of SLA and affects the cognitive processes of sentence production. Corpora can provide useful information about the frequency of co-occurring words and can therefore tell us about collocational patterning in language production in native (NS) and non-native speakers (NNS). As we saw in Chapter four, this can provide teachers with useful information about aspects of the target language that their learners may still need to acquire. In order to obtain information about the words that collocate most frequently with the three types of "wh" words in the written language produced by NS and NNSs, we will now look at frequency lists for their most common collocations. As with the previous chapters, we will look at the words which occur immediately after the "wh" word. This is therefore an investigation of both colligation and collocation and the ultimate aim is to identify the linguistic features that are semantically associated with the particular "wh" words in each corpus. We have chosen to look at the words immediately following the "wh" words as this often gives us a clear picture of the grammatical-lexical words that the "wh" words are particularly likely to combine with.

<u>What</u>

In the following sections, we look at the frequencies of words occurring immediately after "what" in interrogatives, declaratives and subordinate clauses. The findings will tell us the differences between native speakers and non-native speakers in terms of the patterns of words and in terms of which lexico-grammatical items tend to be over or under-used by non-native speakers in comparison with native speakers.

Table 7.15 shows the frequencies of the words occurring immediately after "what" in interrogatives across the two (native and non-native speaker) written corpora.

LOCNESS			WECCL		
word	**No.**	**%**	**word**	**No.**	**%**
is	15	25.42%	is	41	27.52%
do	7	11.86%	about	14	9.40%
about	4	6.78%	do	11	7.39%
can	3	5.08%	should	9	6.04%
makes	3	5.08%	does	9	6.04%
kind	3	5.08%	will	9	6.04%
part	2	3.39%	can	5	3.36%
drives	2	3.39%	kind	5	3.36%
next	2	3.39%	makes	5	3.36%
more	2	3.39%	shall	5	3.36%
does	2	3.39%	are	3	2.01%
am	2	3.39%	would	3	2.01%
should	1	1.70%	can	3	2.01%
could	1	1.70%	might	2	1.34%
cost	1	1.70%	happened	2	1.34%
type	1	1.70%	you	2	1.34%
isn't	1	1.70%	the	2	1.34%
good	1	1.70%	could	1	0.67%
and	1	1.70%	cost	1	0.67%
are	1	1.70%	type	1	0.67%

Table 7.15 Comparison of the frequencies and percentage of different words occurring after "what" in interrogatives

As Table 7.15 shows, 'be' verbs and lexical items occur more frequently than auxiliaries and modals across the two corpora. On the other hand, the LOCNESS has more occurrences of lexical items in the top ten than the WECCL. (The LOCNESS has six while the WECCL only has two). This reflects the wider variety of word choices that native speakers make. These word choices include verbs, adjectives, nouns, and adjectives. Some examples are as follows:

```
What good will it do me? (LOCNESS)
What causes such disturbance? (WECCL)
```

As we might expect, the writings from non-native speakers tend to be more conservative in terms of the word choices. The most common words occurring after "what" in interrogatives in the WECCL are grammatical words, for example *what is ...* and *what about....* Even though these are abstracted from written texts, they have many characteristics of the types of on-line production that we saw in Chapter 6. These findings are probably simply a reflection of the fact that native speakers have a wider vocabulary than non-native speakers.

When they do use lexical items, non-native speakers are likely to use the pattern *what+ lexical items* which can be categorized into two functions. The first refers to asking what the consequence of an event or activity was. These include question openings such as *what makes...* and *what happened....* The second refers to asking for a detailed classification of an event or activity. These include question openings such as *what type...* or *what kind...* or *what part....* These patterns can also be found in textbooks, and it is more likely that non-native speakers store these patterns in their long- term memory.

It is interesting to note that the use of the negative feature *isn't* is found only in the LOCNESS. Apart from the reason that native speakers have a wider variety and vocabulary size, in most cases, they are more flexible in choosing the patterns that are appropriate to the context. On the other hand, non-native speakers tend to use the patterns that are stored in their long-term memory to build a sentence. For some patterns, for example the negative form, non-native speakers do not appear to be very confident in using it because the form might relate to a different usage in previous held knowledge.

This may suggest that native speaker writers are more flexible in choosing grammatical-lexical items and their use of them is highly associated to the text context. On the other hand, non-native speaker writers may be more likely to focus on the sentence structure rather than the whole paragraph. Complications of this kind may lead to difficulties in non-native speakers' writing.

Frequency of the words occurring immediately after "what" in declaratives across the two corpora

Table 7.16 shows the frequencies of the words occurring immediately after "what" declaratives across the two corpora.

LOCNESS			WECCL		
word	No.	%	word	No.	%
a	1	100%	a	25	100%

Table 7.16 Comparison of the frequencies and percentage of different words occurring after "what" in declaratives

According to Table 7.16, the "what" declaratives occur predominantly in the WECCL. The most frequent word (in fact the only word) is the word *a*, indicating a high frequency of exclamatory expressions. For example:

```
what a stupid unethical theory it is.(LOCNESS)
What a great invention mobile phone is!(WECCL)
```

Because there is only one word occurring immediately after 'what' in declaratives, it is necessary to look further to the right of the word in order to identify any variation between the two corpora. If we look at the next two words occurring after the word "what", it is interesting to note that in the majority of cases native speakers use declaratives in negative situations to express a strong view on an event. For example, in the LOCNESS corpus we have the line: '*what a stupid unethical theory it is*'. On the other hand, non-native speakers almost never produce negative sentences of this sort. Instead, they tend to use declaratives to express positive ideas, which are sometimes used as a kind of compliment, such as '*what a great invention mobile phone is!*' (WECCL). Such positive usages were also found in the EFL textbook data (see Chapter 5).

Feifei Zhang

Frequency of the words occurring immediately after "what" in subordinate clauses across the two corpora

Table 7.17 shows the frequencies of the words occurring immediately after "what" in subordinate clauses across the two corpora.

LOCNESS			WECCL		
word	No.	%	word	No.	%
is	46	16.67%	is	98	19.52%
he	29	10.51%	they	58	11.55%
they	23	8.33%	we	55	10.96%
the	20	7.25%	you	36	7.17%
it	15	5.43%	the	33	6.57%
to	8	2.90%	their	26	5.18%
a	7	2.54%	I	19	3.78%
would	7	2.54%	he	12	2.39%
we	5	1.81%	to	9	1.79%
was	5	1.81%	happened	9	1.79%
happened	4	1.45%	children	8	1.59%
you	4	1.45%	makes	8	1.59%
will	4	1.45%	are	7	1.39%
has	4	1.45%	will	7	1.39%
might	4	1.45%	she	7	1.39%
this	3	1.09%	parents	6	1.20%
could	3	1.09%	would	6	1.20%
she	3	1.09%	should	5	1.00%
had	3	1.09%	a	5	1.00%
man	3	1.09%	was	4	0.80%

Table 7.17 Comparison of the frequencies and percentage of different words occurring after "what" in subordinate clauses

As Table 7.17 shows, compared to the LOCNESS, the WECCL has a wider range of both grammatical words and lexical items. This is interesting as it is the opposite of what was found with the interrogatives. There the native speakers were found to use a wider variety of forms and this was attributed to their larger vocabulary size. Here the non-natives speakers are using a wider variety of forms. The only explanation that we can offer for this is that there are strong conventions in English about which words tend to follow 'what' in subordinate clauses and that native speakers are more aware of these conventions than non-native speakers. It thus appears to be a relatively restricted construction in English. This reflects the tension between creativity and convention in language learning. In some cases learning a language involves increasing the amount of expressions one uses, whilst in others it involves restricting one's usage patterns to those that may be deemed conventional. Both of these types of knowledge are likely to be acquired through language use. As we can see here, the words learners choose reflect the idea that language structures emerge from language use. The sentences are constructed on the basis of a mixture of the over-extended and the creativity of language patterns. As we will see below, transfer from Chinese may also have been a factor here; the sentence can be traced from a Chinese-English translation.

The verb 'be' occurs the most frequently across the two corpora. Examples are shown as follows:

```
What is needed is a large increase in road tax and tax on fuels to make
car travel more expensive. (LOCNESS)
We still lack of social experience and sometimes can't tell what is right,
we still need our parents' help. (WECCL)
```

The WECCL has more lexical items than the LOCNESS, most of them are nouns. This may suggest that non-native speakers tend to use nouns or noun phrases to indicate a main clause. This finding is discussed below.

It was also found that modals are used more frequently in subordinate 'what' clauses in the LOCNESS than in the WECCL. The reason for this may be that non-native speakers are not very confident in using modals in their writing. This is in accordance with what we found for interrogatives. All of this suggests that modals are difficult for non-native speakers, and that they tend to be avoided, for example:

```
It is against human nature to stop at this stage and ask, should I
introduce what could be the greatest medical discovery of our lifetime
when I am not 100% sure of the consequences. (LOCNESS)
It is better for them to know what their children are thinking about
than to teach their children what can be thought about and what can't
be. (WECCL)
```

Apart from modals, it is interesting to note that non-native speakers tend to use more pronouns or nouns at the beginning of the main clause in subordinate clauses such as *That is what parents should do* and *What we do so is to make the public pay special attention to the environmental protection*. In contrast, in the WECCL, the main information does not necessarily appear at the beginning of the sentence. This contrast is illustrated in the following two sentences:

```
What I would like to see, would be consistent train journeys to major
destinations displayed and advertised. (LOCNESS)
I think if we can pick up the rubbish what we see and put it into the
rubbish box. (WECCL)
```

It was found that the phrase *'what's more'* occurs in both corpora, where it is used as a type of conjunction. It suggests that the phrase "what's more" is used more often in academic writing, for example:

```
...Kuwait - and what's more: the operation had the full backing of the
Security Council of the United Nations. (LOCNESS)
What is more, your writing will be improved as well. (WECCL)
```

As we have just seen, the patterns of behaviour differ across both corpora and the differences for extension 2 were almost the complete reverse of the question form. In the case of interrogatives, native speakers tend to use a wider range of word choices, particularly in grammatical-lexical patterns, whereas non-native speakers are likely to use only grammatical items. Such differences were also found in elicited sentences and EFL textbooks. The question forms in non-native speakers' writings are similar to those found in their on-line production. This may suggest that the written texts that non-native speakers produced may be influenced by previous examples that are stored in their long-term memory.

To sum up, in the case of subordinate clauses, non-native speakers use a lot of grammatical-lexical items, in particular nouns. This may suggest that non-native speakers use nouns or noun phrases as the beginning of the main clause, highlighting the topic. The reason for this might be that, in Chinese, subordinate clauses are hardly ever used unless an event or activity is emphasized. This can also be seen as a transfer from L1. In addition, it may suggest that non-native speakers are not familiar with ellipsis and substitution and how main topics are initiated without using main clauses that contain noun or noun phrases.

How

In the following sections, we look at the frequencies of words occurring immediately after "how" in interrogatives, declaratives, and subordinate clauses. The analysis focuses on patterns with types of words that tend to be over-or under-used by native speakers and non-native speakers. We also compare the behaviours of the word "how" with the word "what".

Frequency of the words occurring immediately after "how" in interrogatives across the two corpora

Table 7.18 shows the frequencies of the words occurring after "how" in interrogatives across the two corpora.

LOCNESS			WECCL		
word	No.	%	**word**	No.	%
can	6	19.35%	to	35	29.91%
could	5	16.13%	can	28	23.93%
do	3	9.68%	do	7	5.98%
much	3	9.68%	much	7	5.98%
is	2	6.45%	about	6	5.13%
many	2	6.45%	should	5	4.27%
about	1	3.23%	could	4	3.42%
are	1	3.23%	does	4	3.42%
did	1	3.23%	are	3	2.56%
different	1	3.23%	would	3	2.56%
does	1	3.23%	many	3	2.56%
fair	1	3.23%	will	3	2.56%
far	1	3.23%	did	2	1.71%
has	1	3.23%	is	2	1.71%
in	1	3.23%	was	1	0.85%
should	1	3.23%	in	1	0.85%
			fair	1	0.85%
			different	1	0.85%
			fast	1	0.85%

Table 7.18 Comparison of the frequencies and percentage of different words occurring after "how" in interrogatives

According to Table 7.18, the preposition 'to' in the WECCL is the most frequent word across the two corpora. It is interesting to note that the phrase how to occurs most frequently in the WECCL while, in contrast, the LOCNESS does not have this phrase. Again, such a phrase is likely to be found in the on-line production rather than written texts. The phrase "how to" is more likely translated from Chinese, indicating situations of dealing with or solving some questions or problems, for example:

```
So, how to deal with such a generation gap? (WECCL)
```

In the case of grammatical words, the WECCL has a higher frequency of occurrences than those in the LOCNESS. Grammatical words in "how" interrogatives are somewhat over-used. It seems that non-native speakers over-generalise the use of interrogatives, and are largely unaware of the restrictions and contexts. Examples are shown as follows:

```
And how are they communicating? (LOCNESS)
how is your mood now? (WECCL)
But how does Prozac accomplish this? (LOCNESS)
How do they face it? (LOCNESS)
How do you think of those things? (WECCL)
How did I get there? (LOCNESS)
How do you the "freedom" the children have? (WECCL)
```

As expected, there are occurrences of quantifying words (e.g. much, many) and measuring words (long, fast, different and far). Such combinations can be considered to be somewhat formulaic in that the meanings are determined by the ways in which the words are combined. This may suggest that language is restricted in its collocation and colligation. In addition, L1 transfer may be a factor which brings these words together, for example:

```
How far would you go to be the best athlete in the world? (LOCNESS)
How about your examination today? (WECCL)
How about those low-mark students? (WECCL)
how nice, Ah Rong, you like to walk too? (WECCL)
How much? (WECCL)
```

In terms of modals, native speaker writers tend to use the word to refer to a kind of blaming, for example, How could we ever ban a sport as full of skill and traditional values. Non-native speaker writers are more likely to use the word 'should', which is used as a way of asking or requesting a suggestion or solution, such as how should we bridge the generation gap? This suggests that language is rich in semantic prosodies, and it seems commonly to occur in written contexts. Examples are shown below:

```
then how can we, as civilians, trust in them? (LOCNESS)
how can we solve the problem? (WECCL)
```

Frequency of the words after "how" in declaratives across the two corpora

Table 7.19 shows the frequencies of the words occurring after "how" in declaratives across the two sets of data.

LOCNESS			WECCL		
word	**No.**	**%**	**word**	**No.**	**%**
restricted	1	20.00%	terrible	8	22.22%
fruitless	1	20.00%	convenient	4	11.11%
wrong	1	20.00%	wonderful	4	11.11%
pleased	1	20.00%	nice	3	8.33%
passive	1	20.00%	stupid	2	5.56%
			excited	1	2.78%
			cruel	1	2.78%
			useful	1	2.78%
			good	1	2.78%
			marvelous	1	2.78%
			cheap	1	2.78%
			boring	1	2.78%
			awkward	1	2.78%
			angry	1	2.78%
			glad	1	2.78%
			important	1	2.78%
			eager	1	2.78%
			worried	1	2.78%
			moving	1	2.78%
			annoying	1	2.78%

Table 7.19 Comparison of the frequencies and percentage of
different words occurring after "how" in declaratives

According to Table 7.19, the WECCL has a wider range of adjectives than those in the LOCNESS. In addition, in the LOCNESS, adjectives which have a negative meaning occur more than those with positive meanings. For example:

```
How passive are they. (LOCNESS)
How fruitless and destructive it all is. (LOCNESS)
```

This may suggest that declaratives are more often used to express negative feelings or emotions by native speakers in written texts. On the other hand, adjectives which have positive meanings occur predominantly in the WECCL, suggesting that non-native speakers, to a large extent, use declaratives to express positive feelings or emotions. Examples are shown as follows:

```
How convenient!(WECCL)
How stupid your children handle with an election. (WECCL)
how nice. (WECCL)
How wonderful it would be(WECCL)
How terrible it was. (WECCL)
```

This phenomenon may suggest that non-native speakers somewhat over-generalize the rules of declaratives, in particular in written texts. This difference can be found in EFL textbooks (see Chapter 5). It is likely that textbook writers carefully select the text resources that are somewhat artificial compared with native speakers' use. For second language acquisition, it might be a good idea for some adjectives with their antonyms to be provided, allowing learners to have more choices in what to use. This is similar to what we saw in the section for the word 'what', in that native speakers tend to use 'what' declaratives to express a negative meaning, such as "what an awful day!" while non-native speakers are more likely to use such words to express a positive meaning, such as "what a lovely house".

Frequency of the words after "how" in subordinate clauses across the two corpora

Table 7.20 shows the frequencies of the words occurring after "how" in subordinate clauses across the two corpora.

LOCNESS			WECCL		
word	**No.**	**%**	**word**	**No.**	**%**
long	39	15.66%	to	133	59.91%
our	36	14.46%	important	9	4.05%
even	27	10.84%	much	7	3.15%
because	14	5.62%	can	6	2.70%
these	12	4.82%	you	5	2.25%
more	9	3.61%	far	5	2.25%
well	9	3.61%	the	4	1.80%
cheating	8	3.21%	many	4	1.80%
someone	7	2.81%	we	3	1.35%
to	6	2.41%	people	3	1.35%
that	5	2.01%	I	3	1.35%
animals	5	2.01%	old	3	1.35%
pleased	5	2.01%	it	2	0.90%
sorry	5	2.01%	their	2	0.90%
importantly	4	1.61%	they	2	0.90%
such	3	1.20%	useful	2	0.90%
old	2	0.80%	terrible	2	0.90%
was	2	0.80%	small	1	0.45%
your	2	0.80%	severely	1	0.45%
everyone	2	0.80%	fast	1	0.45%

Table 7.20 Comparison of the frequencies and percentage of different words occurring after "how" in subordinate clauses

According to Table 7.20, the word *to* is the most frequently used word in the WECCL, suggesting that non-native speakers use the phrase "*how to*" to link the main clause while native speakers tend to use the qualifying phrase "how long" to link the main clause. This is similar to what we found in "how" interrogatives, for example:

```
Human brains still work out how to build the computers, how to program
them and, more importantly, how to control them. (LOCNESS)
Because the people around you speak the same language, you can learn
how to speak it easily. (WECCL)
```

It is interesting to note that quite a few lexical items, such as *terrible, important, small,* and *fast* are found in both corpora. For example:

```
Deciding whether it should have been introduced or not is very much a
personal thing and depends on how importantly you rate the points I have
emphasized in this essay. (LOCNESS)
Now you know how important the mobile telephone is, for your life, for
your success.(WECCL)
```

This suggests that both native and non-native speakers store these phrases as a fixed expression which combines the knowledge of using "how" declarative and subordinate clauses.

It is also found that in the LOCNESS, pronouns such as *someone* or *everyone* are used to refer to a single person who is unknown or every person. For example:

```
The woman tells how everyone in Argos repents for their crime, not just
those who were present when it took place. (LOCNESS)
Men were gentlemen in the 60's, felt that the woman was someone special
and usually these men had parents with values that taught their children
the proper traditional techniques on how someone should (and should not)
act on a date. (LOCNESS)
```

This is a common and professional use in written academic writing. In contrast, non-native speakers use pronouns such as *I, you,* or *we* which tend not to be used as frequently in written discourse by native speakers. Why would non-native speakers use more pronouns than native speakers? One of the reasons of this might be that the writing tasks are more likely associated with everyday life. Non-native speakers found it easier to construct the sentences by using their own experiences.

The comparison of the findings of the word "how" and the word "what" gives us a great deal of information about the ways in which native and non-native speakers of English vary in their usage patterns. In the case of "what" interrogatives, native speakers use more lexical items while non-native speakers use more grammatical items. One reason for this could be that native speakers have a larger vocabulary, while non-native speakers appear to over-generalize the rules of interrogatives.

In the case of "how" interrogatives, both native speakers and non-native speakers use grammatical items more than lexical items. For declaratives, it is clear that native speakers are likely to use the sentences to express a negative opinion, while non-native speakers tend to use them to express a positive opinion or emotion in both of the words. So why does there appear to be such a difference? As we saw above, one reason for this could be that non-native speakers get to learn a language largely via textbooks, and the language they learn is somehow artificial compared to that of native speakers as they have more opportunity to access authentic language.

We see a different picture in the case of subordinate clauses because both native speakers and non-native speakers use the words in similar ways. Both sets of speakers are more likely to use more grammatical words than lexical items in the case of "what" subordinate clauses, while lexical items are used predominantly by both native speakers and non-native speakers with regard to the "how" subordinate clauses. One possible explanation may be that language is full of restricted collocation and colligation and both native speakers and non-native speakers are aware of these language conventions and apply them correctly. It is also found that non-native speakers are particularly good at subordinate clauses. One of the reasons might be that the subordinate clauses are considered to be one of the most important grammatical points that both EFL teachers and textbooks focus on, and it may be because these subordinate clauses are studied explicitly under grammar.

When

We now turn to look at words immediately following the word 'when'. We will see the findings with respect to the behaviours of such words, as well as the similarities and differences between native speakers and non-native speakers' usage. The comparison will also be made between the interrogative and subordinate clause and with the behaviour of previous words.

Frequency of the words after "when" in interrogatives across the two corpora

Table 7.21 shows the frequencies of the words occurring after "when" in interrogatives across the two corpora.

LOCNESS			WECCL		
word	**No.**	**%**	**word**	**No.**	**%**
does	2	25.00%	they	2	66.67%
they	2	25.00%	does	1	33.33%
the	1	12.50%			
you	1	12.50%			
that	1	12.50%			

Table 7.21 Comparison of the frequencies and percentage of different
words occurring after "when" in interrogatives

As Table 7.21 shows, the two corpora share two words (*does* and *they*) in the top six. The LOCNESS has a relatively wider variety of words, including pronouns and articles. Examples are shown as follows:

```
When the pound sterling is taken over by the ECU? (LOCNESS)
When they start to eat? (WECCL)
```

Feifei Zhang

Frequency of the words after "when" in subordinate clauses across the two corpora

Table 7.22 shows the frequencies of the words occurring after "when" in subordinate clauses across the two corpora.

LOCNESS			WECCL		
word	No.	%	word	No.	%
the	108	23.23%	you	200	23.28%
he	79	16.99%	we	139	16.18%
it	40	8.60%	they	99	11.53%
they	37	7.96%	I	94	10.94%
a	34	7.31%	the	58	6.75%
you	21	4.52%	he	34	3.96%
people	18	3.87%	it	24	2.79%
there	15	3.23%	a	18	2.10%
I	14	3.01%	children	13	1.51%
one	9	1.94%	your	12	1.40%
she	9	1.94%	there	10	1.16%
an	8	1.72%	people	8	0.93%
their	7	1.51%	my	8	0.93%
we	7	1.51%	she	8	0.93%
this	5	1.08%	their	6	0.70%
in	4	0.86%	the	6	0.70%
faced	3	0.65%	in	6	0.70%
asked	3	0.65%	someone	5	0.58%
his	3	0.65%	something	5	0.58%
both	3	0.65%	one	5	0.58%

Table 7.22 Comparison of the frequencies and percentage of different words occurring after "when" in subordinate clauses

According to Table 7.22, both corpora have relatively high frequencies of pronouns. This suggests that this is an area where learners do not experience difficulties. The corpora share three pronouns in the top six (*you, they,* and *he*). For example:

```
When I receive a paper letter from my friend, I feel very happy and
warm. I can feel that my friends is<gr-are> caring about me, and I am
not lonely. (WECCL)
Paul Bennett, a young striker at York City died during a match a few
years ago when he swallowed his tounge.(LOCNESS)
```

232

In terms of lexical items, two verbs (*faced* and *asked*) are found in the top 20 while there are none in the WECCL. This may suggest that non-native speakers lack the knowledge of writing sentences with the ellipsis of nouns or noun phrases in the subordinate clauses. The explanation might be that the only type of subordinate clause in Chinese highlights the main topic which usually is nouns or noun phrases.

For example:

```
When faced with large traffic jams there is the tendancy to find shortcuts
and this can lead to heavy traffic through rural villages or residential
areas.(LOCNESS)
```

It has also been found that pronouns such as *someone* or *something* occur in the WECCL, while there are none in the LOCNESS. For example:

```
When someone looks pretty or handsome in special clothes, we will tell
him or her you are "Ku Bi Le". (WECCL)
It applies to situations in which the inferior bears fear to talk to the
superior for change when something wrong happens.(WECCL)
```

Some words occurring with a high frequency in the LOCNESS have a relatively low frequency in the WECCL, for example, the words *the*, *one*, and *a*, and vice versa, for instance the word *I*. This could be because the vocabulary size of L2 learners is smaller than that of L1 learners. Some words rarely occur in some collocations and constructions. For example:

```
When the dogs finally find a scent the hunt begins. (LOCNESS)
Occasionaly foxes to manage to escape or hide but in most cases when a fox
is spotted once the dogs reach it, it will be torn to pieces. (LOCNESS)
```

The word *there* occurs in a higher frequency across the two corpora, indicating a condition of a situation. Clearly, we can see that the sentence contains two separate segments: one segment refers to a situation, and the other suggests a solution to the situation. Examples are shown as follows:

```
During the period when there was no computer, we use paper cards. (WECCL)
The Unions can pressure employers on matters of wages and working
conditions when there is a recession on, but they are powerless in
economic crisis. As unemployment rose, wages were held down in the name
of competition. (LOCNESS)
```

In the case of subordinate clauses, the use of words is associated highly with the context and content of the texts. This may cause difficulties for EFL learners in that they need to be aware of the correct form in a different register.

As we saw from the discussion, "when" subordinate clauses are more complicated if compared with "what" and "how" subordinate clauses. One reason for this could be related to the meanings of these individual words. "What" and "how" subordinate clauses are more likely to include the extra information used to decorate or emphasize the main clause, while "when" subordinate clauses contain two segments, namely, the condition and a solution.

Why

In the following sections, we will look at the behaviour of "why" interrogative and subordinate clauses. We will also look at the similarities and differences of the usage between native speakers and non-native speakers, as well as the behaviours with previous words.

Frequency of the words after "why" in interrogatives across the two corpora

Table 7.23 shows the frequencies of the words occurring after "why" in interrogatives across the two corpora.

LOCNESS			WECCL		
word	**No.**	**%**	**word**	**No.**	**%**
should	16	27.12%	do	19	19.19%
do	10	16.95%	don't	16	16.16%
not	7	11.86%	not	13	13.13%
is	4	6.78%	does	7	7.07%
can't	3	5.08%	not	6	6.06%
shouldn't	2	3.39%	can't	6	6.06%
am	2	3.39%	should	4	4.04%
make	2	3.39%	people	3	3.03%
stop	2	3.39%	it	3	3.03%
for	1	1.69%	did	2	2.02%
worsen	1	1.69%	I	2	2.02%
get	1	1.69%	are	2	2.02%
go	1	1.69%	can	2	2.02%
does	1	1.69%	have	2	2.02%
was	1	1.69%	language	1	1.01%
aren't	1	1.69%	my	1	1.01%
are	1	1.69%	shouldn't	1	1.01%
don't	1	1.69%	am	1	1.01%
weren't	1	1.69%	your	1	1.01%

Table 7.23 Comparison of the frequencies and percentage of different words occurring after "why" in interrogatives

According to Table 7.23, the word *do* has the highest occurrence in the WECCL, with approximately 16%, while The LOCNESS has the highest occurrence of the modal word "should", with approximately 27%. This may suggest that non-native speakers are likely to use the auxiliary and native speakers prefer to use the modal in interrogatives. The explanation for this difference could be that "why" interrogatives indicate a polarity intonation which non-native speakers have not picked up. Examples are shown as follows:

```
So why do we still insist on traveling on the road? (LOCNESS)
Why did you copy others? (WECCL)
```

Lexical items are relatively few. The negative form also has a relatively high occurrence across the two corpora. For the word "why", both native speakers and non-native speakers have grasped the negative form here. This may have something to do with the influence of the textbooks as well as the negative polarity of the word "why". Examples are shown as follows:

```
Why not gays in the military? (LOCNESS)
So why can't we have portable <sp-pocketable> telephone? (WECCL)
```

In the case of lexical items, native speaker writers tend to use verbs after the word "why" such as *get*, *make*, and *stop* while there are none in the non-native speakers' writing. Instead, a few abstract nouns such as *people* and *language* are found. The reason for this difference could be that there is L1 transfer. In Chinese, abstract nouns are more likely to be used after the question word "why". The main clauses are linked to the word "why", indicating the reasons or explanations of problems.

Examples of lexical items are shown as follows:

```
Why make life worse than it already is? (LOCNESS)
Why language is created? (WECCL)
```

Frequency of the words immediately after "why" in subordinate clauses across the two corpora

Table 7.24 shows the frequencies of the words occurring immediately after "why" in subordinate clauses across the two corpora.

LOCNESS			WECCL		
word	**No.**	**%**	**word**	**No.**	**%**
they	16	14.81%	I	12	16.44%
people	11	10.19%	the	9	12.33%
the	10	9.26%	they	8	10.96%
we	7	6.48%	we	6	8.22%
it	7	6.48%	you	3	4.11%
he	7	6.48%	it	3	4.11%
there	5	4.63%	there	2	2.74%
many	4	3.70%	generation	2	2.74%
this	4	3.70%	children	2	2.74%
is	3	2.78%	don't	2	2.74%
a	3	2.78%	their	2	2.74%
these	2	1.85%	a	2	2.74%
boxing	2	1.85%	parents	2	2.74%
praying	2	1.85%	people	2	2.74%
would	2	1.85%	he	2	2.74%
so	2	1.85%	do	2	2.74%
I	1	0.93%	some	1	1.37%
depends	1	0.93%	waiting	1	1.37%
work	1	0.93%	her	1	1.37%

Table 7.24 Comparison of the frequencies and percentage of different
words occurring after "why" in subordinate clauses

There are clearly differences in the way that native speaker writers and non-native speaker writers have decided to choose the words occurring after the word "why". As Table 7.24 shows, apart from pronouns frequently occurring across both corpora, in terms of lexical items, verbs in the LOCNESS (*boxing, praying, depends,* and *work*) have a higher frequency than those in the WECCL (*waiting*). It seems that the gerund as a grammatical point specifically occurs in "why" subordinate clauses in native speakers' writing. Why do non-native speakers not use the same pattern? One of the reasons for this could be that native speakers simply have a wider range of vocabulary and they are more aware of the restricted collocation and colligation. Examples are shown as follows:

```
All the suggestions I have made have problems and this is why we still
have problems on our roads today. (LOCNESS)
Reading in English can help us to understand why we say a sentence like
this, not that. (WECCL)
```

It was found that only one abstract noun (*people*) was found in the LOCNESS in the top 20, while both general nouns (*children*, and *parents*) and abstract nouns (*people*, and *generation*) are found in the WECCL, for example:

```
There are various reasons why people in the UK may decide to stop eating
beef. (LOCNESS)
They should think that why children are so anger. (WECCL)
```

It has also been found that the word "*I*" occurs more frequently in the WECCL than it does in the LOCNESS. This may suggest that non-native speakers are not aware of the extent to which the use of the first person pronoun is acceptable in academic writing. There is only one negative form "don't" which occurs in the WECCL. It seems that the negative form is somehow under-used by non-native speakers in this particular construction, and that they are perhaps taught to avoid it.

Compared with the previous words, "what", "how" and "when", the word "why" seems to have a wider range of word choices used by both native and non-native speakers. Several grammatical choices of joining a main clause to a subordinate clause, such as with negative forms, are used quite often in interrogatives and subordinate clauses, while gerunds of nouns becoming verbs are used in subordinate clauses. Although such grammatical choices take more evidence into account in their analysis, it certainly sheds some light on what the authentic language is and how writers express the idea with certain structures. For example, the negative form of the "why" interrogative indicates an intonation of blaming or questioning. This is definitely something of which language teachers should be aware.

Which

We now turn to the behavior of the word "which" in both interrogatives and subordinate clauses. The following sections investigate the similarities and differences between native speakers and non-native speakers in terms of the words occurring after the word "which". We also compare how the behavior of "which" differs from the previous words.

Frequency of the words after "which" in interrogatives across the two corpora

Table 7.25 shows the frequencies of the words occurring after "which" in interrogatives across the two corpora.

LOCNESS			WECCL		
word	No.	%	word	No.	%
is	1	100%	is	8	29.63%
			one	7	25.93%
			may	5	18.52%
			skill	3	11.11%
			would	2	7.41%
			job	1	3.70%
			to	1	3.70%

Table 7.25 Comparison of the frequencies and percentage of different words occurring after "which" in interrogatives

As Table 7.25 shows, compared to the WECCL, only the word *is* occurring after "which" interrogatives is found in the LOCNESS. This may suggest that non-native speakers somehow over-use the interrogative form in written texts. Examples are shown as follows:

```
Which is good news for the majority of the British public? (LOCNESS)
Which is No. 1 in English study? (WECCL)
```

The WECCL has a wider variety, containing 'be' verbs, modals, prepositions, and lexical items. This may suggest that non-native speakers make substantial use of the word *"which"* in the form of interrogatives in written texts as opposed to the fact that it is more likely to be used in spoken contexts. Another possible explanation could be L1 transfer. The sentences can be traced back to Chinese-English translation. Examples are shown below:

```
Which one do you prefer? (WECCL)
Which one do you choose? (WECCL)
```

Frequency of the words after "which" in subordinate clauses across the two corpora

Table 7.26 shows the frequencies of the words occurring after "which" in subordinate clauses across the two corpora.

LOCNESS			WECCL		
word	**No.**	**%**	**word**	**No.**	**%**
is	34	13.99%	is	86	17.34%
would	14	5.76%	can	52	10.48%
are	13	5.35%	are	35	7.06%
the	12	4.94%	they	20	4.03%
have	11	4.53%	we	19	3.83%
has	11	4.53%	will	17	3.43%
can	10	4.12%	has	16	3.23%
will	9	3.70%	makes	11	2.22%
may	8	3.29%	was	9	1.81%
could	7	2.88%	have	9	1.81%
in	6	2.47%	you	8	1.61%
was	6	2.47%	means	8	1.61%
it	4	1.65%	would	7	1.41%
I	3	1.23%	were	6	1.21%
means	3	1.23%	may	6	1.21%
they	3	1.23%	way	6	1.21%
many	3	1.23%	I	5	1.01%
our	3	1.23%	do	5	1.01%
must	3	1.23%	changes	5	1.01%

Table 7.26 Comparison of the frequencies and percentage of different words occurring after "which" in subordinate clauses

Table7.26 shows that modals have a relatively high frequency in terms of grammatical words across both corpora. For modals, the word "*would*" in the LOCNESS has a higher frequency than in the WECCL. The word "*can*" in the WECCL has a higher frequency than in the LOCNESS. For example:

```
The release of exhaust fumes from our vehicles such as C.F.C.s and CO our
depleting the ozone layer which could have disastrous global consequences
in years to come. (LOCNESS)
```

```
Opinions often vary on the new and pop things between parents and
children, such as PC-games, fashionable clothes, pop music, lap-tops,
Dinks, which can lead to the widened gap.(WECCL)
```

Here we come back to the problem of modals that we had before. In the case of "which" subordinate clauses, modals are more likely to be used as a kind of suggestion or an alternative solution for an event, while non-native speakers are more likely to use modals to explain something with positive credit that they strongly believe in. This may also suggest that non-native speakers are not aware of the intonation and extension of the meaning from the modal verbs. This is similar to what we found in "how" interrogatives.

Both corpora have almost the same distribution in terms of grammatical words. The word "*is*" has the most frequent occurrence across the two corpora. For example:

```
This leads to an increase in fare dodging, which is now quite possible
unintentionally - with ticket offices closed at both ends of the journey…
(LOCNESS)
Listening in NMET takes a higher percent, which is just a simple exam
of that.(LOCNESS)
```

The article "*the*" occurs a few times in the LOCNESS while not at all in the WECCL. The reason for this could be that non-native speakers have problems with the definite article. In other words, this is also caused by L1-L2 transfer because there are no articles in the Chinese language.

The WECCL has more pronouns than those in the LOCNESS. For example, "*they* and *we*" in the WECCL have a higher frequency than in the LOCNESS. This again may suggest that non-native speakers are not aware of how to use pronouns in different contexts, particularly in academic writing, for example:

```
Nobody wants a concrete jungle for a country. There is though an optimum
balance which I believe has not yet been reached. (LOCNESS)
Generally speaking, I do not use many new expressions which my parents'
generation do not understand. (WECCL)
```

Non-native speakers use more lexical items than native speakers, in particular they tend to make use of a lot of verbs (*means*, *changes*, and *makes*). This is used to indicate certain degrees of consequences for the main clauses. The possible explanation for this could be that the verbs non-native speakers choose have something to do with the purpose of highlighting topics, for example:

```
…which means construction is stopped until further time when resources
and money again become readily available. (LOCNESS)
It also is the time in which children's character comes into being.
(WECCL)
```

With the analysis discussed above, we can see that the behavior of the word "which" is quite similar to the word "what", although native speakers hardly ever produce "which" interrogatives in written texts. At a theoretical level, such a gathering of words cannot fully explain the behavior of the word "which" used in interrogative and subordinate clauses in general because the texts that are abstracted here are either context-based or topic-given. However, at a practical level, it is useful for language teachers to understand how the word is used in certain contexts and with certain topics. Non-native speakers seem to stick to the spoken structure of "which" interrogatives in the written format. This is similar to what we found in "what" interrogatives. In terms of subordinate clauses, compared with native speakers, non-native speakers tend to use a few verbs to emphasize a kind of degree of consequence for the main clauses. This is different from the previous words.

Where

We now turn to the behavior of the word "where" in interrogatives and subordinate clauses. The identifiable patterns of the word "where" are set to investigate the similarities and differences between native speakers and non-native speakers who tend to over or under-use grammatical-lexical items. We also compare the behaviour of "where" with the previous words.

Frequency of the words after "where" in interrogatives across the two corpora

Table 7.27 shows the frequencies of the words occurring after "where" in interrogatives across the two corpora.

LOCNESS			WECCL		
word	**No.**	**%**	**word**	**No.**	**%**
would	4	33.33%	do	3	42.86%
is	3	25.00%	is	2	28.57%
do	2	16.67%	can	2	28.57%
he	1	8.33%			
she	1	8.33%			
will	1	8.33%			

Table 7.27 Comparison of the frequencies and percentage of different words occurring after "where" in interrogatives

According to Table 7.27, the LOCNESS has a relatively wider range of words than those in the WECCL. Compared to the LOCNESS, non-native speakers seem not to use this word in written texts. Only grammatical words are found across the two corpora. Modals, auxiliaries, and be verbs occur across the two corpora. Pronouns are not found in the WECCL. Why are there such differences? One reason for this could again be that the vocabulary size of L2 speakers is smaller than that of L1 speakers. Non-native speakers have not grasped the interrogative form.

Examples are shown as follows:

```
Where would it stop? (LOCNESS)
```

```
Then, where can we be educated? (WECCL)
where is it all going? (LOCNESS)
Where are you now? (WECCL)
where do I come from? (WECCL)
```

As the data reveals, the word "where" is less frequently used in written contexts. Native speakers have a slightly wider variety of word choices than non-native speakers. Only grammatical words are found associated with "where" interrogatives. This is the opposite of the word "which" as non-native speakers appear to have a wider range of vocabulary in interrogative forms.

Frequency of the words after "where" in subordinate clauses across the two corpora

Table 7.28 shows the frequencies of the words occurring after "where" in subordinate clauses across the two corpora.

LOCNESS			WECCL		
word	No.	%	word	No.	%
the	53	21.99%	he	8	15.69%
they	20	8.30%	you	7	13.73%
he	18	7.47%	I	4	7.84%
everything	11	4.56%	they	4	7.84%
a	9	3.73%	there	3	5.88%
there	7	2.90%	the	3	5.88%
it	6	2.49%	we	3	5.88%
all	5	2.07%	his	2	3.92%
you	5	2.07%	people	2	3.92%
people	4	1.66%	you	2	3.92%
to	4	1.66%	are	2	3.92%
we	3	1.24%	is	2	3.92%
this	3	1.24%	their	1	1.96%
both	3	1.24%	while	1	1.96%
in	3	1.24%	everyone	1	1.96%
new	2	0.83%	and	1	1.96%
even	2	0.83%	everybody	1	1.96%
workers	2	0.83%	produce	1	1.96%
their	2	0.83%	modernization	1	1.96%

Table 7.28 Comparison of the frequencies and percentage of different words occurring after "where" in subordinate clauses

According to Table 7.28, pronouns have a high frequency in the WECCL while the article "the" has the highest frequency in the LOCNESS. This may suggest that non-native speakers somehow over-use pronouns with this particular construction in academic writing. The low occurrence of the definite article is again because of L1 transfer as there are no definite articles in the Chinese language.

For example:

```
They do not put their faith in God (although at his death, Kaliayev turns
to God), yet the acknowledge the presence of some kind of metaphysical,
where they will meet after their deaths. (LOCNESS)
This summer when his father went out to do some business, Wang Liang
felt extremely uncomfortable seeing his step-mother and step-brother in
the house where his mother used to live in, no matter how well his step-
mother treated him and tolerated his unpoliteness.(WECCL)
```

It is interesting that the word *there* occurs a few times in the WECCL and is used as an idiom: where there is a will, there is a way. However, such an idiom cannot be found in the LOCNESS. The possible explanation is that EFL textbooks largely influence learners' production, however the language in textbooks is somewhat artificial compared to authentic language. For example:

```
He blames this on man, and announces univesal guilt to the world, where
there is no more innocence. (LOCNESS)
I think no one wants to live a place where there are quite a lot of
rubbish around us. (WECCL)
```

Pronouns such as *everything* have a high frequency in the LOCNESS while the words *everybody* and *everyone* have a low frequency in the WECCL. This again may suggest that non-native speakers over-use personal pronouns as opposed to a lack of knowledge of certain pronouns such as *everything*. Only abstract nouns such as *people* and *modernization* are found in the top 20 words in the WECCL while the abstract nouns *people* and the general nouns *workers* are both found in the top 20 in the LOCNESS. The reason for this might be that native speakers have a larger vocabulary. For example:

```
In the western world where everyone appeal for the human's right, people
will attach importance to the individual.(LOCNESS)
In a word, Traditions are firm base where modernization<sp-mordernization>
can be founded. (WECCL)
```

As the data shows, the word "where" has a wider range of word choices when used by non-native speakers, which is different from the previous words. Native speakers and non-native speakers are quite similar in the words they use, although we still can detect some interesting points. For example, the verb (*produce*) is found in the WECCL while the preposition (*in*) occurs in the LOCNESS.

The behavior of the word "where" in interrogatives is similar to the word "when", with native speakers likely to produce a wider variety of words than non-native speakers. Textbooks and elicited data also suggest that non-native speakers tend to use this word in spoken contexts. In English, a subordinate clause is normally associated with the framework-content pattern. The first segment of the clause is a signal of the framework within which what we want to say is to be understood. The resting clause can be seen as transmitting what we want to say within this framework. In other words, the topic or themes of the clauses are always in front. In the case of "where" subordinate clauses, the topic or themes often come as the first segment of the clauses and native speakers tend to use the complex noun phrase to introduce the rest of the sentence. This is different from non-native speakers. Instead, they tend to use simple nouns to introduce the rest of the sentence, such as "...*yet the acknowledge the presence of some kind of metaphysical, where they will meet after their deaths*" from the LOCNESS, and "...*Wang Liang felt extremely uncomfortable seeing his step-mother and step-brother in the house where his mother used to live in...*". The reason for this difference might be that the position in the clause in Chinese is normally placed to emphasize an event or a property.

Who

Frequency of the words after "who" in interrogatives across the two corpora

In the following sections, we look at the behavior of the word "who" and how it is used by native speakers and non-native speakers. We also compare such behaviour with the previous words.

Table 7.29 shows the frequencies of the words occurring after "who" in interrogatives across the two corpora.

LOCNESS			WECCL		
word	No.	%	word	No.	%
has	2	28.57%	is	4	30.77%
are	1	14.29%	knows	2	15.38%
would	1	14.29%	can	2	15.38%
was	1	14.29%	feeds	1	7.69%
won	1	14.29%	dig	1	7.69%
isn't	1	14.29%	care	1	7.69%
			will	1	7.69%
			decide	1	7.69%

Table 7.29 Comparison of the frequencies and percentage of different words occurring after "who" in interrogatives

As Table 7.29 shows, there are clear differences between the two corpora. Grammatical words are found in a large proportion with this construction in the LOCNESS, while in the WECCL it has a wider range of words in both grammatical and lexical items. Why is there such a difference? One reason for this might be L1 transfer, and over-generalization of interrogative forms as non-native speakers apply both grammatical-lexical items after the word "who". It could also be that non-native speakers lack the awareness of restricted collocations and constructions.

For example,

```
And who isn't? (LOCNESS)
Who are you supposed to pay? (LOCNESS)
Who is the monitor? (WECCL)
Who should take the responsibility for all these? (WECCL)
Who won, Newcastle or Aston? (LOCNESS)
And who dig the gap? (WECCL)
```

Textbooks and elicited data show that both native speakers and non-native speakers are likely to produce interrogatives in a large proportion. It seems non-native speakers follow the same regularity in written texts.

Frequency of the words after "who" in subordinate clauses across the two corpora

Table 7.30 shows the frequencies of the words occurring after "who" in subordinate clauses across the two corpora.

LOCNESS			WECCL		
word	**No.**	**%**	**word**	**No.**	**%**
are	76	19.49%	only	34	7.11%
is	49	12.56%	is	12	2.51%
has	40	10.26%	are	12	2.51%
have	35	8.97%	support	8	1.67%
had	23	5.90%	play	7	1.46%
were	20	5.13%	believe	7	1.46%
do	16	4.10%	like	6	1.26%
would	12	3.08%	have	6	1.26%
can	12	3.08%	oppose	6	1.26%
was	12	3.08%	often	5	1.05%
should	10	2.56%	think	4	0.84%
will	9	2.31%	also	4	0.84%
did	8	2.05%	play	4	0.84%
could	8	2.05%	run	4	0.84%
don't	7	1.79%	always	4	0.84%
they	7	1.79%	want	4	0.84%
does	5	1.28%	believe	4	0.84%
may	4	1.03%	developed	4	0.84%
not	3	0.77%	believes	4	0.84%

Table 7.30 Comparison of the frequencies and percentage of different words occurring after "who" in subordinate clauses

According to Table 7.30, the words occurring after "who" in subordinate clauses in the LOCNESS are grammatical words while there are a wider variety of lexical items in the WECCL. To some extent, grammatical words are under-used and lexical words are over-used in the WECCL. For example:

```
Also people who are paying for a car's road tax, insurance and depreciation
prefer to use the car. (LOCNESS)
If you are a person who is not interested in English but has to pass
some exams. (WECCL)
```

As we can see from the above examples, the reason non-native speakers over-use lexical items could be that the verbs are used to support and highlight the main idea. Native speakers use more grammatical words to indicate a situation.

Modals are not found in the WECCL with this construction. This again suggests that non-native speakers have difficulties using different types of modals, in particular the intonation and extension of the meanings. With pronouns, there are none for both native speakers and non-native speakers. This may suggest that they have become aware of the restricted collocation and construction.

Whom

In the following sections, we look at the behaviour of the word "whom" and how it is used by native speakers and non-native speakers. We also compare such behaviour with the previous words.

Frequency of the words after "whom" in interrogatives across the two corpora

Table 7.31 shows the frequencies of the words occurring after "whom" in interrogatives across the two corpora.

LOCNESS		
word	**No.**	**%**
is	2	100%

Table 7.31 Comparison of the frequencies and percentage of different words occurring after "whom" in interrogatives

According to Table 7.31, only the word 'is' is found occurring after "whom" in interrogatives in the LOCNESS, and there are none in the non-native speakers' corpus. This may suggest that non-native speakers have not grasped the interrogative form of "whom", for example:

```
For whom is there a payoff? (LOCNESS)
```

There may be two reasons for this phenomenon. The first is that the word "whom" has fewer occurrences in textbooks and natural language; the second is that learners simply cannot produce sentences that contain "whom".

The interrogative "whom" sentence is not found in the WECCL and it is also found less frequently in textbooks and learners' production. This is a phrase that learners are clearly not aware of. It was under-represented in the textbook corpus as well.

Frequency of the words after "whom" in subordinate clauses across the two corpora

Table 7.32 shows the frequencies of the words occurring after "whom" in subordinate clauses across the two corpora.

LOCNESS			WECCL		
word	**No.**	**%**	**word**	**No.**	**%**
he	6	33.33%	you	5	55.56%
they	4	22.22%	their	1	11.11%
we	3	16.67%	I	1	11.11%
the	1	5.56%	to	1	11.11%
actions	1	5.56%	may	1	11.11%
equality	1	5.56%			
are	1	5.56%			
I	1	5.56%			

Table 7.32 Comparison of the frequencies and percentage of different words occurring after "whom" in subordinate clauses

According to Table 7.32, only the pronoun "I" occurs in both corpora. For example:

```
I'm guilty of being like society and not rewarding teachers whom I didn't
like.(LOCNESS)
If I want to send an important letter to whom I'd like him to receive
soon, I will choose E-mails of course.(WECCL)
```

Only grammatical words are found in the WECCL, while the LOCNESS has a wider variety. Two nouns (*actions* and *equality*) are found in the LOCNESS, while the modal (*may*) is found in the WECCL. For such differences, one reason for this could be that native speakers have a larger vocabulary size and they are more aware of the restricted collocations and constructions. Examples are shown as follows:

```
If an egg is donated by a friend, the donater could want rights over a
child whom they may see as their own. (LOCNESS)
You want to receive a paper card from whom you hope and send a paper
card to whom you want. (WECCL)
```

Again, the "whom" subordinate clause has a lower frequency in both native speakers and non-native speakers than other "wh" words. This is found in accordance with textbook data and elicited sentences. Clearly, compared with other "wh" words, learners seem to have less confidence in using the word. The reason may not be the difficulty of usage, but that it occurs less frequently in textbooks and elicited data.

Whose

Frequency of the words after "whose" in interrogatives across the two corpora

In the following sections, we look at the behaviour of the word "whose" and how it is used by native speakers and non-native speakers. We also compare such behaviour with the previous words.

Table 7.33 shows the frequencies of the words occurring after "whose" in interrogatives across the two corpora.

WECCL		
word	No.	%
fault	1	100%

Table 7.33 Comparison of the frequencies and percentage of different words occurring after "whose" in interrogatives

According to Table 7.33, only the word "fault" is found occurring after "whose" in interrogatives in the WECCL. It may be suggested that native speakers rarely use "whose" interrogatives in written texts. This is the opposite of the behaviour of the "whom" interrogatives, for which there are none in non-native speakers' corpus.

For example:

```
Whose fault it is? (WECCL)
```

Frequency of the words after "whose" in subordinate clauses across the two corpora

Table 7.34 shows the frequencies of the words occurring after "whose" in subordinate clauses across the two corpora.

LOCNESS			WECCL		
word	**No.**	**%**	**word**	**No.**	**%**
life	2	9.09%	duty	2	16.67%
role	1	4.55%	major	1	8.33%
ideas	1	4.55%	looking	1	8.33%
lives	1	4.55%	phone	1	8.33%
financial	1	4.55%	degree	1	8.33%
views	1	4.55%	boyfriend	1	8.33%
decision	1	4.55%	son	1	8.33%
orders	1	4.55%	name	1	8.33%
function	1	4.55%	formal	1	8.33%
loyalty	1	4.55%	job	1	8.33%
underlying	1	4.55%	workplace	1	8.33%
laws	1	4.55%			
power	1	4.55%			
intention	1	4.55%			
acts	1	4.55%			
ends	1	4.55%			
judgements	1	4.55%			
sole	1	4.55%			
father	1	4.55%			

**Table 7.34 The frequencies of the words occurring after "whose"
in subordinate clauses across the two corpora**

According to Table 7.34, lexical items are the most frequent words occurring after "whose" across the two corpora. Most lexical words are abstract nouns in the LOCNESS which are more likely to describe a person's spirit such as *judgements*, *sole*, *intention*, *loyalty* and *decision*, while most lexical words related to personal life are found in the WECCL such as *duty*, *major*, *phone*, *workplace*, *son*, and *boyfriend*. This is a concrete versus abstract difference. It is also found in accordance with learners' on-line production. Examples are shown as follows:

```
Sisyphus is a demigod who dies and on whose orders his wife throws his
body into the street without burial. (LOCNESS)
And also, mobile phones are very useful to those whose workplace can't
stay at one place, especially to the journalists. (WECCL)
```

We have discussed the frequency lists of words occurring after "wh" words in three types of sentences, encompassing what the frequency of co-occurring words can therefore tell us about collocational patterning, as well as how these patterns are under- or over-used with reference to native speakers and non-native speakers.

As the discussion reveals, there are five possible explanations for the different use of words occurring immediately after "wh" words: the vocabulary size of L2 speakers is smaller than that of L1 speakers; non-native speakers' lack of awareness of restricted collocations and constructions; L1 transfer; over/under-generalization of rules and textbooks.

The above explanations also suggest that language is rich in collocational restrictions and that the use of different grammatical-lexical items indicates different types of polarity. In addition, in non-native speakers' writing, the use of fixed expressions memorized as formulaic chunks also suggests that language structures emerge from language use.

The data also suggest that language learning needs to be considered at three levels: the level of language description, such as the use of grammatical-lexical items, the skills of language use, such as how to use a particular grammatical-lexical item in different contexts and how language teachers should create activities for some low frequency words and their usage. This learning process can be seen as a gradual and dynamic process, suggesting that language teachers and textbook writers should be concerned more with the learning procedures which may have some direct bearing on such matters.

After investigating the words occurring on the right immediately after the "wh" words, it is worthwhile investigating their association patterns on the left and the differences between native speakers and non-native speakers with reference to written discourse.

7.5 Discussion

7.5 1 Prototypes

Table 7.35 shows the distribution of "wh" words as prototypes and extensions.

Wh-word	LOCNESS (%)			WECCL (%)		
	P	E1	E2	P	E1	E2
what	14	0	86	16	2	82
how	19	1	80	29	8	63
when	1	0	99	0	0	100
which	0	0	100	4	0	96
who	10	0	90	3	0	97
whom	10	0	90	0	0	100
why	30	0	70	59	0	41
whose	0	0	100	8	0	92
where	5	0	95	11	0	89
average	10	0	90	14	1	85

Table 7.35 Distribution of prototypes and extensions across the two corpora

According to Table 7.35, Extension 2 subordinate clauses are largely produced in both native speakers and non-native speakers' written texts almost all the "wh" words, except the word "why" in the WECCL. This may suggest that, although in both textbooks and elicited data prototypes are predominant, there are more extension structures across the two corpora as this kind of sentence structure is largely produced in written texts. Why there is such a difference? The possible explanation might be that textbooks tend to provide more prototype structures because it is easier for human mental representation processing. Learners' production is largely influenced by textbooks. Both of them have almost the same distribution of sentence structures. In the case of written texts, subordinate clauses are largely found, which may be related to the characteristics of the written texts, particularly academic writing, which is the type of language within the written corpus.

Extension 1 declaratives are found predominately in the WECCL. This is in accordance with what we found in textbook data and elicited data. This may suggest that learners' production is influenced by exemplars provided in textbooks. Such schemas are more likely to be stored in learners' long-term memory.

7.5.2 *Frequency Of Words Occurring Immediately After Wh-Words Across The Two Corpora*

We have discussed the words occurring immediately after "wh" words with reference to three types of sentences across the two corpora. The investigation set out to compare the difference and similarities between native speakers and non-native speakers in terms of the usage of different groups of words, as well as how lexical-grammatical items tend to be over or under-used.

The findings suggest that there are five possible explanations for the different use of words occurring immediately after "wh" words: 1 the vocabulary size of L2 speakers is smaller than that of L1 speakers; 2 non-native speakers' lack of awareness of restricted collocations and constructions; 3 L1 transfer; 4 over/under-generalization of rules and 5 textbooks.

For the first explanation that the vocabulary size of L2 speakers is smaller than that of L1 speakers, evidence can be found from "what" interrogatives. In the case of the word "what", there are a wider variety of word choices that native speakers make. These word choices include verbs, adjectives, nouns, and adjectives. On the other hand, non-native speakers tend to be more conservative in terms of their word choices. The most common words occurring after "what" in interrogatives in the WECCL are grammatical words, for example *what is …* and *what about….*

For the second explanation of non-native speakers' lack of awareness of restricted collocations and constructions, the example can be found from "what" subordinate clauses, where non-native speakers seem to over-use grammatical-lexical words. This may due to the fact that there are strong conventions in English about which words tend to follow 'what' in subordinate clauses and that native speakers are more aware of these conventions than non-native speakers.

For the third explanation that of L1 transfer, examples can be found from "what" subordinate clauses. In the case of "what" subordinate clauses and "how" interrogatives, non-native speakers use many grammatical-lexical items, in particular nouns. The reason for this might be that, in Chinese, subordinate clauses are hardly ever used unless an event or activity is emphasized. This can also be seen as a transfer from L1.

For the fourth explanation, that of over/under generalization of the rules, the example can be found from "how" interrogatives where the use of modal verbs can typically describe this problem. In most cases, non-native speakers lack the awareness that different modals indicate different kind of intonation and extension of the meanings.

For the last explanation relating to the influence of textbooks, evidence can be found from "what" declaratives and "how" declaratives, in which non-native speakers are more likely to produce sentences containing positive feelings or emotions, while such sentence structure is largely used to express negative meaning in native speakers' written texts.

The above findings also suggest that language learning needs to be considered at two levels: the level of language description, such as the use of grammatical-lexical items, the skills of language use, such as how to use a particular grammatical-lexical item in different contexts and how language teachers should create activities for some low frequency words and their usage.

The findings for textbook data suggest that textbook writers tend to introduce simple and easily memorable linguistic grammatical-lexical construction at learners' beginning stage, and gradually add more complex sentence structures as learners' proficiency levels increase.

In the case of elicited data, prototypical structures largely occur across all four groups of participants (three groups of non-native speakers and one group of native speakers). It is more likely that learners stored the prototypical exemplars that provide in textbooks in their long-term memory, and produce them in a similar context as their previously stored experience. This may suggest that when elicited data have been collected, learners explicitly construct the sentences from their previously memorised experience. In other words, the way learners construct sentences can be considered to be combined both explicit and implicit knowledge. We have discussed the idea that L2 learning process can be seen as a gradual and dynamic process, and language teachers and textbook writers should be concerned more with the learning procedures which may have some direct bearing on such matters. In the case of native speakers, the prototypical effect seems even stronger because native speakers construct sentences largely on the basis of their linguistic knowledge or daily life experience. In other words, they may construct the sentence by using their implicit knowledge.

Chapter Eight

Conclusion

8.1 Introduction

As we saw in the introduction to this study, when referring to knowledge of Language Chomsky (1986) coined the terms "E-language and I-language" (1986:24). He explained that analysis of a language system should be focused on the actual use and understanding of language rather than how language should be used . Between e and i language, there is always an ineliminable gap or an irreducible otherness. Taylor (2010) suggests a new relationship between E and I language. He sees E-language as the product of I –language of individual speakers, while I-language of individual speakers is the product of their exposure to E-language (Taylor 2010).

There is one important parameter that relates to both types of language and this is *input*. It is believed that individuals learn a language via speech signals and written texts, which are both considered to be forms of external input. To be more explicit, E-language can be considered to be the language input that individual speakers are exposed to as well as language production that individual speakers produce. On the other hand, I-language can be considered to be the result of the digest processing of the language input in the individual speaker's mind. Taylor points out that in order to understand certain features of E-language, some features of I-language should be an integral part of an analysis. These include features such as "the frequency of occurrence of its various items, their collocations and co-occurrence patterns, their contextual situatedness, and the ubiquity of the idiomatic and the formulaic" (Taylor 2010:29).

Language teachers are interested in the ways in which individuals process in their minds, a fact which reflects the idea that language acquisition actually takes place in a person's mind. Unfortunately, we cannot look into the human mind. However, we can obtain indirect evidence of a learner's I-language by analysing and understanding the language that they produce. This is one of the most important tasks for L2 language researchers and teachers.

Cognitive linguistics studies language and the mind, and how they interact with each other. It emphasizes that language is learned from individuals' exposure to language experience, the processing of language input and the use of language in different social contexts (Robinson and Ellis 2008).

These ideas are complementary and, to a large extent, account for the way we learn and use language on the basis of our daily experience. Learning a language involves intricate cognitive processes such as memory, attention and awareness, which in turn involve category formation and induction (Carrol 2001).

In this study we have examined the similarities between two types of E-language (textbook data and language corpora) and a type of language that in some ways could be considered to be a reflection of I-language, i.e. elicited data. We have looked at patterns of prototypicality for "wh" sentences in these three types of language as produced by native and non-native speakers.

8.2 Summary of the main arguments and findings that have been presented in the study

To illustrate my central arguments clearly, this study started, in Chapter one by elucidating some key concepts in Second Language Acquisition research. In chapter one, we investigated the relationship between L2 language acquisition, input, and mind. We saw that, L2 language acquisition process, in contemporary theories, is considered to be a dynamic and complex system, in which a number of variables within the system continuously interact, thus leading the system as a whole to change over time. Such change in the system results from complex interactions between the environment and principles of self-organization. In other words, language learning is considered to be an outcome of the interaction between external input, such as speech signals or written texts, and internal cognitive processes, such as attention and awareness. This, in turn, can be considered to reflect the internal structure of the relationship between E and I language. The relationship between i and e language can be understood as the way individuals process language input in their minds. More specifically, we looked at how language is used and reflected on the basis of our daily experience. For example, when we are exposed to language input, we tend to focus on those features that are salient, ignoring or missing less salient features. We can recognise items quicker if we have encountered them frequently enough in previous experience.

Having explained the idea that L2 learning is a dynamic and complex system, and the relationship between e and i language, Chapter two, "The developing language system in the minds of the learners", set out to discuss the idea that in a multilingual context individuals create and develop an implicit linguistic system, in which they process external L2 input in similar ways to those in which they process their L1. L2 instructed classroom input plays an important role in L2 language teaching and learning processes. Unlike other types of input, textbook input can be considered to be one of the most widely used resources that language learners have access to. In many language teaching contexts (such as in Chinese schools and universities), learners memorise extensive examples of target language provided in textbooks. Thus the patterns of learners' L2 production are often similar to the examples provided in textbooks. In other words, textbooks, to some extent, influence the way learners process or produce i and e language. During the L2 acquisition process, cognitive processes such as noticing, attention and awareness, perform the role of filter between L2 input and L2 acquisition. While it is hard to describe precisely the exact ways in which these individual cognitive processes work, this study focuses on the frequency and salience of the input, and one particular cognitive process, i.e. categorization, wh ich is considered to be the "explanatory cornerstone of language learning" (Ellis cited in Ortega 2009: 113). Chapter two discussed the relationship between input and cognitive processes and indicated the extent to which language knowledge is thought to reside in the mind. One of the founding theories of Cognitive Linguistics (CL), namely, categorization and prototype theory was discussed with regards to both traditional views and more up-to-date views.

Chapter three provided a more detailed discussion of the cognitive linguists' view of lexical semantics. The literature reviews the cognitive semantics that lexical items can constitute a complex category, which is named the radial category (Lakoff 1987). It has been pointed out by Evans and Green that radial categories are also conceptual categories in which a range of concepts is organised in relation to a central or prototypical sense. This chapter also reviewed two main approaches to semantic categories involving, polysemy. Based on the theory of principled polysemy, a corpus-based study was conducted in order to identify the different sentence constructions in which the "wh" words occur. Finally, the acquisition order for "wh" words and structures, by both native speaker infants and second language learners were discussed.

After having discussed the acquisition order for "wh" words and structures by second language learners, we turned in Chapter four to discuss the situation of English language teaching and learning in China with reference to the three different age groups (junior, senior and university). The chapter focused on the current situation of English language teaching and learning in Mainland China. Several issues such as the background of the three different age groups, the purpose of their English language study, the syllabus and teaching methodologies were discussed respectively. The discussion drew a picture of the enormous energy and enthusiasm in English language teaching and learning in China. English is not only considered to be a national compulsory subject, but also a world language that shapes the learners' future careers. Yet, due to the constraints of several examinations under the education system, current English language teaching and learning methodologies and the four aspects of language skills (reading, writing, speaking, and listening) will undoubtedly be reconsidered and structured within the syllabus.

The aim of the study was to compare the use of "wh" sentences across three sets of data: textbook data (from textbooks used by Chinese learners of English), elicited data produced by native speakers of English and Chinese learners of English (where participants were asked to produce five sentences for each wh- word), and written corpus data produced by native speakers of English and Chinese learners of English. The comparison was conducted in order to assess the influence of textbook data (a type of E-language) on the formation and production of "wh" categories in written English and elicited sentences produced by Chinese learners of English (compared with those produced by native speakers of English). We were interested in prototypicality patterns across the three data sets.

Chapter 5 provided a corpus-based analysis of "wh" sentences in EFL textbooks. We analysed the polysemous nature of each "wh" word on the basis of its usage (prototype interrogatives, extended declaratives, and extended clauses). The data shows that for the lowest proficiency textbooks (JTD), prototypes dominate for seven of the nine wh-words (*what, how, which, who, why, whose, where*). For secondary school textbooks (STD), only two words (*how* and *why*) have more prototype structures. For university textbooks (UTD), only two words (*what* and *why*) are found to contain more prototypical structures. Extension 2, i.e., subordinate clausal usage of wh-words, predominates for seven of the nine wh-words in both STD and UTD. The findings suggest that textbook writers tend to provide more prototypical examples at low level proficiency. This is considered to be suitable based on our cognitive understanding of everyday life. It also suggests that the most frequent and salient features of linguistic elements have the most prototypical effect in our minds and in turn are easier to access and less susceptible to change in mental representation (Biber 2008). We also analysed the words occurring immediately after "wh" words in the three types of sentences. The findings show that when teaching the interrogative form, textbooks focus almost exclusively on grammatical words, particularly at the beginner level. In contrast, lexical items have low frequency in lower level textbooks, although for certain word there is a tendency for the occurrence of fixed-expressions and collocations. For example, the word "what" combines with a number of fixed-expressions and collocates such as *what time... what color...* and *what happened...* It was also found (in subsequent chapters) that such formulaic language that is provided in textbooks is stored in learners' long-term memory, and that this sort of language has a high frequency in learners' on-line production.

Chapter Six provided a corpus-based analysis of data elicited from Chinese speaking learners of English and Expert users of English. The structure of the analysis followed a similar pattern to Chapter five. Firstly, we analysed the polysemous nature of each "wh" word on the basis of their usage. The findings show that the prototypical structure is very strong in both native speakers and non-native speakers' data at 92% for JED, 65% for SED, 73% for UED, and 89% for native speakers. Four groups of participants consistently produced the prototypical structures when asked to write "wh" sentences, the prototypical structures are therefore a key cognitive process in human being's minds, regardless the proficiency level of the language. Non-native speakers constantly produced language that was stored in long-term memory. This was manifested by the fact that large amounts of similar examples occurred in a high frequency across the three groups of non-native participants. This may suggest that textbooks influence learners' production, and prototypical examples tend to be stored in learners' long-term memory as a result of repetition by language teachers or memorisation by the learners themselves. In the case of native speakers, the prototypical sentences seemed to consist largely of idiomatic sequences. Native speakers tended to use such prefabricated chunks of language in high frequency. This may suggest that native speakers are aware of collocation restrictions, and such prefabricated chunks of language occur frequently in their daily communication. This being the case, the frequency of linguistic units may somewhat influence the prototypical effect. In light of this, we investigated the words occurring immediately after "wh" words in terms of three types of sentences.

Finally, Chapter Seven analysed the wh-sentences from the both native and non-native speakers written corpora, namely the LOCNESS and the WECCL. Following a similar format as the previously two chapters, the analysis focused on the authentic language corpora in an attempt to see to what extent the prototypes and extension structures were reflected in naturally occurring language. The findings show that Extension 2 subordinate clauses are largely produced in both native speakers and non-native speakers' written corpora, except for the word "why" in the WECCL. This may suggest that, although in both textbooks and elicited data prototypes are predominant, there are more extension structures across the two corpora, as this kind of sentence structure is largely produced in written texts. Although the the written texts in both corpora were not strictly 'academic writing', our findings suggest that the sentences tended to contain predominantly complex structures. It seems that subordinate clauses tend to occur more frequently in written texts than in spoken texts because grammar in written language tends to have a unique structure according to recurring principles. So far, we can see that the written corpus data contrasts markedly with the textbook data and the elicited data. One possible reason for this difference might be that textbooks tend to provide more prototype structures because these lend themselves more easily to human mental representation processing. Learners' production is largely influenced by textbooks. Both of them have almost the same distribution of sentence structures. In the case of written corpora, subordinate clauses predominate, a fact that may be related to the characteristics of the written texts, particularly in academic writing. The second focus of this chapter was on the investigation of the words occurring immediately after "wh" words, with reference to three types of sentences across the two corpora. We compared the differences and similarities between native speakers and non-native speakers in terms of their usage of different groups of words, as well as how looking at lexical-grammatical items tended to be over or under-used. The findings show that there are five possible explanations for the different use of words occurring immediately after "wh" words: 1 the vocabulary size of L2 speakers is smaller than that of L1 speakers; 2 non-native speakers' lack of awareness of restricted collocations and constructions; 3 L1 transfer; 4 over/under-generalization of rules and 5 textbooks.

The above findings have useful pedagogic implications. The findings suggest that prototypes are particularly salient across the textbook data and elicited data. Textbooks are likely to be used to develop our explicit knowledge because the examples provided are stable, discrete and context-independent structures. These examples are largely considered to be the prototypical structures and are easily stored in an individual's memory. Learners understand the linguistic structures via schemas that derive from the best example of a category. In addition, during the process of categorization, learners not only remember a number of exemplars, but also tend to search for similarities between the new exemplar and ones that are already held in their memory.

On the other hand, L2 acquisition involves combining both explicit and implicit knowledge. In contrast with explicit linguistic knowledge, implicit linguistic knowledge is represented in terms of flexible and context-dependent categories and is subject to exemplar-based categories. We saw that extension 2 subordinate clauses predominate in both corpora, which may suggest that although prototypical structures predominate in learners' elicited production possibly as a result of the use of the explicit language knowledge, within certain genres, for example, written texts, the sentence structures tend to be more complex and learners are sensitive to this. This finding also suggests that the close relationship between textbook as a type of e language and learners' production as a type of i language.

The study focuses on explaining the way we learn L2 language using environmentally adaptive input (in countries such as China, widely used textbooks can even 'create' the target-language environment) and cognitive abilities (such as memory, attention and awareness). Explicitly, from the perspective of cognitive linguists, we learn language while processing input (either written or spoken), and the sentence structures emerge from the language used in different social contexts.

For L2 teaching and learning, we should bear in mind the idea that learning a second language is a dynamic, complex and developing process. Although cognitive abilities are emphasized in the L2 teaching and research domain, it is a challenging task for L2 researchers and teachers to understand clearly what cognitive abilities are involved in acquiring linguistic knowledge. So far we seem only to have identified learners' use different types of memory. There is still not enough evidence and analysis of how attention, awareness and forgetting are involved in the L2 language acquisition process.

8.3 *Limitations and Recommendations*

Due to the scale and word limit of the study, this book can only provide a study of the "wh" words in written contexts (textbooks, elicited sentences, and written corpora). Yet, looking back at the study that I have worked on over the past few years, there is still much room for improvement. For instance, it would have been, perhaps, a better idea to collect more native speakers' elicited sentences. In doing so, I might have been able to provide a more detailed study of native speakers' polysemous usage of "wh" sentences. First of all, it would be interesting to look at the formulaic language that occurs in native speakers' data. Second, in addition to analysing the prototypical structures used in different types of data and word frequency occurring immediately after "wh" words, it would be a more complete study if we could also analyse the preferred patterns of the three types of "wh" sentences using corpus methodology. In recent years, theorists have begun to suggest that cognitive linguists and corpus linguists work more closely together but there is much more to be done in this area.

There is also more scope for cross-linguistic studies in this area. Numerous studies have investigated grammar patterns in individual languages, but few have examined the patterns that non-native speakers are likely to use, and compared these with the patterns that native speakers are likely to use. As well as studying grammar patterns occurring immediately after the node, such studies could usefully explore those patterns that occur before the node. In conclusion, an analysis of more data produced by native speakers, and a more in-depth study of the grammar patterns surrounding the three types of "wh" sentences would both be topics worthy of further research.

References

Achard, M. and Niemeier, S. (2004). *Cognitive Linguistics. Second Language Acquisition, and Foreign language Teaching.* Berlin: Mouton de Gruyter.

Achard, A. (2008). '*Teaching* construal: Cognitive Pedagogical Grammar'. In Robinson, P and Ellis, N (eds) *Handbook of Cognitive Linguistics and Second Language Acquisition.* Routledge: New York and London.

Adamson, H. D. 1989. 'Variable rules as prototype schemas' in S. Gass, C. Madden, D. Preston, and L. Selinker (eds.): *Variation in Second Language Acquisition, Volume II: Psycholinguistic Issues.* Clevedon, Avon: Multilingual Matters.

Akmajian (1984). Sentence types and the form-function fit. *Natural Language & Linguistic Theory.* (2): 1-23.

Alexander, R.J. (1984a). Fixed expressions in English: A linguistic, psycholinguistic and didactic study. *Anglistik und Englischunterricht* (6): 171-188.

Aston, G. (1997). 'Enriching the Learning Environment: Corpora in EFL' In Wichmann, A., Fligelstone, S. McEnery, T. and Knowles, G. (eds.) *Teaching and language corpora.* Harlow: Addison Wesley Longman: 51-64.

Athanasopoulos, P. (2006). Effects of the grammatical representation of number on cognition in bilinguals. *Bilingualism: Language and Cognition.* (9): 89–96.

Baddeley, A. (1992). Working memory. *Science.* 225 (5044): 556-559.

Barlow, M. and Kemmer, S. (2000) *Usage-Based Models of Language.* Stanford, CA: CSLI Publications,

Barnbrook, G. (1996). *Language and computers: a practical introduction to the computer analysis of language.* Edinburgh: Edinburgh University Press.

Barry, C. and Seymour, PHK. (1988). Lexical priming and sound-to-spelling contingency effects in non-word spelling. *Quarterly Journal of Experimental Psychology.* 40A: 5-40.

Bernardini, S. (2004). "Corpora in the classroom: an overview and some reflections on future developments" *How to Use Corpora in Language Teaching,* J.Sinclair (ed) Amsterdam: John Benjamins: 15-36.

Bergen, B. and Chang, N. (2005). Embodied construction Grammar in simulation-based language understanding. In J. O. Ostman and M. Fried (eds.). Construction Grammars: Cognitive Grounding and theoretical Extension 2: 147-190. Amsterdam: John Berjamis.

Berman, (1991). *On the semantic and logical forms of wh-clauses.* PhD study. University of Massachusetts at Amherst.

Biber, D. (1990). Methodological Issues Regarding Corpus-based Analyses of Linguistic Variation. *Literature and Linguist Computing.* 5 (4): 257-269.

Biber, D. (2009). A corpus-driven approach to formulaic language in English. *International Jounral of Corpus Linguistics*. 14 (3): 275-311.

Biber, D., Conrad, S. and Reppen, R. (1994). Corpus-based Approaches to Issues in Applied Linguistics. *Applied Linguistics*.15 (2): 169-189.

Biber, D., Conrad, S., and Reppen, R. (2002). *Corpus Linguistics: Investigating Language Structure and Use*. Cambridge: Cambridge University Press.

Bloom, L., Merkin, S., and Wootten, J. (1982). Wh-questions: linguistic factors that contribute to the sequence of acquisition. *Child Development*. 53: 1084-1092.

Bloom, L. (1991). *Language development from two to three*. Cambridge: Cambridge University Press.

Bot, De K., Lowie, W., and Verspoor, M. (2007). A dynamic view as a complementary perspective. *Bilingualism: language and Cognition*.10 (1): 51-55.

Braidi, M S. (1999). *The Acquisition of Second-Language Syntax*. Arnold: Longman.

Braun, S.(2005). "From pedagogically relevant corpora to authentic language learningcontents", *ReCall* 17 (1): 47-64.

Brown, H. (1994). *Princeples of Language Learning and Teaching*. Oxford: Oxford University Press.

Brugman, C. and Lakoff, G. (1988). Cognitive topology and lexical networks. In S. Small., and M. Tannenhaus. (eds.). *Lexical Ambiguity Resolution*. San Matea, CA: Morgan Kaufman: 477-507.

Bybee, J. (2003). Cognitive process in grammaticization. In Tomasello, M. (ed.) *The New Psychological of Language*, Volume II. Mahwah, N.J: Erlbaum: 145-167.

Bybee, J. (2006). From usage to grammar: The mind's response to repetition. *Language*. 72.

Bybee, J. (2008). 'Usage-based grammar and Second Language Acquisition'. In Robinson, P and Ellis, N (eds.) *Handbook of Cognitive Linguistics and Second Language Acquisition*. Routledge: New York and London: 216-236.

Carroll, E A. (2008). Input and SLA: Adults' Sensitivity of Different Sorts of Cues to French Gender. *Language Learning*. 49 (1): 37-92.

Carroll, J.B. and Sapon, Stanley, M. (1958). *Modern Language Aptitude Test*. New York: The psychological Corporation.

Carrol, S. (1999) Putting 'input' in its proper place. *Second language research*. (15): 337-388.

Carter, R. (1995). *Vocabulary*. Routledge: London and New york.

Carter, R. (1998). 'Orders of reality: CAMCODE, communication, and culture' *ELT Journal*, 52 (1): 43-56.

Cermák, F. (2002). Today's corpus linguistics. Some open questions. *International Jounral of Corpus Linguistics*.7 (2): 262-282.

Cermák, F.(2009).Spoken Corpora Design: Their Constitutive Parameters. *International Jounral of Corpus Linguistics*. 14 (1): 113-123.

Chikamatsu, N. (1996). The effects of L1 orthography on L2 word recognition: A study of American and Chinese learners of Japanese. *Studies in Second Language Acquisition*. (18): 403-432.

Chomsky, N. (1957). *Syntactic structures*. The Hague: Mouton.

Chomsky, N. (1965). *Aspects of the theory of syntax*. Cambridge, MA: MIT Press.

Clancy, P. (1989). Form and function in the acquisition of Korean wh-questions. *Journal of child language*. (16): 323-347.

Cobb. T. and Horst, M. (2001). 'Reading academic English: carrying learners across the lexical threshold' in J. Flowerdew and M. Peacock (eds.) *Research Perspectives on English for Academic Purposes.* Cambridge: Cambridge University Press: 315-329.

Cook, G. (2001). *Second Language Learning and Teaching.* (3rd ed.) London: Edward Arnold.

Cook, V.J. (1995). *Linguistics and Second Language Acquisition.* New York: St. Martin's Press.

Cook, V. J. (1997). The consequences of bilingualism for cognitive processing. In A. M. B. de Groot & J. F.Kroll (Eds.) *Tutorials in bilingualism: Psycholinguistic perspectives.* Mahwah, NJ: Lawrence Erlbaum Associates: 279-299.

Cook, V. J. (2002). Background to the L2 user perspective. In V. J. Cook (Ed.), *Portraits of the L2 user.* Clevedon: Multilingual Matters: 1-13.

Corder, S.P. (1967). The significance of learner's errors. *IRAL* 5: 161-169.

Cortazzi, M. and Jin, L.X. (2006). English teaching and learning in China: A Bridge to the Future. *Asia-Pacific Journal of Education*, 22 (2): 53-64.

Croft, W. (2003). *Lexical rules vs construction grammar: Syntactic Theory in Typological Perspective.* Oxford: Oxford University Press.

Croft, W. and Cruse, D.A. (2004). *Cognitive linguistics.* Cambridge: Cambridge University Press.

Crystal, D. (1992). *An encyclopedic dictionary of language and languages.* Blackwell.

De Bot, K. (1992). A bilingual production model. Level's 'speaking' model adapted. *Applied Linguistics.* (13) 1-24.

De Bot, K. and Schreuder, R. (1993). Word production and the bilingual lexicon. In R. Schreuder and B.Weltens (eds.). *The bilingual lexicon.* Amsterdam: Benjamins: 191-214.

De Bot, K. Lowie, W. Verspoor, M. (2005). *Second language acquisition: an advanced resource book.* Routledge: New York.

De Cock (1998). 'Corpora of learner speech and writing and EFL' In A. Usoniene (ed.) *Germanic and Baltic linguistic studies and translation.* Proceedings of international conference held at the university of Vilnius, Litlmania. Vilnius: Home Liber: 56-66.

DeGoot, A. (1993). Word-type effects in bilingual processing tasks. In R.Schreuder and B. Weltens (eds.). *The Bilingual lexicon.* Amsterdam/Philadelphia: John benjamins: 27-51.

Dirven, R. and Verspoor, M. (2004). *Cognitive Exploration of Language and Linguistics.* Second Revised Edition. Amsterdam and Philadelphia: John Benjamins Publishing Company.

Doughty, C. and Williams, J. (1998). Pedagogical choices in focus on form. In W. Doughty and J. Williams (eds). *Focus on Form in Classroom Second Language Acquisition.*Cambridge: Cambridge University Press: 197-262.

Doughty, C. (2001). Cognitive understandings of focus on form. In P. Robinson (ed.). *Cognition and Second Language Instruction.* Cambridge: Cambridge University Press: 206-257.

Ellis, N. (1996). Sequencing in SLA: Phonological memory, chunking, and points of order. *Studies in Second Language Acquisition.* (18): 91-126.

Ellis, N. (2002). Frequency effects in Language Processing: A Review with Implications for Theories of Implicit and Explicit Language Acquisition. *SSLA* 24: 143-188.

Ellis, N. (2006). Language Acquisition as Rational Contingency Learning. *Applied Linguistics.* 27 (1): 1-24.

Ellis, N. (2006). Selective attention and transfer phenomena in L2 acquisition: Contingency, cue competition, Salience, interference, overshadowing, blocking, and perceptual learning. *Applied Linguistics.* 27 (1): 1-24.

Ellis, N. (2010). Construction learning as category learning. In Pütz M., and Sicola, L. (eds). *Cognitive Processing in Second Language Acquisition*: 27-48.

Ellis, R. (1990). *Instructed Second Language Acquisition.* Oxford: Blackwell.

Ellis, R. (1997). *SLA research and Language Teaching.* Oxford: Oxford University Press.

Ellis, R. (2001). Introduction: Investigating form-focused instruction. *Language.* 51:1-46.

Ellis, R. (2002). 'The place of Grammar Instruction in the Second / Foreign Language Curriculum' In *New perspectives on Grammar Teaching in Second Language Classrooms.* Hinkel, E., Fotos, S.(ed.) Mahwah: New Jersey: 17-34.

Ellis, R., Basturkmen, H. and Loewen, S. (2002). Doing focus-on-form. *System.* 30 (4): 419-432.

Ellis, R. (2006). 'Current Issues in the Teaching of Grammar: An SLA Perspective.' *TESOL QUARTERLY* 40 (1) 83-107.

Ellis, R. (2008). Usage-based and form-focused language acquisition: The associative learning of constructions, learned attention, and the limited L2 endstate. In Robinson, P and Ellis, N (eds) *Handbook of Cognitive Linguistics and Second Language Acquisition.* Routledge: New York and London: 372-405.

Evan, V. (2005). The meaning of time: polysemy, the lexicon and conceptual structure. Journal of Linguistics. (41): 33-75.

Evans, V. and Green, M. (2006). *Cognitive Linguistics an Introduction.* Edinburgh: Edinburgh University Press.

Evans, V., Bergen, B. and Zinken, Z. (2007). *The Cognitive Linguistics Reader.* London: Equinox.

Flowerdew, J. (1993). 'An educational, or process, approach to the teaching of professional genres'. *ELT Journal AHA:* 305-316.

Flowerdew, L. (2001). "The exploration of small learner corpora in EAP materials design". In M. Ghadessy, A.Henry & R.L.Roseberry (eds.).*Small Corpus Studies and ELT: Theory and Practice.* Amesterdam: John Benjamins: 363-379.

Flowerdew, L. (2009). Applying corpus linguistics to pedagogy. *International Journal of Corpus Linguistics.* 14 (3): 393-417.

Fillmore, C. N. (1982). Frame semantics in Linguistics Society of Korea (ed.). *Linguistics in the Morning calm.* Seoul: Hanshin publishing: 111-137.

Fillmore, C. N., Kay, P. and O'Conner, M.K. (1988). Regularity and idiomaticity: the case of let alone. *Language.* 64 (3): 501-538.

Firth, J.R. (1957). *Papers in linguistics.* Oxford: Oxford University Press.

Foster, P. (1976). Bilingual Education: An Educational and Legal Survey. *Journal of Law & Education.* (5) HeinOnline.

Foster, P. (1985). Lexical acquisition and the modular lexicon. *Language and cognitive processes.* (1): 87-108.

Foster, P. (2001). 'Rules and routines: a consideration of their role in task-based language production of native and non-native speakers.' In Bygate, M. Skehan, P. and Swaini, M.(eds) *Researching Pedagogic Tasks: Second Language Learning, Teaching and Testing.* London: Longman. 75-93.

Freeman, Larsen D. (2002). *Making Sense of Frequency.* Cambridge: University of Cambridge.

Garnham, A. (1985) *Psycholinguistics: Central Topics*. London: Methuen.

Gass, Susan, M. (1997). *input, interaction, and the second language learner*. Lawrence Erlhaum Associates.

Gass, Susan, M. and Mackey, A. (2002). Frequency effects and second language acquisition. *Studies in Second Language Acquisition*. (24): 249-260.

Gass, Susan, M. and Mackey, A. (2006). *Input, Interaction and Output: An Overview*. John Benjamin.

Gavioli, L. (2001). "The learner as researcher: introducing corpus concordancing in the classroom". In G. Aston. Houston, (ed). *Learning with Corpora*. TX: Athelstan: 108-137.

Geeraerts, D. (1988). Introduction: Prospects and problems of prototype theory. In *Linguistics*.27: 587-612.

Geeraerts, D. (1993). Vagueness's puzzles. Polysemy's vagaries. *Cognitive Linguistics*. 4 (3):223-272.

Geeraerts, D. (1997). *Diachronic Prototype Semantics: A Contribution to Historical Lexicology*. Oxford: Clarendon Press.

Geeraerts, D. (1997). *Diachronic Prototype Semantics: A Contribution to Historical Lexicograghy*. Oxfod: Clarendon Press.

Gibbs, R.W. (1994). *The Poetics of Mind*. Cambridge: Cambridge University Press.

Gibbs, R.W. and Horter, C. (1995). The cognitive psychological reality of image schemas and their transformations. *Cognitive Linguistics* 6 (4): 347-378.

Gilquin, G. (2004). *Corpus-based cognitive study of the main English Causative verbs. A syntactic; semantic, lexical and stylistic approaches*. PhD. Dissertation, Centre for English Corpus Linguistics, Université catholique de Louvain.

Gilquin, G. (2006). The place of prototypicality in corpus linguistics: Causation in the hot seat. In Gries, Th S, and Stefanowitsch (eds). Corpora in Cognitive Linguistics. Berlin and New York: Mouton de Gruyter: 159-191.

Goldberg, A.E. (1995). *Constructions: a construction grammar approach to argument structure*. Chicago: Chicago University Press.

Goldberg, A.E. (1999). The emergency of the semantics of Argument structure constructions. In Brian MacWhinney (ed.) Lawrence Erlbaum Associates: Mahwah: 197-212.

Goldberg, A.E. (2003). Constructions: A new theoretical approach to language. *Trends in Cognitive Science*. 7 (5):219-224.

Goldberg, A.E. (2006). *Construction; A Construction grammar Approach to Argument Structure*. Chicago: University of Chicago Press.

Goldberg, A.E. and Casenhiser, D. (2004). Learning argument structure generalizations. *Cognitive Linguistics*.15 (3):289-316.

Goldberg, A.E. and Casenhiser, D. (2005). Fast mapping between a phrasal form and meaning. *Developmental Science*. 8 (6): 500–508.

Goldberg, A.E. and Casenhiser, D. and White, T. (2007). Constructions as categories of language: the role of order on construction learning. *New ideas in Psychology*.25 (2): 70-86.

Goldberg, A.E. and Casenhiser, D. (2008). *Construction learning and Second Language Acquisition*. In Robinson, P and Ellis, N (eds.). *Handbook of Cognitive Linguistics and Second Language Acquisition*. Routledge: New York and London: 197-215.

Granger, S. (2002). "A bird's eye view of learner corpus research", In S. Granger, J. Hung and S. Petch-Tyson (eds.). *Computer Learner Corpora, Second Language Acquisition and Foreign Language Teaching.* Amsterdam: John Benjamins: 3-33.

Grauberg, W. (1997). *The Elements of Foreign Language Teaching.* Clevedon.

Greenbaum, S, (1970). *Verb-Intensifier Collocations in English.* The Hague: Mouton.

Gregg, K. (1984). Krashen's monitor and Occam's razor. *Applied Linguistics.* (5): 79-100.

Gries, Stefan Th. (2003). Towards a corpus-based identification of prototypical instances of constructions. *Annual Review of Cognitive Linguistics* 1:1-28.

Gries, Stefan Th. (2006). Corpus-based methods and cognitive semantics: The many senses of to run. In Gries, Stefan Th. and Anatol Stefanowitsch (eds.) *Corpora in Cognitive Linguistics: Corpus-based Approaches to Syntax and Lexis.* Berlin and New York: Mouton de Gruyter: 57-98.

Gries, Stefan Th. (2008). 'Corpus-based methods in analyses of Second Language Acquisition data'. in Robinson, P and Ellis, N (eds) *Handbook of Cognitive Linguistics and Second Language Acquisition.* Routledge: New York and London: 406-431.

Gries, Stefan Th (2008). Dispersions and adjusted frequencies in corpora. *International Journal of Corpus Linguistics.* 13 (4): 403-437.

Gries, Stefan Th, and Stefanowitsch, A (2003). Collostructions: investigating the interaction of words and constructions. *International Journal of Corpus Linguistics.* 8 (2): 209-243.

Gries, Stefan Th, and Stefanowitsch, A (2006). *Corpora in Cognitive Linguistics: Corpus-Based Appraches to Syntax and Lexis.* Berlin and New York: Mouton de Gruyter.

Groenendijk, J. and Stokhof, M. (1982). On the Semantics of Questions and the Pragmatic of Answers. In Fred Landman, Frank Veltman (eds.). *Varieties of Formal Semantics. proceedings of the fourth Amsterdam Colloquium.* Foris Publications-Dordrecht: 3-73.

Groom, N. (2005). Pattern and meaning across genres and disciplines: An exploratory study. *Journal of English for Academic Purposes.* 4 (3): 257-277.

Guariento, W. and Morley, J. (2001). Texts and Tasks in Authenticity in EFL Classroom. *EFL Journal.* 55 (4).: 347-353.

Hahn, A. (2000). Grammar at its best: the development of a rule- and corpus-based grammar of English tenses. In L. Burnard& T. McEnery (eds.), *Rethinking Language Pedagogy from a Corpus Perspective.* Hamburg: Peter Lang: 193-206.

Hales, T. (1997). Exploring data-driven language awareness. *ELT Journal, 51* (3): 217–223.

Hanks, P. (1987). 'Definitions and explanations' in Sinclair (ed.): 116-136.

Hart, N. (2002). Intra-group autonomy and authentic materials: a different approach to ELT in Japanese colleges and universities. *System* 30(1): pp 33-46.

Herdina, P., and Jessner, U. (2002). *A dynamic model of multilingualism: Changing the psycholinguistic perspective.* Clevedon, UK: Multilingual Matters.

Hinkel, E., and Fotos, S. (2002). *New perspectives on Grammar Teaching in Second Language Classrooms.* Mahwah: New Jersey.

Hintzman, D.L. (1986). 'Schema abstraction' in a multiple-trace memory model. *Psychological Review* 93 (4): 411-428.

Hoey, M. (1991). *Patterns of lexis in text.* Oxford University Press.

Hoey, M. (1998). 'Introducing Applied Linguistics: 25 years on' *The pit Corder lecture at the BAAL Annual meeting.* University of Manchester.

Hudson, R. (2008). Word Grammar, Cognitive Linguistics, and second language learning and teaching. In Robinson, P and Ellis, N (eds) *Handbook of Cognitive Linguistics and Second Language Acquisition*. Routledge: New York and London: 89-113.

Hulme, C., Roodenrys, S., Schweickert, R., Brown, Gordon D.A., and Martin, S., Stuart, G. (1997).Word-frequency Effects on Short-Term Memory Tasks: Evidence for a Redintegration Process in Immediate Serial Recall. *Journal of Experimental Psychology: learning, Memory, and Cognition*. 23 (5): 1217-1232.

Hunston, S., Francis, G., and Manning, E. (1997). Grammar and Vocabulary: showing the connections. *EFL*. 51 (3): 208-216.

Hunston, S. and Francis, G. (1996). *Pattern Grammar: A corpus-driven approach to the lexical grammar of English*. John Benjamins Publishing Company: Amsterdam/Philadelphia.

Hunston, S.and Francis, G. (1998). 'Verbs Observed: A corpus-driven pedagogic grammar' *Applied Linguistics* 19: 45-72.

Hunston, S. (2002). *Corpora in Applied Linguistics*. Cambridge: Cambridge University Press.

Hunston, S. and Mason, O. (2004). The automatic recognition of verb patterns: A feasibility study. *International Journal of Corpus Linguistics*. 9 (2): 253-270.

Hunston, S. (2008) Starting with the small words: patterns, lexis and semantic sequences. *International Journal of Corpus Linguistics*. 13 (3): 271-295.

Hyland, K (2002). Options of identity in academic Writing. *EFL Journal*. 56 (4): 351.

Hymes, D. (1971). *Competence and performance in linguistic theories acquisition: Models and methods*. 3-28.

Jackendoff, R. (1983). *Semantics and Cognition*. Cambridge: Cambridge University Press.

Jackendoff, R. (2002) *Foundations of Language: Brain, Meaning, Grammar*. Oxford: Oxford University Press.

Janda, L. (2000). *Cognitive linguistics*. SLING2K Workshop.

Jiang, N. (2000). Lexical representation and development in a second language. *Applied Linguistics*. 21 (1): 47-77.

Johns, T. & P. King. (1991*). Classroom Concordancing*. Birmingham: University of Birmingham.

Kennedy, G. (1998). *An introduction to corpus Linguistics*. (1ˢᵗ ed.). London, England: Longman.

Kilgarriff, A. (1996).*Using word frequency lists to measure corpus homogeneity and similarity between corpora*. University of Brighton.

Kirsner, R. S. (1993). 'From meanmg to message m two theories Cogmtive and Saussurean views of the Modern Dutch demonstratives', In R A Geiger and B Rudzka-Ostyn (eds.). *Conceptualizations and mental processing in language*. Mouton de Gruyter, Berlin: 81-114.

Koffka, K. (1935). *Principles of Gestalt Psychology*. New York: Harcourt, Brace & World.

Kohn, K. (2006). *Corpus Technology and Language Pedagogy: Introduction*. B. Sabine., K. Kohn., & M. Joybrato (eds). Peter Lang.

Kovecese, A. and Szabo, P. (1996). Idioms: A view from Cognitive semantics. *Applied Linguistics* (17): 326-355.

Krashen, S.D. and Terrell, T.D. (1983). *The Natural Approach: Language Acquisition in the classroom*. San Francisco: Alemany Press.

Krashen, S.D. (1985). *The input Hypostudy*. Longman: London and New York.

Kruschke, J.K.(1992). ALCOVE: An exemplar-based connectionist model of category learning. *Psychological Review*. (99): 22-44.

Labov, W. (1973). The boundaries of words and their meanings. In *Bailey and Shuy* 340-73.

Lakoff G. (1977). Linguistics Gestals. *CLS* (13): 236-287.

Lakoff G. and Johnson, (1980). *Metaphors we live by*. Chicago and London: Univeristy of Chicago Press.

Lakoff G. (1982). *Categories and Cognitive Models*. Monograph reproduced by Linguistic Agency University Trier.

Lakoff G. (1987). *Women, Fire, and Dangerous Things. What Categories Reveal about the mind*. Chicago/ London: The University of Chicago Press.

Langacker, R.W. (1986). Abstract motion. *Proceedings of the Twelfth Annual Meeting of the Berkeley Linguistics Society*. 455–471.

Langacker, R.W. (1987). *Foundations of Cognitive Grammar. Volume 1: Theoretical Prerequisites*. Stanford: Stanford University Press.

Langacker, R.W. (1987). *Foundations of Cognitive Grammar. Volume 2: Descriptive Applications*. Stanford: Stanford University Press.

Langacker, R.W. (1990). *Concept, image and symbol: The cognitive basis of grammar*. Berlin and New York: Mouton de Gruyter. Cognitive Linguistics Research 1.

Langacker, R.W. (1995). Raising and transparency. *Language*. (71): 1-62.

Langacker, R.W. (1997b). A dynamic Account of the grammatical function. In Bybee, J., Haiman, J. and Thomas, SA. (eds.). *Essays on language function and language type dedicated to T. Givon*. Amsterdam and Philadelphia: John Benjanmins: 249-273.

Langacker, R. W. (2000). Virtual reality. *Studies in the Linguistic Sciences*, (29):77-103.

Langacker, R. W. (2000). A dynamic usage-based model, in M. Barlow and S. Kemmer (eds.). *Usage-Based Models of Language*. Stanford, CA: CSLI Publication: 1-64.

Langacker, R.W. (2008). Cognitive Grammar as a basis for language instruction. In Robinson, P and Ellis, N (eds) *Handbook of Cognitive Linguistics and Second Language Acquisition*. Routledge: New York and London: 66-88.

Lantolf, P J. (2007). Sociocultural source of thinking and its relevance for second language acquisition. *Bilingualism: Language and Cognition*. 10 (1): 31-33.

Larsen-Freeman, D. and Long, M. (1991). *An Introduction to Second Language Acquisition Research*. London and New York: Longman.

Leaver, B.L., Ehrman, M. and Shekhtman, B. (2005). *Achieving success in second language acquisition*. Cambridge: Cambridge University Press.

Lee, D (2001). *Cognitive Linguistics: An Introduction*. Oxford: Oxford University Press.

Leech, G. (1992). 'Corpora and theories of linguistic performance' in Svartvik (ed.): 105-122.

Lengyel, Z. and Navracsics, J. (2007). *Second Language Lexical Processes: Applied Linguistic and Psycholinguistic Perspectives*. Multilingtual Matters LTD: Clevedon, Buffalo, and Toronto.

Lennebery, Eric, H. (1967). *Biological Foundations of language*. New York.

Levclt. W.J.M. (lYY3). Timing in speech production: With special reference to word form encoding. *Annals of the New York Academy of Sciences*.

Lieven, E. V. M., Behrens, H., Speares, J., & Tomasello, M. (2003). Early syntactic creativity: A usage-based approach. *Journal of Child Language*. 30 (2).

Little, D. (1997). Responding authentically to authentic texts: A problem for self-access language learning. In Benson, P. (ed.). *Autonomy and independence in language learning.* Longman: London and New York: 225-236.

Littlemore, J. and Low, G. (2006). Figurative Thinking and Foreign Language learning. Basingstoke. UK: Palgrave MacMillan.

Long, M. H. (1985). A role for instruction in second language acquisition: Task-based language teaching. In K. Hyltenstam & M. Pienemann (Eds.). *Modeling and assessing second languages acquisition.* Clevedon, England: Multilingual Matters: 77-99.

Long, M. H. (1988). 'Instructed interlanguage development' In Beebe, L. (ed.) Issues in second language acquisition: Multiple perspective. Rowley, MA: Newbury House: 115-141.

Long, M. H. (1991a). Focus on form: A design feature in language teaching methodology. In K. de Bot, R. P. Ginsberg, & C. Kramsch (Eds.). Foreign language research in cross-cultural perspective. Amsterdam: John Benjamins: 39- 52.

Long, M. H. (1996). The role of linguistic environment in second language acquisition. In W. C. Ritchie & T. K. Bhatia (Eds.), *Handbook of second language acquisition.* San Diego, CA: Academic Press: 413-468.

Lorenz, G. (1999). *Adjective Intensification-Learners versus Native Speakers: A Corpus Study of Argumentative Writing.* Amsterdam: Rodopi.

Loschky, L. (1994). Comprehensible input and second language acquisition. *Studies in Second Language Acquisition.* 16(3): 303-323.

Lyons, J. (1996). On competence and performance and related notions. In G.Brown, K. Malmkjaer and J. Williams (eds.) *Performance and competencein second language acquisition.* Cambridge: Cambridge University Press. 11–32.

Mair, C. (1994). Is *see* becaming a conjunction? The study of grammaticalization as a meeting ground for corpus linguistics and grammartical theory. In Udo Fries, Gunnel Tottie, and Pter Schneider (eds), *Creating and Using English Language Corpora. Papers from the Fourteen International Conference on English Language research on Computerized Corpora. Zürich 1993,* 127-137. Amsterdam/Atlanta, GA: Rodopi.

Malinowski, B. (1923). The problem of meaning in primitive languages. In C.K. Ogden & I.A. Richards (eds.) *The meaning of meaning.* London: Harcourt Brace: 296-336

Manzanares, J.V.and López, A.M.R. (2008) what can language learners tell us about constructions. *Cognitive Approaches to Pedagogical Grammar.* A Volume in Honour of René Dirven Edited by De Knop, Sabine;, and De Rycker, Teun Berlin, New York (Mouton de Gruyter):197–230.

Mason, O. and Hunston, S. (2004) The automatic recognition of verb patterns: a feasibility study. *International Journal of Corpus Linguistics,* 9 (2): 253-270.

McCarthy, M. J. (1995). Conversation and literature: tense and aspect. In J. Payne (Ed.). *Linguistic approaches to literature.* Birmingham: University of Birmingham, English Language Research: 58-73.

McCarthy, M. J. (1998). *Spoken language and applied linguistics.* Cambridge, UK: Cambridge University Press.

McCarthy, M. J., and Carter, R. A. (1995). What is spoken grammar and how should we teach it? *ELT Journal,* 49, 207–218.

McCarthy, M. J., and Carter, R. A. (1997). Grammar, tails and affect: Constructing expressive choices in discourse. Text, 17, 405–429.

McCarthy, M. J., and Carter, R. A. (2006). *Cambridge Grammar of English: a comprehensive guide to spoken and written. English grammar and usage.* Cambridge: Cambridge University Press.

McEnery, T. and Wilson, A. (1996). *Corpus Linguistics.* Edinburgh: Edinburgh University Press.

McKay, S. (1980). Teaching the syntactic, semantic and pragmatic dimensions of verbs. *TESOL Quarterly.*14(1):17–26.

McLaughlin, B. (1978). The Monitor model: Some methodological considerations. *Language Learning.* (28): 309-332.

McLaughlin, B. (1980). Restructuring. *Applied Linguistics.* 11 (2): 113-128.

McLaughlin, B. (1987). *Theories of second-language learning.* London: Edward Arnold.

McLaughlin, B. (1990). "Conscious" versus "Unconscious" Learning. *TESOL Quarterly Volume.* 24 (4): 617-634.

Meunier, F. (2002). 'The pedagogical value of native and learner corpora in EFL grammar teaching' In S. Granger, J. Hung & S. Petch-Tyson (eds). *Computer Learner Corpora, Second Language Aacquisition and Foreign Language Teaching.* Amsterdam: John Benjamins: 119-141.

Meunier, F. and Granger, S. (2008). *Phraseology in Foreign Language Learning and Teaching.* Amsterdam/ Philadelphia: John Benjamins

Miller, G. A., Leacock, C., Tengi, R., and Bunker, R.S. (1993). A semantic Concordance. *Proceedings of the ARPA workshop on human language technology.* San Francisco, Morgan Kaufman.

Milton, J. (1999). *WordPilot 2000.* Compulang:Hong Kong.

Mitchell, T. F, (1971). 'Linguistic "goings-on": collocations and other lexical matters arising on the syntagmatic record'. *Archivum Linguisticum* 2 (N.S.), 35-69.

Mukherjee, J. (2004a). "The state of the art in corpus linguistics: three book-length perspectives". *English Language and Linguistics* 8(1): 103-109.

Nation, I. S. P. (2001). *Learning vocabulary in another language.* Cambridge: Cambridge University Press.

Nesselhauf, N. and Römer, U. (2007). Lexical-grammatical patterns in spoken English: A case of the progressive with future time reference. *International Journal of Corpus Linguistics.* 12 (3): 297-333.

Nizegorodcew, A. (2007). *Input for Instructed L2 Learners: The relevance of Relevance.* Multilingtual Matters LTD: Clevedon, Buffalo, and Toronto.

Nosofsky, R.M. (1988). Similarity, Frequency, and Category Representations. *Journal of Experimental Psychology: learning, memory and cognition.* 14 (1): 54-65.

Nunan, D. (1991). *Language teaching methodology: A textbook for teachers.* Prentice Hall: New York.

Nunan, D. (1999). *Second Language Teaching and Learning.* Heinle & Heinle Publishers.

Ortega, L. (2009). *Understanding Second Language Acquisition.* A Hodder Arnold Publication.

Partington, (1998*). Patterns and meanings: using corpora for English language research and teaching.* Benjamin: Amsterdam.

Pawley and Syder (1983). Natural selection in syntax: Notes on adaptive variation and change in vernacular and literary grammar. *Journal of Pragmatics.*7 (5):551-579.

Piaget, J. (1968). On the development of memory and identity. Clark University Press (Worcester, Mass).

Pinker, S. (1999) *Words and Rules: The Ingredients of Language*. New York: Basic Books.

Purpura, J. E. (2004). *Assessing Grammar*. In J. Charles Alderson and Lyle F Bachman (eds.). Cambridge: Cambridge University Press.

Radden, G. (1992): The Cognitive Approach to Natural Language. In: M. Pütz (ed.). *Thirty Years of Linguistic Evolution. Studies in Honour of René Dirven on the Occasion of his Sixtieth Birthday*. Philadelphia u.a., John Benjamins, 513-541.

Raimes, A. (1993). Out of the woods: Emerging traditions in the teaching of writing. In S. Silberstein (ed.). *State of the Art TESOL Essays*. Washington, D.C.:TESOL.

Randall, M. (2007). *Memory, psychology and second language learning*. Amsterdam: Benjenmin.

Robinson, P. (1995). Attention, Memory, and the "Noticing" Hypostudy. *Applied Linguistics*. 45 (2):283-331.

Robinson, P and Ellis, N (2008). *Handbook of Cognitive Linguistics and Second Language Acquisition*. Routledge: New York and London.

Roehr, K. (2006). Metalinguistic knowledge in L2 task performance: A verbal protocol analysis. *Language Awareness*. 15(3): 180-198.

Roehr, K. (2008). Metalinguistic Knowledge and Language Ability in University-Level L2 Learners. *Applied Linguistics*. 29 (2): 173-199.

Rosch, E. (1973). 'Natural categories'. *Cognitive Psychology* (4): 328-50.

Rosch, E. (1975a). 'Cognitive reference points'. *Cognitive Psychology*. (7): 532-47.

Rosch, E. (1975b). 'Cognitive representations of semantic categories'. *Journal of Experimental Psychology: General*. (104): 192-233.

Rosch, E. (1975c). 'Universals and cultural specifics in human categorisation'. In R. W. Brislin, S. Bochner, and W.J.Lonner (eds.). *Cross-cultural Perspectives on Learning.*. New York: John Wiley: 177-206

Rosch, E. (1976). 'Structural bases of typicality effects'. *Journal of Experimental Psychology: Human Perception and Performance* (2): 491-502.

Rosch, E. (1977). Human Categorization.' In N. Warren (ed.) *Studies in Cross-cultural Psychology*. London: Academic Press: 1-49.

Rosch, E. (1978). 'Principles of Categorization'. In E. Rosch and B.B.Lloyd (eds.). *Cognition and Categorization*. Hillsdale, Mich.: Lawrence Erlbaum: 27-48.

Rothkopt, E.Z. (1971). Incidental memory for location of information in text. *Journal of verbal learning and verbal behaviour*. 10 (6): 608-613.

Rowland, C.F., Pine, J.M., and Theakston, A. (2003). Determinants of acquisition order in wh-questions: re-evaluating the role of caregiver speech. *Child Language*. 30: 609-635.

Rutherford, W. (1987). *Second Language Grammar: Learning and Teaching*. Longman: UK.

Sandra, D. (1998). *On Monosemy: A Study in Linguistic Semantics*. Albany: State University of New York.

Saville-Troike, M. (2006). *Introduction to Second language Acquisition*. Cambridge: Cambridge University Press.

Schacter, D.L. (1987). Implicit memory: history and current status. *Journal of Experimental Psychology: learning, memory, cognition*. 13 (3): 501-518.

Schmidt, R.W., and Frota, S.N. (1986). 'Developing basic conversational ability in a second language: A case study of an adult learner of Purtuguese.' In Day, R. (ed.)*Talking to learn: Conversation in second language acquisition.* Rowley, MA: Newbury House: 237-326.

Schmidt, R. (1990). The role of consciousness in second language learning. *Applied Linguistics* (11): 129-88.

Schmidt, Hans-Jorg. (2000).*English Abstract Nouns as Conceptual Shells: From corpus to cognition.* Berlin: Mouton de Gruyter.

Schulze, R. and Römer, U. (2008) Pattens, meaningful units and specialized discourses. *International Journal of Corpus Linguistics.* 13 (3): 265-270.

Scott, M. (2005). *WordSmith Tools: Version 4.0.* Oxford: Oxford University Press.

Selinker, L. (1972). *Interlanguage. International Review of Applied Linguistics.* (10): 209-231.

Siegler, R.S. and Svetina. M. (2002). A microgenetic/cross-sectional study of matrix completion: comparing short-term change and long-term change. *Child Development.* 73: 793-809.

Sinclair, J.M. et al (1990). Collins *CoBuild English Grammar.* London: HarperCollins.

Sinclair, J. M. and A. Renouf. (1988). 'A lexical syllabus for language teaching' in R. Carter and M. McCarthy (eds.). *Vocabulary and Language Teaching.* London: Longman: 140-160.

Sinclair, J.M. (1991). *Corpus, Concordance, Collocation.* Oxford : Oxford University Press.

Singleton, D. (1999). *Exploring the second language mental lexicon.* Cambridge: Cambridge University Press.

Skehan, P. (1998). *A Cognitive Approach to Language Learning.* Oxford: Oxford University Press.

Slobin, D. A. I. (1979). *Psycholinguistics.* (2nd Ed.) London:L Scott, Foreman, and Company.

Summers, D. (1996) Computer lexicography: the importance of representativeness in relation to frequency, in: J. Thomas and M. Short (eds), *Using corpora for language research: studies in the honour of Geoffrey Leech.* London: Longman: 260–266.

Swain, M. (1985). Communicative Competence: some roles of comprehensible input and comprehensible output in its development. In S. Gass and C. Madden (eds.). *Input in Second Language Acquisition.* Cambridge, MA: Newbury House: 235-253.

Sweetser, E. (1986). Polysemy vs abstraction: Mutually exclusive or complementary? In V. Nikiforidon, M. and Varclay, M. Niepokuk, and D. Feder (eds.). *Proceedings of the 12th Annual meeting of the Berkeley Linguistics Society.* Berkelay: Berkelay Linguistics Society: 528-538.

Szirmai, M. (2001).Corpus Linguistics in Japan: Its Status and Role in Language Education. In Lewis, P (ed.). *The changing face of CALL: a Japanese perspective.* Swets & Zeitlinger publishers: 91-107.

Talmy, L. (1978). Figure and ground in complex sentences. In Joseph, H. Greeberg. (ed.). *Univercal of human language. Syntax.* Stanford: Stanford Univeristy Press: 625-649.

Talmy, L. (1988). The relation of grammar to cognition-a synopsis. In Rudzka-Ostyn: 165-205.

Talmy, L. (2000). *Towards a Cognitive Semantics.* Cambridge: Cambridge University Press.

Talmy, L. (2008). Aspects of Attention in Language. In Robinson, P and Ellis, N (eds) *Handbook of Cognitive Linguistics and Second Language Acquisition.* Routledge: New York and London: 27-38.

Taylor, J.(1995). *Linguistic Categorization.* (2nd ed.) Oxford: Oxford University Press.

Taylor, J.(1998). Syntactic Constructions as Prototype Categories. In Tomasello, M. (ed.). *The new psychology of language: cognitive and functional approaches to language structure.* Lawrence Erlbaum Associates. Mahwah: New Jersey: 177-202.

Taylor, J. (2002,2003). *Cognitive grammar.* Oxford: Oxford University Press.

Taylor, J. (2008). Prototypes in Cognitive Linguistics. In Robinson, P and Ellis, N (eds) *Handbook of Cognitive Linguistics and Second Language Acquisition.* Routledge: New York and London: 39-65.

Taylor, J. (2008). Language in the mind. In De Knop, S., Boers, F., & De Rycker, T. (Eds.) *Fostering language teaching efficiency through cognitive linguistics.* Walter de Gruyter GmbH&Co. KG, Berlin/ New York: 29-57.

Terrell, T. (1986). Acquisition in a natural approach: The binding/accessing framework. *The Modern Language Journal.* (70) iii.

Teuburt, W. (2005). My version of Corpus linguistics. *Cognitive Linguistics.*(10): 1-13.

Thelen, E. and Smith, L.B. (1994). *Dynamic Systems Approach to the Development of Cognition and Action.* Cambridge, MA: The MIT Press.

Tomasello, M. (2000). First steps in a Usage based theory of language acquisition, *Cognitive Linguistics.* (11): 61-82.

Tomasello, M. and Lieven, E. (2008). Children's first language acquisition from a usage-based perspective. In Robinson, P and Ellis, N (eds) *Handbook of Cognitive Linguistics and Second Language Acquisition.* Routledge: New York and London: 168-196.

Tomlinson, B. (2001). *Developing materials for language teaching.* London: Continuum.

Tomlinson, B. (2003a). Humanizing the coursebook. In B. Tomlinson (Ed.). *Developing materials for language teaching.* London: Continuum: 162-173.

Tomlinson, B. (2003b). Frameworks for materials development. In B. Tomlinson (Ed.), *Developing materials for language teaching.London*: Continuum: 107-129.

Troike, Saville M (2006). *Introduction Second Language Acquisition.* Cambrdige: Cambridge University Press.

Tsohatzidis (1990). *Meanings and prototypes: Studies in linguistic categorization.* Routledge: London.

Tyler, A. and Evan, V. (2003). *The Semantics of English Prepositions: Spatial Scenes, Cognition and the Experiential Basis of Meaning.* New York and Cambridge: Cambridge University Press.

Tyler, A. and Evans, V. (2007). Reconsidering Prepositional Polysemy Networks: The case of *over.* In Evans, V, Bergen, B., and Zinken, J. (eds). *The Cognitive Linguistics Reader.* London: Equinox: 186-237.

Tyler W.D. and Marslen-Wilson, L.K. (1981). Central process in speech understanding. Philosophical Transactions of the Royal Society of London. Series B, Biological Sciences. *The Psychological Mechanisms of Language.* (295), No. 1077: 317-332

Ungerer, F. and Schmid, H.j. (2006). An *Introduction To Cognitive Linguistics.* (2ed.). Pearson: Longman.

Ur, P. (1996). *A course in language teaching.* Cambridge: Cambridge University Press.

Van Geert, P. 1994. 'Vygotskian dynamics of development,' *Human Development.* (37): 346–65.

Vanpatten, B. (1996). *Input Processing and Grammar Instruction.* New York: Ablex.

Vanpatten, B. (2003). *From Input to Output: A teacher's Guild to Second Language Acquisition.* William R. Glass.

Verspoor, M. and Lowie, W. (2003). Making sense of polysemous words. *Language learning.* (53): 547-586.

Verspoor, M. and Lowie, W. and Van Dijk. (2007). A Dynamic Systems Theory approach to second language acquisition. *Bilingualism: Language and Cognition.* 10 (1): 7–21.

Vygotsky, L. S. (1980). *Mind in Society: The Development of Higher Mental Processes.* Boston, MA: Harvard University Press.

White, R. and Arndt, V. (1991). *Process Writing.* London: Longman

White, L., Spada, N., Lightbown, P.M., and Ranta, L. (1991). Input enhancement and L2 question formation. *Applied linguistics.* 12 (4): 416-432.

Williams, R. (1981). Lexical familiarization in content area textbooks. In L. Chapman (Ed.), *The reader and the text.* London: Heinemann Educational Books Ltd: 49-59.

Wichmann, A., Fligelstone, S., McEnery, T, and Knowles, G (1997). *Teaching and language Corpora.* Longman: London and New York.

Widdowson, H.G. (1979). *Explorations in Applied Linguistics.* Oxford: Oxford University Press.

Willis, D. (1990). *The lexical syllabus: A new approach to language teaching.* Collins ELT.

Wong, L-Y M. (2009). Gei constructions in Mandarin Chinese and bei constructions in Cantonese. *International Journal of Corpus Linguistics.* 14 (1): 60-80.

Yip, V. (1989) 'Grammatical consciousness-raising and learnability' in T. Odlin (ed.) *Perspectives on Pedagogical Grammar.* Cambridge: Cambridge University Press: 123-138.

Zanuttini, R. and Portner, P. (2003) Exclamative Clauses: At the Syntax-Semantics Interface. *Language.* 79 (1). Linguistic Society of America.

Printed in the United States
By Bookmasters